ALPHA BRAVO DELTA
GUIDE TO

DECISIVE 20TH-CENTURY

AMERICAN
BATTLES

ALPHA BRAVO DELTA
GUIDE TO

DECISIVE 20TH-CENTURY
AMERICAN BATTLES

W. THOMAS SMITH JR.

ALPHA

A member of Penguin Group (USA) Inc.

This book is for Dad, the late William Thomas "Bill" Smith.

When I was a boy, Dad's stories of famed Revolutionary War guerrilla Francis Marion ignited within my soul a passion for American military history that will never be extinguished.

This is also for my brother, the late Michael Robert Smith, who enjoyed my retelling of those stories.

International Standard Book Number: 1-59257-147-6
Library of Congress Catalog Card Number: 2003110665

05   04   03   8   7   6   5   4   3   2   1

Interpretation of the printing code: The rightmost number of the first series of numbers is the year of the book's printing; the rightmost number of the second series of numbers is the number of the book's printing. For example, a printing code of 03-1 shows that the first printing occurred in 2003.

Printed in the United States of America

CONTENTS

FOREWORD

BY BRIG. GEN. DAVID L. GRANGE

No other armed force in the world has seen action outside of its own country more than that of the United States in the 20th century. No other country has sent its military abroad more often to defeat tyranny, free the oppressed, and control the spread of fascism and communism.

W. Thomas Smith Jr. has captured the history, commitment, sacrifice, and decisive victories of the U.S. armed forces around the globe, from the Boxer Rebellion in China in 1900 through Task Force Ranger in Somalia in 1993. America's military has served her country well on land, at sea, and in the air like no other nation during this period of history.

Alpha Bravo Delta Guide to Decisive 20th-Century American Battles provides an excellent reference to America's conflicts in the last century. In each case, Mr. Smith brings each conflict alive in a lively, entertaining, and highly readable manner

In the last century, American wars were won, lost, or resulted in a stalemate, though most battles were won by the United States and its allies. The Marines holding the wall in Peking, China, set the tone of America's military for the next century of warfare. Eighteen years later, the "doughboy" was in France proving his worth, beginning with the first American victory by the 1st Division's 28th Infantry "Black Lions" at Cantigny.

Two decades later, American forces were called upon again to defend its shores against the most ruthless enemies in this country's history. After setbacks at Kasserine Pass in North Africa, "Blood and Guts" Patton won the first U.S. victory of the European campaign at El Guetter. Paratroopers of the 82nd and 101st Airborne Divisions assaulted inland ahead of history's largest amphibious assault—the Normandy Invasion. The 1st Infantry Division, the "Big Red One," assaulted Omaha Beach with elements of the 29th Infantry Division. American rangers earned their motto "Rangers Lead the Way" at Omaha Beach and on the cliffs at Pointe du Hoc. The 4th Infantry Division successfully assaulted Utah Beach and linked up with airborne units. Normandy opened the way for successful offensive operations across Europe. The Germans later surprised Allied forces in a last-ditch winter attack primarily against American forces in Belgium. But the determination of seasoned army units, tough leadership at all levels, and the eventual introduction of air support the Allied Forces prevailed and won the Battle of the Bulge. The fall of Nazi Germany followed.

In the Pacific, naval forces, both sea and air, turned the tide against the Japanese during the battles of Coral Sea and Midway, followed by army and Marine victories at Guadalcanal, Tarawa, Iwo Jima, and Okinawa.

When the Korean War began, an ill-prepared American military was faced with stopping the spread of communism on the Korean Peninsula. Rushed to the scene with a military unprepared, the American GI barely held on until an offensive could be launched by MacArthur at Inchon. Combat continued up and down the Korean Peninsula until an armistice was reached for a temporary end of the "Forgotten War."

A decade later, U.S. advisers found themselves in the jungles of Vietnam. Again, the reason was to stop communism on the fringes of the great nations competing for regional influence. U.S. forces won almost every battle, but a lack of political will to take the battle to the enemy's center of gravity lost the war. Many future senior officers learned from the extensive sustained combat and disappointments and applied these lessons to future operations. Hard-learned lessons of leadership, training, and survival were borne in blood by veterans battle-hardened in places like Chu Lai, the Ia Drang Valley, and Dak To.

The American military was determined from the strategic defeat in Vietnam to regroup and rebuild. An all-volunteer force replaced the draft. With the resourcing and moral support of the new administration, the military picked itself up and prepared for the battlefields of the future. Operations like Urgent Fury, El Dorado Canyon, and Just Cause were all fought against repressive dictatorships or supporters of terrorism. All of these successful operations culminated in Operation Desert Storm, which drove the Iraqi army out of Kuwait. The U.S. military was again the most respected in the world.

As we move into the 21st century our enemies continue to attack, but with the vast capabilities developed during the last century, and with rapidly evolving technologies currently being developed, the United States will persevere in the face of often terrifying odds. Those who have served their nation and survived the conflicts of the past century understand the lessons learned on those battlefields and the sacrifices that will be necessary to be victorious in the future. Success in Afghanistan and Iraq are only the first of more battles to come in the new century. The American people demand future success from their military, just as they have over the last 100 years—and nothing less.

Brig. Gen. David L. Grange
Brig. Gen. David L. Grange is a CNN military analyst and the former commanding general of the 1st Infantry Division.

INTRODUCTION

On February 15, 1898, the battleship USS *Maine* was quietly anchored in Havana Harbor. It was just before 9:40 P.M., and the Cuban port was unusually still. In recent days, the city of Havana had been the scene of a number of riots between opposing political factions in Cuba's ongoing quest for independence from Spain. But on that evening, the only sounds were of distant Latin music emanating from one of the waterfront bars and the slow, deliberate footsteps of a lone U.S. Marine guard as he paced along his watch section of the warship's primary weather deck.

Below decks, most of the crew—except for a handful of watch-standers—were sound asleep in their hammocks. A few were playing cards, reading, or squaring away their uniforms for the following morning's muster and inspection. U.S. Navy captain Charles Sigsbee, the *Maine*'s skipper, was relaxing in the aft section of the ship writing a letter home.

Topside, the lone Marine guard paused momentarily. He looked toward the city's twinkling lights, listened to the distant music, then resumed his measured pace along the main deck.

All at once a terrific explosion ripped through the front of the ship. The entire bow disintegrated. Almost everyone in the forward third of the vessel was instantly killed. Black smoke and seawater began pouring into the remaining spaces. The dying ship, its bulkheads groaning under the stress of collapse, was then rocked by a series of jarring secondary explosions. Making his way to the main deck, Captain Sigsbee stumbled through pitch black passageways, bumping into unseen sailors and Marines. They, too, were groping in the darkness. "Abandon ship," Sigsbee ordered. He did not need a damage report to know the *Maine* was doomed.

Indeed, five tons of gunpowder had suddenly ignited, and within minutes, the entire ship was resting on the bottom of the harbor. More than 260 officers and men were blown up or drowned. Survivors were plucked from the water by the crew of the nearby American steamer *City of Washington* and a Spanish warship, *Alfonso XII*.

Despite the Spanish rescue efforts, most Americans believed the explosion to be the work of Spanish saboteurs. American newspapers screamed for vengeance. It was enough to propel America into a war with Spain.

The war only lasted for four months, but America emerged from the conflict as a growing world power. And for the first time in its brief history, America had extra-continental protectorates and a need to be able to defend them.

When the 20th century opened two years later, U.S. military forces comprised a small expeditionary army and a sizeable navy, both of which had begun to exert their influence around the world. The U.S. Army and Navy (including the navy's infantry and security arm, the Marine Corps) were certainly formidable and respected particularly in the Western Hemisphere. But the European military powers, with their long-standing traditions and vast colonial possessions, still controlled much of the globe. That would change over the next several decades as a result of stagnant foreign economies, American industrialization and seemingly endless resources, and two world wars.

But in 1900, despite the defeat of the Spanish, the American armed forces were still viewed as the stepchildren of the great Western military powers. That year, the combined numbers of the U.S. Army, Navy, and Marine Corps were approximately 126,000 officers and men. Many of them had seen action in the Spanish-American War or were veterans of the 19th-century Plains Indian Wars. In some cases, a few of the old hands had fought in the American Civil War. Those numbers would increase to about 200,000 by the time the great European war erupted in 1914. And at the close of hostilities in 1918, some 4.4 million Americans would be in uniform. The numbers fluctuated over the next several decades. At the end of World War II in 1945, some 12 million soldiers, sailors, airmen, and Marines were under arms. And by the year 2000, there were just under 1.4 million service personnel stationed around the globe.

The 20th century was a period in which battlefield technologies developed almost exponentially. In previous centuries, military innovations evolved at a set, almost leisurely pace. When the 20th century opened, the world's air forces were nothing more than small corps of observation balloonists. The navies' new steam ships, with their newly armored hulls, were still captained by officers who had cut their teeth under sail. On the ground, horse cavalry was still the preferred arm of shock. Artillery caissons were still horse-drawn. But the accuracy and rate-of-fire of the field gun itself—with its new rifled, breech-loading capabilities and stabilizing hydraulic-recoil features—had increased to a point that artillery had truly become the "King of Battle." Wheeled vehicles with internal-combustion engines had been invented, but were not mass-produced until the first decade of the century. And the track-propelled tank, essentially a mobile bunker, would not be invented—much less fielded—for several more years. In 1900, much of America's infantry, the "Queen of Battle," was still armed with single-shot rifles, whereas the European armies had adopted new magazine-loading repeaters. The machine gun was still in its infancy.

In 1800, perhaps even 1700, soldiers might very well have envisioned the battlefield technologies of 1900. Scientists and engineers most assuredly did. But no one in 1900 could have fathomed the stunning technological wizardry with which wars would be fought in 2000. When the 20th century closed, America's armed forces were fielding jet fighters achieving near-hypersonic speeds which could be launched and recovered from giant, nuclear-powered aircraft carriers. Highly maneuverable helicopters, bristling with all manner of guided weapons, could hover above and support racing tanks armed with computerized attack systems. Leviathan-size submarines prowled the oceans. Precisely targeted weapons could be brought to bear against land-based enemy targets from a sailor keying in coordinates on a distant warship. And motorcycle-riding special force soldiers—equipped with night vision goggles, range-finding binoculars, and palm-top computers—could race far ahead of advancing armies. If the soldier became lost, he needed only to glance at his GPS (global positioning system) rangefinder, which would pinpoint his exact location on Earth from a satellite orbiting in space. Beyond that, the U.S. arsenal of 2000 included lasers, particle beam weapons, and the darkest weapon of all—intercontinental ballistic missiles tipped with multiple, independently targeted nuclear warheads.

Technology aside, in many ways the U.S. armed forces of 2000 were not unlike American military forces of 1900. Both were characterized by small, Spartan forces of tough professionals. They were led by a core group of experienced senior officers and noncommissioned officers who—as privates, seamen, lieutenants, and ensigns—had served in much larger services. Moreover, both the campaigns of the first and last decades of the 20th century were characterized by specially tasked expeditions aimed at either capturing outlaw leaders or dictators, quelling uprisings, or attempting to keep the peace and protect U.S. nationals and interests in troubled underdeveloped countries.

The difference was that when the century opened, the great world powers were not yet convinced of the American warrior's combat prowess. In the eyes of the military leaders of Great Britain, France, Germany, Russia, Japan, and a smattering of other kingdoms and smaller empires, the American armed forces had yet to prove themselves worthy of sitting at the big table. One hundred years later, no force on Earth could reasonably expect to prevail militarily in a general war with the United States.

As such, the 20th century was a period in which American military power came of age. In doing so, 20th-century American combatants found themselves fighting some of the bloodiest, most decisive battles in all of history. The battles were decisive in the sense that one side was victorious, the other either soundly defeated or so badly crippled it was forced to withdraw in the face of its opponent. Other factors which played a role in determining a battle's decisiveness included dramatic political or social change brought about by a battle's outcome or an innovative change in the nature of armed combat.

Most, though not all, of the decisive 20th-century American battles were victories. The reasoning is simple: America's armed forces have defeated practically every foe faced on land, at sea, and in the air. The nation may have lost one war, Vietnam, but even that war was not lost on the battlefield. And many of the great decisive U.S. victories of the last century were fought in Southeast Asia.

America's first decisive action of the century was fought in 1900 in Peking (Beijing), China. There an allied force with a strong American military presence defeated a numerically superior force of Chinese revolutionaries. Soon thereafter, a series of brushfire wars ignited throughout the western hemisphere, followed by the two great world wars, the "forgotten war" in Korea, the politically botched war in Vietnam, and several post-Vietnam campaigns, including the so-called "mother of all battles" in Iraq.

When the century closed, the world's inhabitants still continued to live in the risk-shadow of total nuclear annihilation. Granted, the Cold War—the dangerous military competition which had long existed between the Western allies and the Eastern Bloc nations—was over. But the collapse of the Soviet Union and the Eastern Bloc heralded the beginning of a new, far more ominous threat—one which would soon manifest itself in a dramatic September-morning terrorist attack on American soil.

The U.S. Army, Navy, Air Force, and Marine Corps were as prepared for any eventuality as any previous American armed forces had been. And, in fact, more so than most. But the new world order was unlike anything anyone could have predicted. America would soon find itself groping in the void: Fearful of the proliferation of weapons of mass destruction, attacking isolated threats from one end of the globe to the next, and soon fighting a somewhat unpopular Gulf War II.

Fortunately for the free world, America now fields a military force that is both strong and flexible. It is capable of rendering humanitarian assistance anywhere in the world. As a combatant force it is unmatched. And with its very heart and soul forged in the great, decisive battles of the last century, that military force will continue to keep the wolf away from the door for at least another 100 years.

Acknowledgments

There are far too many to thank for their assistance in the research and the writing of this book. However, I am particularly indebted to my agent, James C. Vines in New York, and my editors at Alpha Books—Gary Goldstein in New York and Tom Stevens in Indianapolis. Others deserving special recognition include Dr. Richard Walker, former U.S. ambassador to South Korea; Lt. Gen. John Bruce Blount (U.S. Army, ret.), former chief of staff of Allied Forces Southern Europe; Brig. Gen. David L. Grange (U.S. Army, ret.), CNN military analyst; Col. David H. Hackworth (U.S. Army, ret.), author and syndicated columnist; Col. John W. Pierce (U.S. Army, ret.); Lt. Col. Heath L. McMeans Jr. (U.S. Marine Corps, ret.); Maj. Charles Pollard Andrews (U.S. Army, ret.); Dan Crawford of the Marine Corps Historical Center in Washington, D.C.; Prof. Keiko Uesawa Chevray of Columbia University's Department of East Asian Languages and Cultures in New York; my friends and colleagues at the American Society of Journalists & Authors in New York; Tracie Thompson at the Columbia (S.C.) World Affairs Council; and the incredibly helpful librarians and library assistants at the University of South Carolina's Thomas Cooper Library, the Richland County Public Library, and the South Carolina State Library in Columbia.

Battle perspectives were gleaned from far too many individuals to list by name. However, a few include the previously mentioned officers. The book is also a reflection of my previous interviews and conversations with combat veterans including Gen. William C. Westmoreland, former U.S. Army chief of staff; Eugene Germino, former U.S. Army officer during World War II; the late Romey Germino, former U.S. Army artillery forward observer during World War II; Charles Shields Micol, former U.S. Army medical corpsman during World War II; the late Benjamin Milton Smith Jr., former U.S. Army infantryman during World War II; Robert W. Hughes, former U.S. Marine rifleman during World War II; Charles T. Noulles, former U.S. Army Air Forces bomber crewmember during World War II; Michael E. Thornton, former U.S. Navy SEAL and Congressional Medal of Honor recipient in Vietnam; Patrick Cleburne "Clebe" McClary, III, former U.S. Marine reconnaissance officer in Vietnam; Gilbert Bagnell, former U.S. Army interrogator in Vietnam; John Temple Ligon, former U.S. Army artillery officer and Airborne Ranger in Vietnam; the countless U.S. Marines and sailors with whom I served years ago; and many others.

I would like to thank my immediate family, including Mom, Alba Antoinette "Tita" Smith Rowell; Lt. Col. Howard Tobias Rowell

(U.S. Air Force Reserve, ret.); Annette Smith Fowler; James David Smith; Michael Paul Fowler; and William Maxwell Fowler; as well as so many in my extended family for their unwavering support on all fronts. I would also like to thank my eternally patient magazine and newspaper editors— Gordon Witkin of *U.S. News & World Report*, Jeff Stinson at *USA Today*, and others—for hanging tough with me despite months of manuscript work which kept me out of the news fray.

Beyond that, there is an army of friends and supporters who in some way assisted with the work or deserve special recognition for simply keeping my spirits from flagging, sometimes unwittingly. A few of those include Mary Ann Bagnell, Edmund Bagnell, Debbie Jones Hart, Kenney DeCamp, Daniel Patrick "Danny" Smith, Aida Rogers, Bill McDonald, Donna Bunting, Rachel Haynie, Candy Rikert, Joanna Harvey, Bill Webber, Danelle Germino Haakenson, and Uncle Woody and Aunt Sandy's girls.

Although it would be almost an independent work to recognize everyone, special thanks to all those not named in Columbia, Charleston, Aiken, and Myrtle Beach, South Carolina; Raleigh and Durham, North Carolina; Omaha, Nebraska; Chicago; Washington, D.C.; New York; and New Jersey, who in some way contributed to the completion of this book.

I would also like to thank the untold numbers of 20th-century American warriors whose deeds and sacrifices have not only provided me with so much grist for the word mill, but allowed all American authors the freedom to write with accuracy and without fear of political or ideological persecution. Few scribes in history have been so fortunate. And finally thanks to God, for without Him, this work would not have been possible.

PART 1

THE BOXER REBELLION THROUGH WORLD WAR I

CHAPTER 1

THE BOXER REBELLION

(MAY 1900–FEBRUARY 1901)

The 20th century opened with one of the most dramatic albeit little-known victories in American military history, the Boxer Rebellion in Peking (modern Beijing), China, in 1900. The rebellion was the direct result of unwanted and increasing foreign influence in China during the 19th century. Japan and many of the European powers had essentially divided the nation into "spheres of influence" wherein they claimed exclusive trading rights within those spheres and forced Chinese citizens to make concessions against their will. The United States, a relative newcomer as a power on the world stage, instead proposed an "open door" policy in which all nations would share the wealth of China. But the attempt to control China was destined for bloody conflict.

Violence erupted in early 1900 when a secret society of Chinese warriors known as the "Righteous and Harmonious Fists" (the Americans and British called them "Boxers") began terrorizing Christian missionaries and their Chinese converts in the northern regions of the country. Believing they had divine powers and could not be stopped by foreign weapons, the Boxers roamed the countryside, burning churches and homes and killing Christians with impunity. Their ultimate goal was the expulsion of all "foreign devils" from China, and the Boxers were willing to over-throw China's ruling Qing dynasty to do so. The Qing empress, Tzu Hsi, was initially opposed to the Boxers, but her advisers convinced her that an alliance with the society would strengthen her throne and ultimately eliminate foreign influence throughout China.

On May 28, the Boxers torched several train stations along a Belgian-constructed railroad between the capital at Peking and the town of Paotingfu. They then struck at Fengtai, a primary rail junction near Peking. Fearful that Tzu would not protect foreign diplomats from the Boxers, the European legations in Peking cabled for military assistance on May 30.

The following day, a small contingent of American Marines and sailors from both the USS *Oregon* and the USS *Newark* were ordered to Peking to establish a legation guard for the protection of foreign diplomats. The American troops, under the command of American Marine captains John "Handsome Jack" Myers and Newt Hall, soon found themselves besieged—along with other Western troops and the diplomats they were charged with protecting—behind the walls of the legations building. The Marine position was atop the southwest corner of the wall surrounding the legation square. Russian, German, and British troops defended other positions at the entrances and on the walls.

As foreign troop numbers swelled in the nearby city of Tientsin, the Boxers increased their level of violence, and on June 9, they began openly attacking foreign property in Peking. At the legations complex, British foreign minister Sir Claude McDonald was barely able to send a distress wire before the telegraph lines were cut.

On June 10, a multinational force of some 2,500 troops under the command of Vice Adm. Sir Edward Seymour of the Royal Navy left Tientsin for Peking. But after several days of fighting, the initial attempt to relieve the legations was repulsed by both the Empress's army and a strong force of Boxers. On June 22, Seymour's multinationals retired to Tientsin.

Meanwhile, the embattled American Marines and sailors in Peking were running out of ammunition and time. On June 27, the Boxers launched a fierce attack against the American position in the Legation Square but the attackers were beaten back. On July 1, the Boxers broke through the German defenses and forced the Americans to fall back. The Marines then counterattacked and regained their position. The following day, the Boxers moved a wooden tower against the wall. That night the tower was destroyed by a team of American and British Marines.

McDonald wrote, "Captain Myers's post on the wall is the peg which holds the whole thing together."

On August 5, an international coalition of nearly 19,000 men—including a force of 3,000 American soldiers, sailors, and Marines under the command of U.S. Army major general Adna Chaffee—left Tientsin for Peking. En route, they clashed twice with sizeable Chinese forces. In both battles, including a Chinese cavalry attack, the multinationals beat the enemy back in heavy fighting. And on August 13, the allied force reached the gates of Peking. The foreign legations were relieved.

Over the next several months, the number of international troops in China continued to grow. The Boxers were pursued into the backcountry where they were destroyed piecemeal by American and allied forces. On February 1, 1901, the Boxers were officially abolished by Chinese mandate, and on September 7, the Peace Protocol of Peking was signed. The Boxer Rebellion was over.

CHAPTER 2

INTRODUCTION TO WORLD WAR I

World War I, which began in the summer of 1914, was—and will forever be regarded as—one of the great calamities unleashed upon humankind. Ten million combatants were killed in just over three years. And the numbers of wounded, maimed, and emotionally wrenched were far greater. It was initially a European war, but by the close of hostilities in late 1918, it had involved nearly 40 nations, including the United States.

The war's political, economic, and military origins are complex, dating back to a period in the 19th century when a newly industrialized Europe was struggling with issues of empire, boundaries, holdings, and a growing sense of nationalism. Germany had defeated France in 1870 and subsequent disputes over territory created a tremendous animosity between the two nations. Great Britain still ruled the seas, but on the continent Germany was rapidly emerging as a great military power. Alliances were created to balance the power in Europe. But the tension was volatile.

When problems began surfacing in Europe, the continent's American offspring, the United States, was still licking its wounds from a devastating civil war and expanding its westward territories. The relatively new nation had no real interest in the affairs of the "old world." Europe's problems were Europe's, and the average American wanted no part of them. That perception slowly began to change in the summer of 1914.

On June 28, Archduke Franz Ferdinand, heir to the Austria-Hungarian throne, was assassinated by a Serbian nationalist while touring the Bosnian capital of Sarajevo. The archduke's death set off a disastrous chain of events leading to a massive mobilization of European armies and ultimately a world war.

U.S. president Woodrow Wilson was initially opposed to war. He believed it was not America's fight, but a "natural raking-out of the (European) continent's pent-up jealousies."

When Wilson was nominated to a second term, his campaign slogan was "He kept us out of war." But his isolationism began to thaw on May 1, 1915, when a German U-boat torpedoed RMS *Lusitania*, a British ocean liner en route from New York to Liverpool. The ship sank within minutes, taking 1,195 civilian men, women, and children—including 123 Americans—to the bottom.

Then, on January 16, 1917, the British Admiralty intercepted a coded message from German foreign minister Alfred Zimmermann to Mexican President Venustiano Carranza, which proposed a German-Mexican alliance. The message also stated that Germany would begin unrestricted submarine warfare in February. Additionally, if the United States did not remain neutral, a Mexican declaration of war against its northern neighbor would be greatly rewarded. Such rewards would include German support for Mexico in the conquest of previously lost territory in Texas, New Mexico, and Arizona. Carranza rejected the offer, and the British released the message to Wilson, who made it available to the American press.

On January 31, 1917, Germany announced the renewal of unrestricted submarine warfare. This included attacks against neutral American vessels. Three days later, the United States broke diplomatic relations with Germany, expelled all German diplomats from the country, and ordered the U.S. ambassador to Germany home.

On April 2, Wilson asked Congress for a declaration of war. On April 6, Congress voted on and granted the declaration—an act that ultimately sent 112,000 American men and boys to their graves.

Wilson entered the war with great personal reservation. Unlike his allies who fought for the continued existence of their nations and colonial holdings, Wilson, ever the idealist, fought for a "new world order." He wanted his soldiers to fight a "war to end all wars; in order to make the world safe for democracy."

On June 17, 1917, Wilson's new world army under the command of Gen. John Joseph "Black Jack" Pershing began landing on the shores of France. Several days later, Pershing, nicknamed "Black Jack" because he had previously commanded black troops, met with French officers in Paris. There, he proclaimed, "Lafayette, we are here," referring to the Marquis de Lafayette who as the French liaison to Gen. George Washington served the patriot cause during the American Revolution.

Over the next several months tens of thousands of American soldiers organized into the American Expeditionary Force (AEF) poured onto the continent. The "doughboys" were a welcome site to British and French troops who had been bled white by nearly three years of bitter combat at places which now have ominous-sounding names like Ypres, Verdun, and the Somme.

American soldiers in the AEF were affectionately known as "doughboys." The origin of the moniker is still debatable. The most popular explanation suggests the buttons on the soldiers' uniforms resembled a type of deep-fried dumpling then known as a doughboy. A second explanation suggests that uniform polish of the period appeared doughlike when it became wet. A third explanation suggests that during the Mexican War, infantryman often used flour to cover the blemishes on their white belts. This is quite possible given that many historians believe the term *doughboy* was coined as early as the mid-19th century.

America's commitment to pulling its share of the war load was never in question. How American forces would be led and deployed was. Whether American units would be broken up and absorbed into the armies of France and Great Britain was often the subject of debate. Ultimately, Pershing agreed that the AEF would fall under the umbrella of French armies and corps. American units would, however, retain their identities and exist as full American divisions. In time, those divisions would prove their worth, and by war's end the AEF was fighting as an independent Army of the United States.

In 1918, the last year of World War I, a number of decisive battles were fought, pitting the AEF and its veteran European allies against the Imperial German Army. Though not nearly as experienced as its friends or foes, the AEF quickly adapted to the harsh realities of 20th-century combat, and American soldiers and marines were soon moving against the enemy as the spearhead of the allied armies.

For the most part, World War I was viewed by Americans back home as something of a lark—a brief adventure where American farm boys and factory workers were able to spend a year enjoying French wine and French women and maybe killing a few Germans on the side. But it was far more than that. Of the approximately four million Americans who swelled the ranks of the armed forces, over two million served "over there." Of that number, more than 112,000 Yanks died (half were killed in action, half died of disease and other causes) and another 234,000 were wounded. Casualties suffered by the British, French, Italians, Russians, and Germans were appallingly greater—a terrible result of mixing 18th-century linear tactics and 19th-century massed formations with 20th-century weapons.

Making matters worse, of the average 200 men in a 1918 American infantry company, 180 were young, inexperienced recruits. And, with the exception of the Marines, many American soldiers had never fired a weapon in training. They learned quickly in the killing fields of France.

At ground zero, infantrymen on both sides lived for months in freezing, wet, rat-infested trench works. If disease didn't kill them, there was a good chance the enemy's high-explosive shells or poisonous gas would. The trench dwellers were also subjected to sniper fire or the occasional enemy trench raiders—fierce fighting commandos who would slip into the opposing force's works at night, and then attack them with pistols, knives, brass knuckles, and entrenching tools before the defenders knew what had hit them.

When the trench dwellers were ordered to attack the enemy's works, they had to climb up and over their own breastworks and into the open where the enemy's machine guns were trained on them. Those who survived the first few minutes usually found themselves advancing in line with their buddies, bayonets fixed to the upper receivers of their bolt-action rifles.

The lines, led by whistle-blowing officers, moved across an open muddy field often strewn with rotting corpses and unexploded munitions. As they advanced, the enemy poured a murderous fire into their ranks. Bullets and red-hot shell fragments whistled past their heads. Unfortunate souls around them were ripped to shreds. When one man fell, another rushed forward to plug the gap. If the attackers survived to reach the enemy's lines, they had to struggle through rolls of barbed wire, and then rush the enemy with the bayonet. Once within the enemy's trenches, the fighting devolved into a grisly close-quarters action.

To make life easier for the attacking force, a technique known as a creeping or rolling barrage was implemented. This technique consisted of a forward-rolling curtain of exploding shells moving just in front of a line of advancing soldiers. The gunners would shell an identified line of enemy trenches and then lift and move to the next at the moment the attacking infantrymen had reached the first line. Ideally, the line of shellfire moved 50 yards (or less) in front of the attackers.

The reality was that battlefield communications in World War I had not advanced much beyond combat communications during the American Civil War. Thus the artillery fire was based on a calculation of the speed at which the infantrymen were expected to advance from one point to the next. This was determined to be 50 yards per minute. But battery commanders, fearing they might kill friendly forces, often ordered their gunners to increase the distance of the intervals and shorten the time of each barrage. The result was that the barrages hit far behind enemy trenches, which were still strongly defended while the attackers were exposed without adequate covering fire. Worse, the barrages often ceased completely while the attackers were struggling to get through barbed wire defenses.

Historian John Keegan wrote:

> The simple truth of 1914–18 warfare is that the massing of large numbers of soldiers unprotected by anything but cloth uniforms— however they were trained, however equipped—against large masses of other soldiers protected by earthworks and barbed wire, and provided with rapid fire weapons; was bound to result in very heavy casualties among the attackers.

When there was a lull in the fighting, soldiers attended to housekeeping matters: cleaning weapons and equipment, reconstructing trench works, bailing water, tending the wounded, and burying the dead. They entertained themselves by writing letters, playing cards, sharing stories, and dreaming about girls back home. Occasionally, they would be treated to a "dogfight" between opposing airplanes above the lines.

The airplane, still in its infancy, debuted in World War I. In the early years, airplanes were used strictly for reconnaissance purposes. But by 1918, aircraft on both sides were fitted with machine guns and bomb racks, and aviators became full-fledged combatants tasked with bombing and strafing enemy ground forces and attacking their warplanes and obser-vation balloons. The airplanes fought either in groups or as lone hunters.

Despite the carnage, the war was a watershed event in American mili-tary history. America, as a nation, marshaled all of its expansive resources for a global cause, and the American soldier, for the first time, began to develop a reputation for courage and tenacity often unmatched by his allies or his enemies. Beyond that, America's officer corps, under the lead-ership of Pershing, demonstrated to its allies that administrative efficiency in modern warfare was every bit as important as battlefield heroics.

CHAPTER 3

CANTIGNY

(MAY 28–31, 1918)

The crossroads town of Cantigny, in France's Somme River region about 60 miles north of Paris, was the site of America's first action of the war and a decisive victory for the "doughboys" of the American Expeditionary Force. The battle—involving some 4,000 soldiers of the soon-to-be-famous 1st Infantry Division, also known as "the Big Red One"—resulted in the defeat of a far more experienced German army under the command of Gen. Oskar von Hutier.

Cantigny, having been occupied by Hutier's forces since March, was situated on a commanding plateau overlooking the wooded countryside. From that position the Germans were able to both observe the Allied movements below them and conceal German movements in the rear.

The Americans, under the command of Lt. Gen. Robert Lee Bullard, had received orders to move up and into a line of trench works within striking distance of the plateau in April. Prior to their deployment, they were addressed by General Pershing: "You are now to go against a victorious enemy under new and harder conditions," said Pershing. "All our Allies will be watching to see how you conduct yourselves. I am confident that you will meet their best hope." They did indeed, and beyond what even Pershing believed possible.

Once in the trenches, the Americans began to suffer under the strain of a near-constant artillery barrage of shells carrying both high explosives and poisonous gas. The Germans knew the doughboys had positioned themselves to attack. And it was later discovered that the German artillerists had been specifically ordered to "target Americans" in an attempt to kill or break the spirits of the doughboys whom the German commanders were beginning to fear. Rumors had been circulating throughout the ranks of the German army that the Yanks, though untested, were natural warriors. A demoralizing rumor for the German soldier, and it proved to be true.

On the eve of the attack, Gen. Erich von Ludendorff (technically, Field Marshal Paul von Hindenburg's subordinate quartermaster general) launched his Third Great Offensive aimed at winning the war by year's end. Ludendorff's attack was different from his previous two—the first in March, the second in April—which had been launched to destroy French and British armies. The Third Great Offensive, launched across the Chemin des Dames ridgeline, had as its primary objective the seizure of the Marne River crossings and ultimately Paris. As a result, French general Henri Philippe Pétain withdrew much of his artillery, which was slated for support of the Americans. More than 350 heavy guns remained, but would have to be pulled out of action as soon as the Americans achieved their objectives at Cantigny.

The American attack could have been cancelled justifiably, and in hindsight perhaps should have been. But Pershing viewed it as an opportunity to demonstrate to both the Allies and the enemy that AEF could fight.

In the early morning hours of May 28, the Germans were awakened by a fierce artillery bombardment, which lasted for the better part of an hour. Then at 6:45 A.M., whistles were blown along the American trench lines, and soldiers from the division's 28th Infantry Regiment clambered over the top and into the open. The Americans advanced over a distance of 1,600 yards in three waves at marked intervals behind a "creeping barrage." In addition to French artillery, the attacking waves of American infantry were supported by French aircraft, tanks, and mortar and flamethrower teams. By 7:20 A.M., the German trench lines were reached and the enemy routed.

"We laid down and started to shoot and it was our good fortune that the second wave reached the place at this time," American sergeant Boleslaw Suchocki would later write.

"About twenty Dutchmen came out of the holes, threw down their rifles and stood with their hands up. The doughboys didn't pay any attention to this but started in to butcher and shoot them. One of the doughboys on the run stabbed a Dutchman and his bayonet went clear through him."

In the town, minor fighting occurred as the doughboys flushed the Germans from their hiding places in shops and houses. French soldiers with flamethrowers were called up to assist in clearing the cellars of buildings.

Lt. Clarence Huebner, who would command the 1st Infantry Division in the next great war, watched in horror as one of his badly burned enemies rushed from a flamed-out cellar. It was "just as I had seen rabbits in Kansas come out of burning straw stacks," he recalled. The German ran a few yards, then dropped dead. The incident was not isolated.

Cantigny was seized in less than 45 minutes, and 240 German soldiers had been captured. The Americans quickly constructed a line of trenches, laid barbed wire, positioned machine guns, and reinforced former German positions in preparation for German counterattacks. That night, Bullard received a message from Pershing directing "in most emphatic terms, that the 28th must, under no conditions, quit the position it had taken." In Bullard's mind, the message implied a lack of faith on the part of Pershing and his French and British counterparts in the fighting prowess of American soldiers. The doughboys proved otherwise.

By early evening of May 30, seven violent German counterattacks had been launched against the AEF. At least three of the attacks were battalion-strength. But in all cases, the enemy was beaten back with machine guns, rifles, and light artillery.

The AEF's most serious problem was the enemy artillery, which relentlessly pounded the American positions. The French heavy artillery had been withdrawn after the Americans seized the town. The Germans knew it, and their cannoneers were allowed to fire with impunity. When the smoke cleared, the doughboys had suffered more than 1,600 casualties, including 199 killed. But the U.S. Army held the town.

During the night, much of the weary 28th Infantry was relieved by soldiers of the 16th Infantry Regiment, also of the Big Red One. The following day, the remaining companies of the 28th were relieved by the 16th.

The green American army had proven its mettle against a battle-hardened foe. "The moral effects to flow from this proof of the reliability of the American soldier in battle far outweigh the direct action itself," said Bullard.

The 28th became known as the Lions of Cantigny. Eventually adopting as its regimental insignia the heraldic black lion and white shield of France's Picardy Province, the "Lions of Cantigny" became known as simply the Black Lions.

Despite its loss at Cantigny, the German high command was not convinced of the doughboy's combat prowess. Cantigny was an American cakewalk in the minds of German generals: The AEF had yet to experience losses suffered on the scale of its allies or its enemies, and therefore the American soldier was still overrated. That disregard would transform into a healthy respect near the town of Château-Thierry.

CHAPTER 4

CHÂTEAU-THIERRY

(MAY 31–JULY 10, 1918)

Following the American victory at Cantigny, American Army and Marine forces became involved in a three-battle campaign to save Paris. The campaign, which lasted a total of 41 days, resulted in the defeat of Imperial German forces near Château-Thierry, a Marne River town some 35 miles from the French capital. The battles include the defense of the Marne River line, the battle of Belleau Wood, and the capture of Vaux.

DEFENSE OF THE MARNE RIVER LINE

The brief defense of the Marne River in late-spring 1918 ushered in one of the defining campaigns of modern American military tradition—Château-Thierry.

On May 30, as the U.S. 1st Infantry Division was strengthening its newly won positions at Cantigny, the 3rd Division was being rushed toward the Marne River in order to stem the tide of German forces advancing toward Paris in Ludendorff's Third Great Offensive.

Launched on May 27, Ludendorff's attack struck the French 6th Army between Rheims and Soissons and pressed toward the Marne River. The French 6th Army, under Gen. Denis Auguste Duchene, quickly fell back on the Marne and began preparing its defenses in the area around Château-Thierry. There, the German army had reached its deepest point in France and was poised to either cross the river or seize one or more of its bridges. The French were desperate. Under-strength and demoralized, many French officers and rank-and-file soldiers were close to panic.

"C'est terrible! C'est affreux!" shouted two French officers rushing into AEF headquarters. Pershing's chief of operations, Col. Fox Conner, purportedly had to calm them down "as if they were children." Conner then picked up the telephone and requested 3rd Division headquarters.

The American 3rd—under the command of Brig. Gen. Joseph Dickman, a 61-year-old veteran of the American Plains Indian wars—had had little training in trench warfare. But with the Germans driving hard toward the Marne, the 3rd was soon making its way from Château-Villain to Château-Thierry by train, a journey faster than marching, but requiring several days. The French railway service had been slowed by fears of the German advance.

The division's 7th Machine Gun Battalion, however, had its own vehicles, and so arrived 24 hours after vacating its post at la-Ferte-sur-Aube.

Reporting to the French commander on the afternoon of May 31, the 17 squads of the 7th were immediately dispatched to the defense of the Marne bridges at Château-Thierry. First to arrive were 15 doughboys, a recently graduated West Point officer, and two brand-new Hotchkiss machine guns, neither of which had ever fired a shot in anger. The officer, 1st Lt. John T. Bissell, quickly positioned his guns on the south bank of the Marne. Other Americans from the 7th soon arrived.

By dawn of the following morning, the 7th had placed most of its guns on the south bank. A portion of one company was also posted on the north bank where, if the Germans attacked, they were to fight a delaying action. The men on the north bank were also responsible for forward reconnaissance, but were to fall back on the south bank if the enemy attacked in force.

That night, the Americans were hit by a German artillery barrage, wounding 14 machine gunners. But the gunners held their positions.

The following day, the Germans attacked in force. North of Château-Thierry, the enemy smashed into Belleau Wood, seizing the adjacent high ground and the nearby village of Vaux. However, they were unable to break through the 7th's defenses and enter Château-Thierry. The Americans had set up their guns in such a manner that they covered most of the town's streets, and they poured a terrific volume of fire into the advancing enemy. The Germans attempted to screen their movements with smoke, and they constantly pounded the American positions with artillery and mortars. Eventually, numerical superiority prevailed and the doughboys were forced to fall back, but not before the initial infantry elements of the 3rd Division began pouring into the region.

By June 3, the American division's main body arrived at Château-Thierry and began deploying along the line. Pershing later noted, "the conduct of the machine gun battalion in the operation was highly praised by Gen. (Henri) Pétain."

In fact, it had been a remarkable delaying action fought by inexperienced American troops. They not only held their positions until the end, they prevented the Germans from ever crossing the Marne into the southern sector of Château-Thierry. Unfortunately, they received no credit in the American newspapers. The papers instead published headlines that read "Germans stopped at Château-Thierry with help of God and Few Marines." It was an oversight the U.S. Army would never forget. (During World War II, senior army planners deliberately left the Marines out of the European theater fearing that army soldiers might again be upstaged by the leathernecks.) But the worst of the Château-Thierry campaign was yet to come. And the Marines would indeed play a leading role.

BELLEAU WOOD

Part of the Château-Thierry campaign of 1918, the Battle of Belleau Wood was a grim struggle on an old French hunting preserve near the village of Bouresches where American Marines launched their most famous attack of the war. The battle, which began in early June, helped stem the tide of the German push toward Paris. And it signified the coming of age of the modern U.S. Marine Corps.

In late May, while the American 1st Division was mopping up at Cantigny and the 3rd was busying itself with the defense of the Marne River crossings, the American 2nd Division was assembling in Meaux, some 40 miles east of Paris. The 2nd, a hybrid Army-Marine division under the command of U.S. Army major general Omar Bundy, had been previously ordered to relieve the Big Red One at Cantigny. But those orders were cancelled and the division was instead hurried toward the village of Coupru. Once there, they were to reinforce French general Jean Degoutte and his embattled XXI Corps d'Armée.

On the road, the division encountered lines of civilian refugees moving in the opposite direction along with weary French troops falling back from the front. The Frenchmen, pale and hollow-eyed, looked curiously at the fresh-faced Americans who were laughing and singing on the backs of trucks rolling toward the sound of the guns "as if they were going to a party." One of the French soldiers purportedly shouted to a group of Marines, "Turn back, retreat, the Germans are coming." Marine captain Lloyd Williams responded, "Retreat, hell, we just got here." Williams, whose words would be indelibly carved in Marine Corps lore, was later killed in the fighting.

Northeast of Coupru, the Germans were making spirited thrusts along the front and threatened to break the line. The 2nd Division was about to make history.

The 2nd was a unique mix comprised of the 3rd Infantry Brigade (army), the 4th Infantry Brigade (marines), the 2nd Field Artillery Brigade (army), and supporting units.

The 4th Brigade of Marines, commanded by U.S. Army general James G. Harbord, was considered to be "the most professional element of the doughboy army." The brigade was comprised of the 5th and 6th Marine Regiments, commanded by Marine colonels Wendell C. Neville and Albertus W. Catlin respectively, and the 6th Machine Gun Battalion of Marines under the command of Marine major Edward W. Cole.

On June 2, advance elements of German Army Group "Crown Prince" reached Belleau Wood and began digging in opposite Degoutte's XXI Corps. Two days later, the Germans launched a vigorous attack against the XXI Corps, specifically Bundy's division.

Ordered to "hold the line at all hazards," Marines positioned behind their earthworks, adjusted their sights, and waited. Soon, a creeping artillery barrage approached the Allied lines, struck, and passed over the Marines. Behind the barrage, the Germans were seen advancing in orderly assault waves. "The devils are coming," shouted Marine captain John Blanchfield in a thick Irish brogue.

The attack was impressive: A wall of gray-coated Imperial German infantrymen pressed forward with bayonets fixed. But they were soon beaten back by rifle fire from Harbord's Marines, who were knocking down Germans at distances of up to 800 yards. The leathernecks worked over the front ranks and then started on the second, chambering rounds and squeezing triggers just as coolly as they had done on the rifle ranges at Parris Island, South Carolina, and Mare Island, California, where most had mastered their deadly trade. The accuracy of the fire shocked the Germans. The relaxed manner in which the Marines handled their bolt-action rifles while being attacked amazed both the French and American armies.

Degoutte himself was also impressed with the Marines' performance, but he was consumed with far weightier matters: The war was taking a physical and emotional toll on French soldiers. The Germans were within striking distance of Paris. Though repelled by sharpshooting Marines, the enemy's attack appeared to have been a determined assault; and the French general was unsure of what lay before his army in the dark woods.

Degoutte believed he needed to seize the initiative. He would attack before the enemy had a chance to do so again.

No prior reconnaissance had been made of Belleau Wood which the Germans held in great strength, an unfortunate reality for any attacking force. Nevertheless, on June 5, Degoutte ordered Bundy to attack Hill 142, a commanding rise on the eastern edge of the woods.

Just before sunrise on June 6, Harbord's Marine brigade moved forward. The advance elements were four neatly dressed lines of leathernecks from the 5th Marine Regiment under the command of Neville, a future Corps Commandant. With bayonets fixed and front, the Marines crossed a wheat field dotted with bright red poppies and advanced toward the trees. As they neared the woods, the staccato of Maxim machine guns echoed across the front. In the rear, French and Americans soldiers listened nervously to the distant chatter of the guns and the cries of the attacking Marines. According to an after-action report issued by Secretary of the Navy Josephus Daniels, "in the black recesses of Belleau Wood the Germans had established nest after nest of machineguns."

The Marines pressed on, their neatly dressed lines being cut to pieces by the interlocking fire of the German guns. "The Marines fought strictly according to American methods," wrote Daniels. "A rush, a halt, a rush again, in four-wave formation, the rear waves taking over the work of those who had fallen before them, passing over the bodies of their dead comrades and plunging ahead until they, too, should be torn to bits." Casualties mounted.

"In my platoon, there were 52 people," said Merwin Silverthorn, a sergeant in one of the advance elements. "Only six got across the first 75 yards."

Most Marines, however, were able to reach the German positions where they routed or killed the enemy with pistols, grenades, bayonets, rifle butts, and bare hands. Many of the Germans fought back savagely. Others raised their hands and begged for mercy. "Kamerad!" they shouted. Most attempting to surrender were killed.

Whenever a nest was taken, a Marine would man the enemy machine gun and swing it around on another German position. A few German counterattacks were attempted, but quickly smashed.

By early afternoon, Harbord had made the decision to order a second attack in two phases: One would strike the eastern edge of Belleau Wood. The other would target the nearby village of Bouresches. Both, involving battalions of the 5th and 6th Marines, would kick off at 5 P.M.

Floyd Gibbons, a war correspondent for the *Chicago Tribune*, located 5th Marine headquarters and requested permission to go forward with the attack. "Go as far as you like," said Neville. "But I want to tell you it's damn hot up there."

Just before zero hour, a young lieutenant preparing to lead his platoon forward looked at Gibbons. "If I were you I'd be about 40 miles south of this place," the lieutenant said. "But if you want to see the fun stick around. We're going forward in five minutes." Colonel Catlin was heard saying to his men, "give 'em hell, boys."

At 5 P.M. the first waves went over the top. As they crossed one of the wheat fields, the German machine guns began their terrible chatter. The first American elements were instantly cut down, and one of the lines faltered momentarily. Gibbons then watched in amazement as Gunnery Sgt. Dan Daly—a two-time Congressional Medal of Honor winner—dashed out in front, and then turned to face his Marines. "Come on you sons of bitches," Daly roared above the whistling hailstorm of lead. "Do you want to live forever?"

The Marines continued to press the attack. A portion of the woods was gained, as was Bouresches, but at terrible cost. By the end of the day, some

1,087 Marines were dead, wounded, or missing in action. And with only a foothold gained on the edge of the woods, those numbers would rise dramatically over the next 20 days.

The attacks of June 6 would become the stuff of legends. One report, the Navy secretary's, stated that some of the leathernecks were barechested and screaming at the tops of their lungs when they rushed the terrified Germans.

Gibbons, having previously filed a story touting the early successes of the AEF, suffered a serious facial wound during the second attack, which cost him an eye. But his friends at the army's press office received word he had been killed. Gibbons had previously requested that the Marines be identified as a separate force in his story. Army censorship rules forbade any identification of American units, a fact that frustrated many correspondents, particularly those who covered the Big Red One's victory at Cantigny. Gibbon's comrades, however, argued that the Marines were not a unit, but a separate arm of service. That, combined with the belief that Gibbons was dead, resulted in the granting of his request as a final tribute to his service as a reporter.

Gibbons survived, but the natural rivalry between the U.S. Army and Marines was ratcheted up several notches.

The following day, headlines in most of the world's English-language newspapers cheered the Marines' victory, which only contributed to the Corps' already legendary reputation. U.S. Army officers chafed under the glowing—sometimes undeserving—attention given the Marines by the press. For instance, American newspapers referring to the fighting at the Marne River bridges at Château-Thierry (a few days prior to Belleau Wood) published headlines that read "Germans stopped at Château-Thierry with help of God and Few Marines." The Germans in fact had been stopped at Château-Thierry by the 7th machine gun battalion of the U.S. Army.

On June 7 and 8, the Germans counterattacked. The Marines repelled the thrust. On June 13, the Germans attacked with poisonous gas followed by an infantry assault. And for nearly two weeks thereafter both American and German artillery pounded various sectors in and around Belleau Wood. The Marines (though temporarily relieved by a battalion of the army's 7th Infantry Regiment) struggled throughout the period to clear the woods of resisting Germans. Unfortunately for both sides, the latter tenaciously fought to hold the same.

On the evening of June 25, after a fierce artillery pummeling, Neville's Marines moved into the northern sector of the woods where the Germans began surrounding en masse. The following day, Harbord sent a message from General Pershing's headquarters. It read, "Woods now U.S. Marine Corps' entirely."

The downside of Belleau Wood was that by the end of the battle, five thousand men of the original 8,000-man Marine brigade were either dead or wounded. That number was greater than the cumulative losses suffered by the Corps since its founding in 1775. The Corps would not suffer as many casualties in a single fight until the Battle of Tarawa in 1942.

Elliott D. Cooke, a U.S. Army officer, would later write, "a bitter price to pay for a piece of woods that stank of high explosive, crushed shrubbery, and scattered human flesh. Dead men littered the ground and lay hidden in every thicket and rocky cleft. Even the living walked out in a sort of shell-shocked daze." But Belleau Wood would forever belong to the Corps.

Degoutte, promoted to commanding general of the French 6th Army, changed the name of the woods from "Bois de Belleau" to "Bois de la Brigade de Marine." And the Germans—believing the Marines to be something akin to "shock troops"—nicknamed their foes *teufelhunden* (translated into English, devil dogs).

"The Marines are considered a sort of elite Corps designed to go into action outside the United States," read a German intelligence report following the battle. "The high percentage of marksmen, sharpshooters, and expert riflemen, as perceived among our prisoners, allows a conclusion to be drawn as to the quality of the training in rifle marksmanship that the Marines receive. The prisoners are mostly members of the better class, and they consider their membership in the Marine Corps to be something of an honor. They proudly resent any attempts to place their regiments on a par with other infantry regiments."

Days after the battle, Assistant Secretary of the Navy Franklin Delano Roosevelt authorized the wearing of Marine Corps emblems on the collars of enlisted men's uniforms (a privilege previously reserved for officers) in recognition of "splendid work" at Belleau Wood.

"It took them 20 days to go through that forest," Marine Corps Commandant Gen. Charles C. Krulak said during a memorial service on the edge of Belleau Wood in 1998. "Twenty days of little sleep, little food, poison gas, machine gun fire, artillery, loneliness and death. In those 20 days, they beat back five German counterattacks, fighting off more than four divisions of crack German troops. They did it with their rifles, their bayonets and sometimes with their fists."

CAPTURE OF VAUX

The capture of the town of Vaux was a "perfectly executed" operation and the closing shots of the Château-Thierry campaign.

While the 2nd Division's Marine Brigade was slugging it out in Belleau Wood, the 3rd Brigade (army) was also suffering heavy losses on the southeastern stretch of the XXI Corps' line. And they had gained little ground to show for it.

Shelling was incessant. On June 21, the Germans launched a three-day series of devastating gas attacks, inflicting 170 casualties on members of the brigade's 9th Infantry Regiment. And morale was being sapped along the lines.

Despite the fact that the Germans had been driven from the field during the defense of the Marne River and the seizing of Belleau Wood and Bouresches, they had not withdrawn from the region. French general Stanislas Naulin, having recently assumed command of the XXI Corps, expressed his concern to General Bundy about what he perceived to be a dangerous "gaping hole" existing in the lines near the town of Vaux. The German army's position was such that it controlled two hills on either side of Vaux—Hill 204 on the right and Hill 192 on the left—as well as a grove of trees, La Roche Wood, left of town. Vaux was not simply a place on the map where two opposing armies faced one another: It was a critical point which had to be taken in order to protect the AEF's interior lines and ultimately Paris.

Unlike Belleau Wood, however, the infantry tasked with seizing the town would not advance blindly for lack of intelligence. Colonel Arthur Conger, the 2nd Division's newly joined intelligence officer, thoroughly interrogated refugees from Vaux and captured German prisoners. In so doing, his office was able to piece together raw information and draw accurate diagrams detailing practically every inch of the town, including building floor plans and the disposition of enemy troops. Conger's work was considered nothing short of a "little masterpiece."

The battle commenced on July 1 at 5 A.M. when Allied artillery opened fire on the German positions at Vaux. For the next 12 hours the firing intensified. At 5 P.M., advance elements of the 23rd Infantry formed their lines for attack. At 5:57, the shelling began to take the form of rolling barrage, moving 100 yards every 2 minutes toward the German lines. Three minutes after the barrage began, American infantry stepped off toward Vaux advancing close behind, but well out of range of the barrage.

The 23rd advanced quickly toward Hill 192 and La Roche Wood. The 9th Regiment advanced on the town and a French regiment moved against and took Hill 204.

The artillery proved to be very effective. The Germans caught in the open were either dead or dying. Others who had taken cover attempted to resist the American infantry advance after the artillery had passed beyond them. But their positions were quickly flanked and captured. In less than an hour, AEF forces had seized their objectives, including a railroad line east of town, and were busy digging in preparation for an enemy counterattack.

The capture of Vaux signaled the end of the Château-Thierry campaign. Ludendorff's Third Great Offensive had been halted. The Americans had proven they could fight. But the toughest fighting for the AEF would begin in two weeks.

CHAPTER 5

SECOND MARNE TO MEUSE-ARGONNE OFFENSIVE

(JULY 15–NOVEMBER 11, 1918)

Following the American victories at Château-Thierry, American soldiers and Marines participated in a series of three final engagements which ultimately battered the German army to its knees. The battles include Second Marne, St. Mihiel, and Meuse-Argonne.

SECOND BATTLE OF THE MARNE

The Second Battle of the Marne was a turning point in the war, which began with a German offensive followed by a major Allied offensive. The seesaw battle, which lasted from mid-July to mid-September, drove the Germans back to pre-1914 positions. (First Marne took place in September 1914, more than two years before the United States entered the war.) And having proven their worth during the Château-Thierry campaign, American soldiers would find themselves among the advance elements during Second Marne.

Seeds for Second Marne were sown in May when Allied forces began developing a plan to attack and reduce a rounded salient (or bulge) in the lines along the Marne River. The salient, which was approximately 30 miles wide, pushed 25 miles deep into the Allied front, thus making the lines more difficult to defend. Additionally, German infantry was still within striking distance of Paris. If the salient broke, the Allies would be hard-pressed to prevent the enemy from advancing on the French capital.

In order to reduce the salient, a two-pronged attack plan was proposed which would drive the Germans back to a more linear position. In early July, however, intelligence reports indicated the Germans were planning an all-out attack. The decision was then made to let the Germans attack. The Allies would prepare their lines to absorb the shock. They would let the Germans exhaust themselves against stiff Allied resistance. When the weary Germans fell back on their own lines, the Allies would counter-attack.

The battle opened on July 15 with the launching of the German attack. Referred to as the *Friedensturm*, or Peace Offensive, by German general Erich Ludendorff, the attack against the Allied lines was something of a last-ditch effort that failed miserably two days after it began.

Striking in two wings from the east side of the salient, Ludendorff hoped to cross the Marne, trap Allied forces on the southern side, seize a vital stretch of railroad, and gain access to the Surmelin Valley. From there, he would be able to launch an attack on the French capital.

It was not to be.

The Germans struck the Allies along a bend in the Marne which was defended by Brig. Gen. Joseph Dickman's U.S. 3rd Division, specifically the 30th and the 38th Infantry Regiments. The 30th, under the command of Col. Edmund Luther "Billy" Butts, was positioned on the extreme left of a mile-and-a-half stretch of the Marne that blocked the passage into the Surmelin Valley. In the center was the 38th under Col. Ulysses Grant McAlexander. On the extreme right was an independent French division.

McAlexander was a warrior in the purest sense of the word. Armed with a Springfield rifle instead of the standard officer's pistol, he ordered his men not to let "anything appear on the other side (of the river) and live."

Just after midnight on July 15, the Germans began crossing the Marne on small boats and across hastily constructed pontoon bridges. The 3rd Division's machine guns opened up. Several enemy boats were capsized and a substantial number of enemy soldiers were forced off the bridges and into the water where they had to swim to the opposite side. At 3:30 A.M., the Allies were hit by a creeping barrage with German infantry following close behind.

The French line collapsed and many of the French soldiers fled to the rear in a panic. The 30th was also beaten back, but only temporarily. With both forces withdrawn, the 38th's flanks were dangerously exposed. Fighting in three directions, McAlexander's men held. In one instance, a single doughboy company launched a violent bayonet attack against the Germans who were pressing them on the right. Still, the eventual outcome seemed grim for the men of the 38th. According to one French officer, "having received orders to hold on at any cost, they got killed only after having accounted for at least three times as many as the enemy."

Late that afternoon, Butts's 30th Infantry pushed the advancing enemy into the 38th's positions where the two divisions were able to crush them. The Germans were halted and driven back. It was their final offensive of the war.

"I have never seen so many dead," Lt. Kurt Hesse of the German 5th Grenadiers would later write. "I have never seen such a frightful spectacle of war. On the other bank the Americans, in close combat, had destroyed two of our companies. Lying down in the wheat, they had allowed our troops to approach and then annihilated them at a range of 30 to 50 yards. 'The Americans kill everyone,' was the cry of fear on July 15—a cry that caused our men to tremble for a long time."

> For their stalwart stands, the 30th and the 38th Infantry Regiments earned for the 3rd Division the title Rock of the Marne.

Ludendorff's *Friedensturm* was stopped cold by the Americans. The Germans were tired, demoralized, frightened, and sick, their ranks having been ravaged by an influenza epidemic. Making matters worse for the enemy, on the night of July 17, American soldiers and Marines—the 28th, of Cantigny fame; the 42nd, also known as the Rainbow Division; and the "Rock of the Marne" 3rd, among others—moved into position for a massive attack aimed at cutting the highway leading from Soissons to Château-Thierry. The doughboys' movements were concealed by both the darkness and a torrential downpour of rain.

The Rainbow Division was named by Brig. Gen. Douglas MacArthur, who once said the 42nd Division stretched "like a Rainbow from one end of America to the other."

The following morning, a brief though devastating artillery barrage commenced. When the barrage lifted, 24 Allied divisions, including 9 American divisions led by the 1st and 2nd Infantry Divisions advanced toward the German army. The 1st was under the command of Maj. Gen. Charles P. Summerall. The 2nd was under the command of Maj. Gen. James Harbord, former commander of the famous 4th Brigade at Belleau Wood. The attack was to be known as the Aisne-Marne Counteroffensive (or the Second Battle of the Marne).

The fighting was sharp along the entire front, with much the fighting being done by the 1st and 2nd. By nightfall, the enemy had been driven back in some places as much as five miles.

Over the next few days, AEF forces began encountering near-fanatical resistance.

On the morning of July 19, a message was wired from one future Marine Corps commandant to another. It was destined to become one of the legendary dispatches in American military history. The message read:

> To: Major [Thomas] Holcomb. I am in an old abandoned French trench bordering on road leading out from your C.P. [command post] and 350 yds. from an old mill. I have only two men out of my company. We need support, but it is almost suicide to try and get here as we are swept by machine-gun fire and a constant barrage is on us. I have no one on my left and only a few on my right. I will hold. [Clifton] Cates, 2nd Lt.

The fighting along the front stiffened over the next month, ultimately devolving into a bloody slugfest. Fresh American divisions, including the "Rock of the Marne," were hurled forward against the enemy.

By early August, the Germans had stemmed the American and French advance along the Vesle River. The Germans then began terrorizing Allied troops with numerous mustard gas attacks. But the Marne salient had been substantially reduced, the Germans fell back toward the Chemin des Dames, and the threat to Paris had been all but eliminated.

American casualties suffered during Second Marne were heavy. Of the 250,000 men involved in the fight, some 50,000 were dead or wounded. On the plus side, the American soldier had established himself as a tenacious warrior, worthy of the respect of any combatant anywhere in the world.

That respect was finally justified on August 10 when the AEF was reorganized as an independent army with Pershing as commander.

ST. MIHIEL

With the salient reduced in the Marne region, the Allies focused their attention on the Somme and St. Mihiel. The Somme was primarily a British, Australian, and Canadian operation wherein German forces were beaten back, thus reducing a salient in the Amiens region. At St. Mihiel, Pershing and his newly created 1st Army were tasked with eliminating another salient—25 miles wide and 15 miles deep—which had been formed along the lines in late 1914.

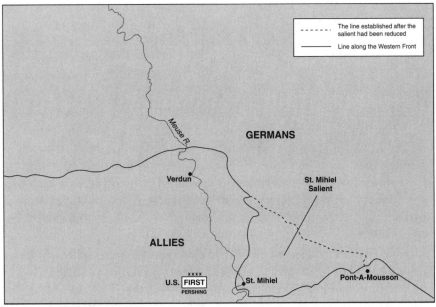

The St. Mihiel Offensive.

Leaving a few American divisions under French command defending the Vesle River, Pershing established 1st Army headquarters in the

St. Mihiel region, south of Verdun, in mid-August. Soon thereafter, he was joined by three U.S. Infantry Corps. The force included I Corps, composed of the 2nd (including two Marine brigades), the 5th, the 82nd (which would become the 82nd Airborne Division in World War II), the 90th, and the 78th Infantry Divisions; IV Corps, composed of the 1st (the Big Red One), the 42nd (the Rainbow Division), the 89th, and the 3rd (Rock of the Marne) Infantry Divisions; and V Corps, composed of the 4th and the 26th Infantry Divisions, and the 15th French Colonial Division. Pershing also commanded a French Colonial Corps.

St. Mihiel proved to be one of the most significant battles of World War I. No contest in the war was regarded as more successful or definitively complete than the attack on the salient. It was also the first battle of the war in which an independent American army engaged the enemy, and small unit leaders were able to operate under their own initiative. The latter was accomplished as a result of senior commanders devising for and providing junior officers with clear, concise operational orders, and then giving those young officers the freedom to act.

Pershing initially lacked tanks and artillery—he received both from the British and the French—but what he lacked in weaponry, he more than made up for in tough men and talented officers. One of the better-known combat commanders at St. Mihiel was Lt. Col. George Smith Patton Jr., destined for eternal glory as the bold "Blood and Guts" general of the next great war.

In February, Patton had established the AEF's Light Tank School near Langres. With no tanks in the American arsenal, he and his students trained in plywood simulators. A turret mounted on top was fitted with a medium machine gun. The entire contraption was mounted on a rocking mechanism to simulate movement over rugged ground while trainees fired at stationary targets. Patton was a strict taskmaster, demanding of his men perfection in everything from tactical maneuvers to clean uniforms and crisp salutes.

In late March, Patton received his first shipment of Renault light tanks from the French. A second shipment followed within two months. By June, Patton had established two tank battalions, the 326th and 327th, making him the commanding officer of the 1st Tank Brigade. At St. Mihiel, he would direct his men from the front.

Another St. Mihiel commander destined for fame in the next great war was newly promoted Brig. Gen. Douglas MacArthur. Having commanded troops in defense of the Marne River, he was known for his rakish appearance, elegant manners, and utter fearlessness in the face of the enemy. He often led his men on trench raids, personally armed with nothing more than a riding crop. His distinctive attire—sweaters, satin neckties, and jaunty caps (he never wore a helmet or a gas mask)—earned him such affectionate monikers as "Beau Brummel" and "D'Artagnan of the AEF."

A third commander who would achieve fame was quiet Col. George Catlett Marshall Jr., the future Army chief of staff who would become famous for his Marshall Plan, which rebuilt Western Europe after World War II. Known as the "wizard" for his mastery of operational detail, Marshall was responsible for planning much of the attack against the St. Mihiel salient.

At 1 A.M. on September 12, Allied artillery consisting of 2,800 guns began pounding the German positions. At 5 A.M., the guns ceased fire, and a brigade of MacArthur's Rainbow Division clambered over the top and began moving toward the enemy lines. Lurching forward in support were the men and machines of Patton's 1st Tank Brigade which quickly bogged down in the mud.

Overhead, biwinged bombers and pursuit planes were throttling forward of the American ground formations. The aircraft, part of an enormous Allied air armada of some 1,500 planes, were flying at treetop level. Heavy, blowing rain and fog greatly reduced visibility along the front edge of the salient, grounding most of the planes on the first day. But several hundred eager pilots, dismissing the poor weather conditions, flew their craft low and managed to strafe and bomb German trenches, roads, and concentrations of troops and vehicles. They were also able to knock down a few enemy planes and observation balloons, as well as reconnoiter the enemy's front and rear areas.

Commanded by U.S. brigadier general William "Billy" Mitchell, the air armada was composed of American, British, French, and Italian squadrons. And as such, it was the largest concentration of air power that had ever been assembled.

As the sun crept over the trees, the first lines of advancing American riflemen appeared to those in subsequent lines as something akin to a pageant. "West and east, the waves of assault rolled steadily forward with a power and irresistibleness that made this scene more resemble an especially staged spectacle than an important operation," said U.S. Army major Walter Wolf. "It was just like a picture."

Strategically, St. Mihiel appeared to be a relatively painless operation. German leadership was ineffective along the front and German ranks by September had thinned dramatically. Prior to the attack, the Germans had begun withdrawing toward the better-prepared defenses of the Michel Line on the back edge of the salient. Consequently, when the Americans struck, the already-withdrawing Germans were forced to fight a difficult rearguard action.

At the tactical level, the situation was far different. Weather and terrain were major obstacles for the advancing Americans. Like the pilots, the soldiers were hampered by rain and fog. The rain also turned the ground into a thick muck that slowed the infantry and, at times, became impassable for the tanks. Additionally, the Germans had previously dug an extensive network of—and their defenses were well fitted with—wire obstacles and machine gun nests.

On the afternoon of the first day, Patton and MacArthur met on the battlefield, and according to one account:

> The lieutenant colonel [Patton] sported a Colt .45 pistol with an ivory grip and his engraved initials. A pipe was clenched in his teeth. The brigadier [MacArthur] wore a barracks cap and a muffler his mother knitted for him. As they spoke to each other, a German artillery barrage opened up and began marching towards their position. Infantrymen scattered and dove for cover, but the two officers remained standing, coolly talking with each other.

The performance of the Americans at St. Mihiel astounded their allies. A British officer touring a field which had been recently crossed by doughboys advancing under fire was taken aback by the bodies which he said, "lay in long orderly lines, a tribute to the high spirit and splendid courage with which they had advanced to certain death." And in many instances, death was almost certain.

The horror of the action made more of an impression on American Marine general John A. Lejeune, who commanded the Army's 2nd Division at St. Mihiel, than did the operation itself. Years later, he recalled, "In war, if a man is to keep his sanity, he must come to regard death as being just as normal as life and hold himself always in readiness, mentally and spiritually, to answer the call of the grim reaper whenever fate decrees that his hour has struck."

By mid-September, 7,000 doughboys were either dead or wounded in the U.S. Army's largest military operation since the Civil War. But the victory at St. Mihiel was considered a textbook operation. Some 16,000 Germans had been captured along with 250 artillery pieces, and the salient had been eliminated. The opposition was tough, but the American soldier proved himself to be just as formidable. Pershing attributed the army's success to the American character. "Americans were the products of immigrants who had possessed the initiative and courage to leave the Old World … to make a mighty nation out of a wilderness," he confided to Brig. Gen. Dennis Nolan, his chief of intelligence. "Americans had the willpower and spirit that Europeans lacked."

Pershing was clearly pleased with the performance of his soldiers, but he knew there was no time for glory-basking. A far greater challenge was just 60 miles up the road.

MEUSE-ARGONNE

An epic clash of arms often described as "the big show," the six-week-long Meuse-Argonne Offensive was the greatest battle of World War I in which the Americans participated. The battle began with approximately 600,000 doughboys and marines. Before it was over U.S. ranks swelled to more one million men.

In the weeks prior to the offensive, French marshal Ferdinand Foch had planned a grand Belgian-British-French-American attack: In Foch's words, a "tout le monde à la bataille." The goal was to simultaneously strike the Germans with 220 Allied divisions (including 42 U.S. divisions) along various sectors of the western front, thus driving the enemy behind his own borders before winter.

The U.S. Army's objective was to capture the rail hub at Sedan, thus cutting the German army's rail net, which supported its troops in France and Flanders. This would force the enemy to fall back on German territory in the sector.

The majority of the Americans tasked with seizing the rail hub were fresh from the fighting at St. Mihiel. Having been regrouped, most without rest, roughly 500,000 doughboys were marched 60 miles to a line just north of the medieval fortress town of Verdun. There, the new lines extended approximately 30 miles from the Meuse River to the Argonne Forest. Though overseen by Pershing, the shifting of forces from St. Mihiel to the Meuse-Argonne sector was planned and directed almost entirely by Col. George Catlett Marshall, the U.S. Army's future chief of staff. It was considered one of the great logistical feats of the war.

Opposing the Germans was the U.S. 1st Army. This included the American I Corps, composed of the 92nd, the 77th, the 28th, and the 35th Infantry Divisions; V Corps, composed of the 91st, the 37th, and the 79th Infantry Divisions; and III Corps, composed of the 4th, the 80th, and the 33rd Infantry Divisions. Supporting the infantry were dismounted cavalry troopers operating as scouts; a brigade of Renault tanks; and 821 biplanes, 604 of which were flown by American pilots. The Americans outnumbered the Germans nearly eight to one. But the terrain was rugged. The enemy was defending strong positions he had been fortifying for nearly four years. And he was initially determined to hold.

Though officially launched on September 26, the Meuse-Argonne Offensive began with an intense artillery fire which opened up on the German positions at 11:30 P.M. on September 25. The barrage ceased briefly at some point after midnight, and then resumed at 2:30 on the morning of September 26. Three hours later, the shelling ceased, whistles were blown along the American lines, and, with bayonets fixed, the doughboys went over the top and began their assault against the enemy lines.

The III Corps quickly penetrated the Germans' 1st defensive line and struck the second in the Argonne Forest. But the V Corps encountered stiff enemy resistance at a lookout position near the village of Montfaucon d'Argonne, where German forward observers were directing their own artillery against the doughboys. After a day and a half of fierce fighting, the Americans drove the Germans from the lookout position and captured Montfaucon. But the delay in the advance enabled the Germans to regroup and avoid being routed. Additionally, the Americans had advanced so quickly they had literally outrun their supporting artillery: The cannoneers finding it difficult to move their guns across the rugged terrain. The ground had been churned "as if by a giant's plow" by shelling going back to the bloody Battle of Verdun in 1916. Wire entanglements, shattered trees, and new growth added to the morass, which had to be crossed.

On September 28, the artillery caught up with the infantry, and the Americans pushed the enemy back nearly two miles along the entire front, bringing the III and V Corps within striking distance of the German third—the fabled Hindenburg (or Seigfried)—line. Desperate to stop the advance, German commanders cannibalized other units on the front and hurried fresh divisions toward the Americans in the Meuse-Argonne area. For the next several days, the advance ground down to a grisly slugfest with casualties mounting on both sides.

On October 1, Pershing received a message from Foch suggesting that fresh French troops be sent forward into the area between the French 4th Army and the American 1st Army. The two armies were linked on the extreme American left which was positioned in the forest. In Pershing's mind, the idea was a veiled attempt to break up his new independent army and bring American units back under the umbrella of the French Army. The general, rejecting the offer, ordered his left wing—the 77th Infantry Division—forward "without regard of losses and without regard to the exposed conditions of the flanks." The order proved costly.

Two days later, a German counterattack surrounded elements of three battalions of the 77th Infantry Division. The combined elements became known as the Lost Battalion. The Americans fought ferociously, but they had no blankets or overcoats, and they began to run short of food, ammunition, and medical supplies. The wounded were often patched up with bloody bandages removed from the dead. Worse, the Americans were unable to get water. Thirst-crazed soldiers crawled into the open toward a nearby stream where German machine gunners cut them to pieces. To prevent this, U.S. major Charles S. Whittlesey posted guards with the order to shoot any man who ventured toward the stream.

American pilots attempted to drop supplies to the battalion, but the drops fell too short and landed within the German lines.

When all seemed lost, the Germans demanded the battalion's surrender. Whittlesey allegedly replied, "Go to hell." Another story suggested he said, "Come and get us."

On October 4, the American army resumed the offensive and attempted to gain ground along the entire front, but the gains were minimal in the densely wooded Argonne, and the losses high. The Germans also rushed more of their most experienced troops into the fray. Within days, I Corps was reinforced with the 82nd Infantry Division.

On October 7, the 82nd battled its way toward—and successfully relieved—the Lost Battalion. During that same action Pfc. Alvin C. York, a Tennessee backwoodsman and one-time conscientious objector, became the ranking man in his platoon after the unit suffered heavy casualties. Seizing the initiative, York led a seven-man team of doughboys against a strong German position. The team killed at least 25 Germans and captured 4 officers, 128 soldiers, and more than 30 machine guns.

York, an expert rifleman, later described the action as something akin to a Tennessee turkey shoot. "Every time one of them raised his head, I just teched him off," he said.

Bypassing the rank of corporal, Pfc. York was promoted to sergeant and awarded both the American Congressional Medal of Honor and the French Croix de Guerre. Personally decorating York with the latter, Foch said, "What you did was the greatest thing accomplished by any private soldier of all the armies of Europe." Whittlesey also received the award for his stalwart defense as commander of the Lost Battalion.

For two weeks following the relief of the Lost Battalion, U.S. forces pressed the Germans. But the latter continued to resist and launched several counterattacks. By October 10, the Allies had punched through the Argonne, and were advancing through open country, but the AEF was temporarily slowed. Four days later, a sharp attack by the Americans resumed against the Germans, but the advance again stalled.

French premier Georges Clemenceau began to question Pershing's leadership and the ability of the AEF to operate as an independent army. Having no grasp of conditions at the front, the premier believed the Americans were moving too slowly against the enemy. Foch knew better. He was a pure warrior who had both an intuitive feel for the battlefield and a tremendous respect for Pershing and the AEF. He also knew that the enemy had nearly exhausted his reserves hurling every man forward into the fight against the Americans. Consequently, Foch refused to back Clemenceau's move to have Pershing relieved.

During that same period, Pershing reorganized the 1st Army and relinquished his command to Lt. Gen. Hunter Liggett. The U.S. 2nd Army was created and command of it was given to Lt. Gen. Robert Lee Bullard. Both the 1st and 2nd Armies were brought under the Army Group command of Pershing.

By mid-October the British army on the Allied wing had broken through the Hindenburg Line.

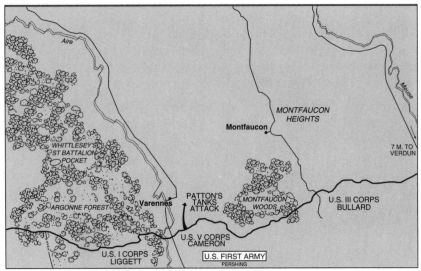

The Meuse-Argonne Offensive.

On November 1, the Americans began a rapid advance against the final German defenses.

"While the high pressure of these dogged attacks was a great strain on our troops, it was calamitous to the enemy," Pershing stated in an after-action report. "His [the enemy's] divisions had been thrown into confusion by our furious assaults, and his morale had been reduced until his will to resist had well-nigh reached the breaking point." Pershing also noted that once an enemy division was engaged, it was almost impossible for German commanders to effect its relief. Without adequate reinforcements, the Germans were forced to break up other tactical organizations and rush them toward crisis points on the line. As a result, the German units on the line quickly thinned and became separated.

On November 6, soldiers of the Big Red One were poised to take the city of Sedan when they were halted. However, the honor of capturing Sedan was to be given to the French Army.

On November 10, Bullard's 2nd Army launched an all-out attack in an attempt to capture the town of Montmedy. The following day at 11 A.M., the Germans surrendered.

In the 6-week offensive, some 27,000 American soldiers had been killed and another 96,000 had been wounded. But the "war to end all wars" was over.

PART 2

WORLD WAR II

CHAPTER 6

INTRODUCTION TO WORLD WAR II

World War II will forever be one the great watershed events in all of history. In terms of military history, the war was unparalleled. The efficiency with which armies, navies, and air forces had evolved to kill their foes was appalling. For the first time in history, massive numbers of casualties were inflicted upon opposing force combatants, their homelands, and even their families without the aggressor actually seeing the results of his own hand. The war was fought on every continent of the globe, claimed more than 57 million lives (half of that number being civilian losses), and ended only when a weapon was employed capable of vaporizing hundreds of thousands of people in less time than it would take to squeeze the trigger of an M-1 rifle.

Many historians and political scientists have since claimed that World War II was simply the catastrophic conclusion of an unresolved World War I—a legitimate argument considering the factors that spawned the second great war. First, Germany was forced to submit to economically ruinous policies of the (peace) Treaty of Versailles. A global economic depression soon compounded the problem. Europe, essentially in a state of political and economic chaos, became a breeding ground for fascism, Nazism (essentially a German adaptation of fascism), and Communism. All three ideological movements glorified military service and tradition, rejected any semblance of an international community, fostered a sense of near-fanatical nationalism, and accepted war as both a natural state of man and a means by which national goals could be achieved. Worse, those movements began to proliferate throughout a world.

The League of Nations, the predecessor organization to the United Nations, had been created after World War I. Its founders hoped that the league would create an international environment wherein nations would strive to work together. But individual state concerns over the growing economic crisis forced countries to look to themselves for salvation.

A brutal military society within Japan assumed control of that nation. The Japanese leadership then came to the conclusion that its military power and influence would have to serve as a means of protecting its own teetering economy. To conquer and to expand was to survive.

GERMANY AND ITALY ADOPT SIMILAR APPROACHES

In 1933, Adolf Hitler, a former corporal in the Imperial German Army, capitalized on Germany's beaten-down soul by promoting the idea that Germans were not only a great people, but were physically, intellectually, and culturally superior to all others. Elections were held and Hitler's National Socialist German Workers Party (Nazis) won a majority of the seats in the Reichstag, or legislature. Hitler, the party's leader, became chancellor (prime minister). The following year, German president Paul von Hindenburg died. The offices of president and chancellor were fused together. Thus Hitler became the undisputed leader, der Führer, of Germany. Rejecting the provisions of the Versailles peace treaty, Hitler reinstated the military draft and began rebuilding the German armed forces.

Italian dictator Benito Mussolini invaded and occupied Ethiopia. The League of Nations voted minor sanctions against Italy, but they were wholly ineffective.

The world was racing toward war. Great Britain was determined to avoid conflict, as was France. Neither trusted the new Union of Soviet Socialist Republics (Communist Russia). And Russia did not trust any nation in the capitalist West, including those of the Nazis and the fascists.

In 1936, Hitler remilitarized the Rhineland. Two years later, he annexed Austria and threatened Czechoslovakia with invasion. The leaders of Britain and France, hoping to avoid war, met with Hitler and Mussolini in Munich, Germany. In an attempt to appease der Führer, they agreed to

Germany's occupation of the Sudetenland (a slice of Czechoslovakia) with the promise from Hitler that his military adventures were over. The following year, Hitler took all of Czechoslovakia and invaded Poland. With German forces moving toward their doorstep, the Soviets began to seize Latvia, Estonia, and Lithuania.

Meanwhile Japan, an aggressive nation ruled by a deified emperor and his warlords, had emerged as a major world military power. If nothing else, that country certainly had the most powerful armed forces in Asia and the western Pacific. Japan invaded and conquered Manchuria, later China proper, and was thrusting throughout the Pacific. Again, the impotent League of Nations took no action.

In late 1940, Germany, Italy, and Japan signed a treaty—the Tripartite Pact—which basically stated that Japan recognized the rights of Germany and Italy to establish a new order in Europe. In turn, Germany and Italy accepted Japan's authority to establish the same in greater east Asia.

When Japan moved into French Indochina (the future Vietnam), the United States embargoed steel, iron, and fuel exports to Japan. The following year, Japanese assets were frozen in the United States, Great Britain, and the Netherlands.

On the morning of December 7, 1941, the Japanese struck the harbor, the main naval base, and an army airfield in Pearl Harbor, Hawaii. The attack, which caught the American military completely by surprise, was devastating. But Pearl Harbor was not an isolated event. Japan simultaneously struck American and British naval and air targets with a dizzying array of attacks throughout the Pacific.

On December 8, President Roosevelt asked Congress for a declaration of war against the Japanese empire. That afternoon Congress officially declared war on Japan. Three days later, Hitler declared that a state of war existed between Germany and the United States. Mussolini and Italy followed suit. The President again went before Congress and asked for declarations of war against both Germany and Italy. His requests were granted, and the United States was at war.

A DIFFERENT WAR

World War II marked a dramatic shift in the way in which America's wars would be fought. For the first time in history, there was an enormous divide between the combat soldier and the support soldier. The latter's sole responsibility was to keep the former healthy, fed, equipped, and in the fight. Most soldiers fell into the support role category. If they did hear shots fired in anger it was usually the distant *whooomp* of artillery shells striking targets miles away. For the front-line combat soldier, life was not only physically and emotionally taxing, it was mentally draining.

Unlike previous wars, World War II placed a new requirement on the individual combat soldier: He would have to have brains as well as brawn to survive contact with the enemy. For centuries, battlefield weapons had been tools that needed only a stout heart, a strong back, and perhaps a little hand-and-eye coordination to employ them. Even after the first practical application of gunpowder in the 15th century, muzzle-loading—later breech-loading—weapons were not complex weapons to operate. However, by World War I, individually served weapons had evolved to the point that a level of cognitive skill was needed to use them effectively.

In the Second World War, the operational art among the lower ranks of the infantry took on a new level of sophistication which had only been seen among special trench-raiding commandos in the previous war. Soldiers in World War II had to know how to operate everything from rifles to grenades to light machine guns and mortars. They also had to be familiar with maps, compasses, and radios. Land navigation skills among the most junior leaders were important. Battlefield medicine had also reached a fairly high level of sophistication and was administered by young medics and hospital corpsmen who marched alongside the riflemen.

The primary tactical lesson of the First World War was that massed infantry forces attacking headlong into interlocking machine-gun fire or long-range rifle fire would suffer unacceptable losses. To counter this in World War II, small maneuvering units led by young corporals and sergeants and even younger lieutenants were deployed across the front. Instead of attacking the enemy in great frontal waves, the preferred method was flanking him, cutting him off from his lines of supply, or bypassing him altogether and then pressing on toward the objective.

On-the-job training was simply not sufficient. Precombat instruction was critical. If the unit leaders—officers or noncommissioned officers—were killed or severely wounded, the most senior private soldier had to immediately assume the reins of command. Such would not be considered a tall order in a small professional army of the late 20th or early 21st century. But soldiers who made up the infantry units of World War II were mostly draftees, many of whom had never finished or even attended high school.

"The skills and imagination expected of a rifleman in 1944 would have reduced most nineteenth-century soldiers to bewildered inaction," wrote author John Ellis in *The Sharp End*, "Yet this war was fought almost entirely by non-professionals, by men conscripted from civilian life and thrown into battle after only three months or so of training."

Unlike World War I, where the initial rally of the call to arms was seen as something of an adventure, soldiers in the Second World War viewed their calling as a solemn duty to destroy the forces of evil. After all, the Japanese navy had struck a peacetime America on her home soil at Pearl Harbor. The Japanese army was brutalizing civilians and prisoners of war throughout its conquered territories in the western Pacific. And word was soon leaking out about the atrocities Hitler was committing against entire segments of the civilian population both in Germany and in Nazi-occupied territories. (That said, the death camps and the extent of the horror committed in such were not fully known until Allied forces found and liberated them near war's end.)

World War II, for the American fighting man, was a global war in the purest sense of the term. True to the Marines' hymn, "in every clime and place" did the soldiers, sailors, airmen, and marines find themselves slugging it out with the enemy.

STRATEGY AND SCOPE

The White House had adopted a policy of "Europe first." The consensus was that Germany posed a greater, more immediate threat to world freedom. It was believed that Japan, also dangerous, could be contained in the western Pacific. When the Allies were done with Hitler, his cronies, and to a lesser extent Mussolini, they planned to sort out the Japanese. In the end, American resources brought to bear in the Pacific were so great that by the time Germany folded in the spring of 1945, Japan, too, was on the verge of collapse.

In the European theater, American combatants fought across the Atlantic Ocean and the Mediterranean Sea, from the deserts of North Africa to the craggy rocks of the Italian boot; from the French coast to the deep black timber of the northern Belgian and German forests.

In Europe, the war was characterized by enormous drives across open countryside. The drives were slowed only by a river here, a hill there, and the myriad towns liberated along the way. At times, the American army advanced so far so fast, it literally outran its supply lines. Fighting was bitter. Drawing almost spiritual strength from their old Prussian military tradition, German soldiers were superbly trained and brave to a fault. And excepting the often irrational orders issued from Berlin, the German armed forces were well led.

In the Pacific theater, Americans battled across the length and breadth of the Pacific Ocean from the Aleutians chain in the far north to the fringes of the Australian waters in the south. In between—particularly the stretch from the Solomon Islands to the Ryukyu Islands—they fought terrible actions on- and offshore from tiny isles and atolls with previously unheard-of names like Tarawa and Tulagi. To a lesser degree, American combatants also found themselves in the vast albeit isolated backcountry of the China-Burma-India theater.

American GIs in the Pacific faced a much different war than those fighting in Europe. The American military leadership adopted a strategy of "island hopping" or leapfrogging from island-to-island. (Who actually conceived the plan is still the subject of debate. The most widely held view is that Gen. Douglas MacArthur came up with the idea. Another belief is that the plan was the brainchild of an officer on the staff of Adm. Ernest J. King. However, British naval correspondent Hector C. Bywater outlined a similar strategy in his 1924 best-seller, *The Great Pacific War*.) "Island hopping" involved striking and seizing one island, then moving on to the next. Islands or certain bases on islands that were deemed to be of over-whelming enemy strength—like the great Japanese strongholds at Rabaul, Truk, and Wewak—were bypassed and isolated from supply convoys, thus reducing their strategic value. This strategy left the bypassed islands or bases to die on the vine without sacrificing the lives of American soldiers, sailors, and Marines who would otherwise have to storm those beaches.

The Japanese were fanatical warriors: In most cases they literally fought to the death. Of the Japanese combat tactics, none was more feared by the Americans than the infamous banzai charge: a suicidal human-wave assault led by sword-wielding officers against American positions. The charging Japanese would rush forward, screaming "Banzai!"—a battle cry meaning "10,000 years," suggesting "may the emperor (or the empire) last 10,000 years." Such attacks were a major gut-check for the American soldiers and Marines. Disregarding their own losses, the Japanese would invariably close with the Americans where the fighting would become hand to hand. To physically prepare themselves for the inevitable assaults, American Marines were known to do pushups and isometric exercises in their fox-holes during lulls in the fighting.

At the tactical level, senior Japanese officers who survived losing battles almost always committed suicide. To them death was preferred over returning home in disgrace or being captured by their foes, also considered shameful. Consequently, American and Allied soldiers who were taken prisoner were viewed as weak-souled cowards who did not deserve to be treated decently. And they were not. Some of the worst atrocities of the 20th century were committed against American prisoners of war by their Japanese captors. Beheadings, forced starvation, and all manner of ingenious methods of torture were common.

In both the Pacific and European theaters, the Allies achieved total supremacy in the air. This enabled pilots and crews to roam above the battle areas and deep behind the enemy's lines, bombing, strafing, transporting troops, and gathering intelligence while simultaneously denying the enemy the ability to do the same. Enormous fleets of strategic bombers were also sent forward against the enemy's great war-making industrial centers.

At sea, the largest and the last of the world's great naval battles were fought. And the great-gunned battlewagons would give way to aircraft carriers, the latter becoming the capital ships of the modern fleets.

In the end, hostilities ceased when atomic bombs were dropped over two Japanese cities. And for the first time in history, military leaders realized that total war was no longer a survivable option.

CHAPTER 7

CORAL SEA

(MAY 3–8, 1942)

In the Battle of the Coral Sea, Japanese naval forces steaming toward Australia were stopped cold by the U.S. Navy in the first-ever great aircraft carrier battle and the first clash in which two opposing naval forces engaged without ever coming within eyesight of one another. But it was not without great cost. Japanese aircraft sank the American aircraft carrier *Lexington* and damaged the *Yorktown*. The Americans sank the Japanese carrier *Shoho*, destroyed much of the carrier *Zuikaku*'s air group, and severely damaged the carrier *Shokaku* and two cruisers.

By the spring of 1942, Japan's armed forces had achieved a string of stunning victories in the Pacific. Following the previous December's attacks on the American military installations at Pearl Harbor and the subsequent captures of Guam, Wake Island, and Hong Kong, the Japanese had seized the Philippines, Malaya, Singapore, the Dutch East Indies, Burma, Siam, and a host of atolls and islands with only minor losses in terms of warships, aircraft, and men. Plans were also in the works for a sweeping westward expansion into India and Ceylon, as was a southward thrust toward Australia. But Isoroku Yamamoto, admiral of the Japanese fleet, had convinced military planners that the destruction of

American ground, naval, and air forces should be their primary objective. Japan could not expect to win a protracted war against the resource-rich United States. The only way to defeat the Americans was to destroy their forces quickly, or damage them so severely that they would have no choice but to agree to a negotiated peace.

Though they had suffered setbacks and had yet to win a significant victory, American forces in the region were growing stronger daily.

U.S. general Douglas MacArthur, the supreme commander of Allied forces in the southwest Pacific, had begun building a base near the harbor town of Port Moresby, New Guinea. The town only had a small port and an airfield. But it was shaping up to become a major military installation. The Japanese had naval superiority in the western Pacific, but senior Japanese commanders knew that if their fleet was going to be able to operate unmolested in the south, it would have to take Port Moresby.

To do so, the Japanese launched Operation Mo, a plan to seize Port Moresby and simultaneously land troops on the island of Tulagi in the southern Solomon Islands. The operation also called for a minor landing in the Louisiade Islands southeast of New Guinea. The operation, under the overall direction of Fourth Fleet commander Vice Adm. Shigeyoshi Inouye, involved two aircraft carrier task forces: The first, under the command of Rear Adm. Aritomo Goto, was composed of the light carrier *Shoho*, four heavy cruisers, and one destroyer. The second, under the command of Vice Adm. Takeo Takagi, was composed of the *Shokaku* and *Zuikaku* (two of the carriers which had participated in the attacks on Pearl Harbor), as well as two heavy cruisers and six destroyers. Also under the task forces were troop freighters and supporting vessels.

The two forces were to strike the islet of Tulagi off Florida Island in the Solomons on May 3, and then turn their attentions toward Port Moresby where they would support the landings slated for May 10. Fortunately, U.S. intelligence forces were able to break the Japanese code, nicknamed Magic, and determine that the Japanese were planning something big around the Rabaul area—probably Port Moresby—in early May.

To counter the threat, the calm and deliberate commander in chief of the U.S. Pacific fleet, Adm. Chester W. Nimitz, ordered two carrier task forces into the region. The first was Task Force 17 under the command of Rear Adm. Frank Jack Fletcher and built around the carrier USS *Yorktown*. The second was Task Force 11 under the command of Fletcher's Naval Academy classmate, Rear Adm. Aubrey W. Fitch. This force was built around the carrier USS *Lexington*, affectionately referred to as *Lady Lex* by her crew.

Nimitz was concerned that the enemy vessels outnumbered his own. But as he told his staff, "we should be able to accept odds in battle if necessary." The admiral was gambling on the fact that his carriers could bring more planes to the fight. He also believed that the resourcefulness of the American sailor and airman would ultimately carry the day.

The battle began on May 3 when Fletcher received word the Japanese were landing on Tulagi. U.S. headquarters at Port Moresby simultaneously received a message that the enemy had captured Florida Island.

On the morning of May 4, the two U.S. task forces launched air strikes against the newly landed enemy forces on Tulagi and their supporting vessels offshore. The strike aircraft included Douglas Devastator torpedo bombers, Douglas Dauntless dive bombers, and Grumman Wildcat fighters. The Wildcat was not nearly as maneuverable as its Japanese counterpart, the Mitsubishi Zero-sen, known simply as the "Zero" or "Zeke" fighter. But the Zero was lightly armored, making it easy to kill the pilot, and a short machine-gun burst into its nonsealing fuel tank would easily set the Zero on fire.

As the American planes reached Tulagi, three enemy seaplanes took to the air, but were quickly knocked down. A handful of Japanese surface vessels were also struck.

Later that day, Task Force 44 under the command of Royal Navy rear admiral J. C. Crace joined Fletcher and Fitch. The British contribution consisted of three heavy cruisers—two Australian and one American— among other vessels. Two days later, the three allied task forces were organized into a single group under Fletcher's Task Force 17. Fletcher now had two carriers, eight heavy cruisers, and eleven destroyers.

On the morning of May 7, Fletcher sent Crace with three cruisers and two destroyers toward the Louisiades to intercept any enemy force en route to Port Moresby. Soon thereafter, the American oiler (refueling vessel) USS *Neosho* and its destroyer escort, USS *Sims*, were spotted by Japanese dive bombers. After a brief fight, the *Sims* was sunk. Only six of her crew survived. *Neosho* was reduced to a drifting mass of black smoke and flame. Believing that *Neosho* was a carrier, Japanese planes continued working her over. Meanwhile, nearly 100 aircraft from Fletcher's task force attacked Goto's force, which was steaming toward the Guadalcanal-Tulagi region, and quickly pounced on the *Shoho*, sinking her within minutes.

"Scratch one flattop," flight leader Lt. Cmdr. R. E. Dixon shouted into his aircraft radio. Crews listening in the radio rooms of both *Yorktown* and *Lexington* began cheering.

Hours later, *Shokaku* and *Zuikaku* launched an attack force aimed at finding and destroying the American fleet. En route, they met and engaged U.S. fighters from the *Yorktown* and the *Lexington.* Several of the Japanese planes were shot down and the engagement broke off.

On the morning of May 8, both fleets dispatched scout planes to locate one another's forces. Though still in overall command, Fletcher relinquished tactical command to Fitch; the latter had more experience in carrier-air operations.

The Japanese had the advantage of being partially concealed by overcast weather conditions, whereas the Americans ships were sailing beneath clear skies.

Japanese planes spotted Fletcher's ships just after sunup. Soon thereafter, *Shokaku* and *Zuikaku* were spotted by an American search plane. The signal went out, "Two carriers, four heavy cruisers, many destroyers ..."

Just after 9 A.M., the battle opened in earnest. Fletcher launched an attack force of dive bombers, torpedo bombers, and fighters against the Japanese carriers. Just after 11 A.M., the American pilots located their targets and attacked.

Shokaku was struck first by aircraft from the *Yorktown.* Planes from the *Lexington* followed suit. Heavily damaged and burning from three direct bomb hits, *Shokaku* was unable to stay in the fight. She would be able to recover her surviving planes after their attack on the American carriers, but launchings would be impossible without repairs in port. *Zuikaku,* having previously launched her planes, managed to slip into a nearby rain squall. She would not be damaged at Coral Sea, but she suffered a significant loss of planes and pilots. In fact, some 40 percent of *Zuikaku*'s planes were destroyed in aerial combat over the American fleet.

Just before 11:30 A.M., the *Yorktown* was attacked and struck by enemy torpedo bombers. One bomb penetrated to the fourth deck, killing sailors and setting fires. Flight operations continued and the fires were brought under control.

The *Lexington* was simultaneously attacked and suffered direct hits from two torpedoes and three bombs. The fires below decks were also quickly brought under control. Flight operations continued, and it looked as if she, too, would survive the engagement. Meanwhile, U.S. Navy antiaircraft gunners were blasting away at the enemy planes swarming above them. The Japanese pilots were aggressive and not afraid to attack close, which enabled them to score direct hits. It also resulted in many of their number being blown out of the sky.

By the early afternoon, Takagi's force had been badly mauled. However, having been misinformed by his aircrews, who reported that both American carriers were lying on the ocean floor, he initially believed he had won the day. *Zuikaku* steamed out of the squall, her sailors disheartened to see their sister ship, *Shokaku*, burning on the horizon. Takagi ordered the crippled *Shokaku* home to Japan. The carrier was listing so severely she nearly capsized en route.

American aircrews returning from the attacks on Takagi's fleet found their *own* carriers smoking but still underway. One of them, the *Lexington*, was doomed.

Just before 1 P.M. the *Lexington*'s captain, Frederick C. Sherman, received an encouraging and somewhat lighthearted telephone call from Cmdr. Howard Raymond Healy in damage control central. "We've got the torpedo damage temporarily shored up," Healy calmly reported. "The fire's out and soon we'll have the ship back on an even keel. But I would suggest, sir, that if you have to take any more torpedoes, you take 'em on the starboard side." All at once, a terrific explosion ripped through the *Lady Lex*. The explosion, caused by igniting fuel vapors, resulted in raging fires which quickly swept throughout the ship's interior spaces. Sadly, Healy was killed. (A newly commissioned destroyer would be named for him the following year.)

Within a few hours, all of the *Lexington*'s planes were transferred to the *Yorktown*, destroyers were dispatched to rescue the crew, and Sherman gave the order to abandon ship. Not long after, the last surviving sailor had vacated the *Lexington*'s decks, fire reached her ordinance magazines, and the ship's stern erupted in a great roiling ball of flame and black smoke. Just after dark an American destroyer fired torpedoes into the burning hulk. Veteran sailors who had served on the *Lexington* since she was commissioned in 1927 reportedly wept as she slipped beneath the surface. She was the first American carrier to be sunk in the war.

Fletcher briefly considered launching a night attack, but Nimitz signaled him from Pearl Harbor. The action had been decided. It was time to withdraw.

When the smoke cleared, Admiral Inouye also recalled his forces. Upon learning of Inouye's recall, Admiral Yamamoto fired back with his own message ordering Goto and Takagi to reverse course and "annihilate the enemy." It was not to be.

By sinking the big carrier *Lexington* and other ships, the Japanese navy won a tactical victory at Coral Sea. But it was a Pyrrhic win. The light carrier *Shoho* was lost and *Shokaku* was badly damaged. The Japanese also lost 77 aircraft and 1,074 men. The Americans lost 66 planes and 543 men.

From a strategic standpoint, the Americans won hands down. According to Nimitz, it was "a victory with *decisive* and far reaching consequences." The Japanese had been halted in the western Pacific. They had failed to destroy Task Force 17. And with *Shoho* sunk, *Shokaku* severely damaged, and *Zuikaku* having suffered substantial losses in aircraft and crews, none of the three carriers would participate in the coming Battle of Midway. Had any one of them been there, the results might have been dramatically different.

CHAPTER 8

MIDWAY

(JUNE 4–5, 1942)

The Battle of Midway was a turning point in the Pacific theater of operations. The Japanese fleet, planning to attack Midway Island, was intercepted, engaged, and soundly defeated by American naval forces. The Americans lost one carrier, the *Yorktown*, but four Japanese carriers were sent to the bottom.

Coming on the heels of the Battle of Coral Sea—where the American fleet had halted the enemy's drive toward Australia—Isoroku Yamamoto, admiral of the Japanese fleet, moved to seize Midway Island, an atoll approximately 1,000 miles west of Hawaii. If captured, Midway would serve as both an advance base for future operations against American military installations at Pearl Harbor, and as an early warning station against any American advances toward the Japanese mainland. Beyond that, Yamamoto hoped to lure U.S. admiral Chester W. Nimitz's Pacific fleet into a great naval battle that Japan would win.

Yamamoto knew that time was critical. American forces in the Pacific had to be destroyed if Japan was going to have any hope of either winning the war or suing for an honorable peace.

To accomplish this, Yamamoto brought to bear a vast armada of some 215 warships, including 4 aircraft carriers, 11 battleships, and a variety of cruisers, destroyers, oilers, and freighters carrying some 5,000 amphibious troops (marines). The force was led by the admiral's flagship, *Yamato*, a 70,000-ton battlewagon and the largest warship of its kind ever built.

Yamamoto's primary strike force would consist of a massive aircraft carrier battle group under the command of Vice Adm. Chuichi Nagumo, the famous Japanese naval air chief who had directed the attacks against Pearl Harbor in December. At Midway, Nagumo's group would be composed of the carriers *Akagi* (Nagumo's flagship), *Kaga, Hiryu*, and *Soryu*, as well as two battleships, two heavy cruisers, one light cruiser, and eleven destroyers. Yamamoto also had a close support bombardment group, under Rear Adm. Takeo Kurita. This group was composed of four cruisers slated to support the landings on Midway Island, which of course never took place.

Opposing Yamamoto's force was Nimitz's fleet, composed of three task forces and their subordinate task groups. Task Force 16, under the command of Adm. Raymond Ames Spruance, was composed of the carriers USS *Enterprise* and USS *Hornet*, as well as five heavy cruisers, one light cruiser, and nine destroyers. Nimitz would have preferred his most experienced carrier commander, Adm. William Frederick "Bull" Halsey Jr., at the helm of Task Force 16, but Halsey was hospitalized in Pearl Harbor with a severe case of dermatitis. Nimitz chose Spruance as Halsey's replacement, on the latter's recommendation. Task Force 17, under the command of Rear Adm. Frank Jack Fletcher, was composed of the carrier USS *Yorktown*, two heavy cruisers, and six destroyers. Task Force 8, under the command of Rear Adm. Robert Alfred Theobald, was composed of 5 cruisers and 10 destroyers.

The first phase of Yamamoto's overall Midway strategy was a decoy invasion of the Aleutian Islands chain in the northern Pacific between Alaska and the Soviet Union's Kamchatka Peninsula. To accomplish this, Yamamoto dispatched Vice Adm. Boshiro Hosogaya to the area with a marginal force composed of two small aircraft carriers, five cruisers, twelve destroyers, six submarines, four troop freighters, and supporting vessels.

YAMAMOTO UNDERESTIMATES HIS OPPONENTS

Yamamoto believed that such a force and the threat of attack would draw Nimitz's fleet north to challenge them. Then with his main force, Yamamoto would attack and seize Midway. Once the Americans discovered that Midway was the primary target, they would reverse course and steam south to confront the Japanese fleet. By that time, Yamamoto surmised, Midway would be in Japanese hands. Then the Japanese fleet would be able to focus all of its attention on destroying Nimitz's carriers. Seizing key islands in the Aleutians would also prevent any future American move on the Japanese mainland from that direction. The only flaw in Yamamoto's overall plan was that it depended entirely on Nimitz reacting the way the Japanese admiral predicted he would.

Unfortunately for Yamamoto, the Americans did not put nearly as much stock in the strategic value of the Aleutians as did the Japanese. And Nimitz was never deceived into believing an attack in the north was anything more than a strategic feint.

Beyond that, Yamamoto underestimated the U.S. Navy's ability to crack the Japanese navy's secret codes. Granted, most of the laurels for America's victory at Midway would justifiably be heaped upon the heads of the American aircrews and sailors. They were the ones who ultimately fought and defeated the enemy. But the enemy's defeat would not have been possible were it not for the efforts of the Pacific fleet's intelligence wizard, Cmdr. Joseph John Rochefort.

Living for weeks in the basement of Nimitz's headquarters at Pearl Harbor, Rochefort and a handful of cryptanalysts deciphered Japanese messages and determined what they were planning based on Rochefort's personal knowledge and intuitive grasp of the Japanese psyche. Often unshaven, disheveled, and with little sleep, Rochefort not only predicted a major Japanese offensive, he accurately predicted the time and place.

As Yamamoto assembled his forces for the Midway campaign, messages between his ships and shore stations indicated that an attack on the Aleutians was a diversion, whereas Midway was the primary target. But the only reference to the primary target was the coded designation "AF." Rochefort cleverly devised a way to determine whether "AF" was in fact Midway. He arranged for the open transmission of a false message stating that Midway's water distillation system had malfunctioned and that the island's garrison was short of fresh water. The ruse worked. The Japanese intercepted the message, and reported in code that "AF" was having water problems. Rochefort immediately informed Nimitz that the Japanese intended to attack Midway.

In late May, Yamamoto steamed east across the Pacific. Spruance and Fletcher raced west from Pearl Harbor toward an area just north of Midway to intercept him.

As both fleets were searching for the other's main force, Yamamoto ordered his force in the northern Pacific to launch the decoy. But Nimitz refused to bite. Knowing full well that the Aleutians invasion was a sideshow, he retained his three aircraft carriers for the Midway battle. He did, however, decide to confront the enemy in the Aleutians, thus sending Theobald's Task Force 8, roughly a third of Nimitz's surface fleet, to defend the approaches to Alaska.

THE ATTACK

On the morning of June 3, Japanese planes bombed the U.S. Navy's Aleutian Islands station at Dutch Harbor. Days later, the Japanese landed troops on and seized the islands of Kiska, Attu, and Agattu (all were regained by U.S. forces the following year).

As Nimitz received word that Dutch Harbor was under attack, the big fight was opening in the central Pacific.

During the predawn hours of June 4, Japanese carrier pilots were treated to a traditional warrior's breakfast. Normally, they were served a small meal before battle. But on this day they received trays of rice, soybean soup, pickles, dry chestnuts, and sake (rice wine). There was a sense throughout the fleet that the fate of Japan hinged on success at Midway. On the *Hiryu*, a senior flight officer urged his men to "put their nerve into it (the battle)."

Meanwhile, anxious American combat pilots scarfed down scrambled eggs, orange juice, and coffee; then hurried to ships' ready rooms for a preattack briefing. On the *Hornet*, Lt. Cmdr. John C. Waldron, who would later lead his torpedo bomber squadron in a courageous albeit suicidal attack, issued his attack plan. Attached was a personal letter to his pilots. "My greatest hope is that we encounter a favorable tactical situation," he wrote. "If we don't, and the worst comes to worst, I want each of us to do his utmost to destroy our enemies. If there is only one plane left to make a final run in, I want that man to go in and get a hit. May God be with all of us. Good luck, happy landings and give 'em hell." As noble and poignant as Waldron's letter was, it reflected the overall mood of the American aircrews on all of the carriers and at Midway.

As their task forces rendezvoused some 200 miles northeast of Midway, Spruance and Fletcher sent patrol planes out to find Yamamoto's fleet.

At 5:34 A.M., an American reconnaissance plane sighted the Japanese fleet some 250 miles west of Midway and signaled, "Enemy carriers!"

Eleven minutes later, the same plane signaled, "Many enemy planes heading Midway!" Admiral Nagumo's carriers had in fact launched 72 bombers and 36 fighters for a strike against the island. The attack was led by the *Hiryu's* flight unit commander, Lt. Joichi Tomonaga.

Eight minutes after the second signal was sent, a radar post on Midway detected incoming aircraft, 93 miles out and closing fast. The alarm was sounded across the island. Marines and sailors either scurried for cover or sprinted toward their antiaircraft gun positions. Pilots hurried toward their aging Brewster Buffalo and Grumman Wildcat fighter planes. Within minutes, the Midway-based fighters were airborne. Thirty miles out, they intercepted the inbound Japanese air group, composed of dive and torpedo bombers and the highly maneuverable "Zeke" fighter. The American planes were vastly outnumbered, and, from the standpoint of aircraft performance, outmatched.

By 6:30 A.M., the enemy had passed through the intercepting planes and bombs were falling on Midway. Twenty minutes later, the only raid to be launched against Midway was over. Sadly, of the 26 planes sent to intercept the Japanese strike, only 9 returned, and 7 of those were badly damaged.

Though the first action was a Japanese victory, the battle was far from over. Nagumo had two primary concerns. First, he believed the U.S. fleet was in the area, but his reconnaissance planes had not yet located any American ships. Second, he was not altogether pleased with the raid: Despite the fact that his aircraft had destroyed several buildings and wiped out most of the American fighters sent up against him, about a third of his 108-plane raiding force had been destroyed. Moreover, he had received a message from Tomonaga, who said the runways on Midway were still operational.

Soon thereafter, the flight leader's assertion was confirmed. A loosely organized series of counterattacks were launched against the Japanese fleet by U.S. Navy, Marine Corps, and Army Air Corps bombers from the island. In all cases, they were beaten back and no hits were scored on Nagumo's vessels.

While the Midway-based planes were attacking the Japanese ships, Spruance's task force was launching 116 aircraft toward the last reported position the enemy carriers were sighted. The American planes included a group of Wildcat fighters, a group of Douglas Dauntless dive bombers, and a group of Douglas Devastator torpedo bombers all launched from the *Hornet* and the *Enterprise*. Flying at different speeds and altitudes, the three air groups became separated. The fighters and dive bombers never located the enemy. The torpedo bombers did, with disastrous results for their aircrews.

At 7:15 A.M., the Japanese admiral issued an order that ultimately altered the course of history. Some 93 Japanese planes, armed with torpedoes and armor-piercing bombs, were standing by to defend against an American sea attack. But with no American ships sighted, Nagumo made the decision to have those planes rearmed with incendiary and high-explosive bombs for a second strike on Midway's airfields. As his sailors busied themselves with rearming the planes, Nagumo received a message from one of his reconnaissance aircraft. The American fleet had been sighted and was on course to intercept him.

Frantically rescinding his previous order, Nagumo directed his air commanders to prepare for a sea attack. This meant that many of the planes that had had their torpedoes replaced with bombs would now have to have the bombs removed and the torpedoes remounted. Switching ordinance was a time-consuming operation, and Nagumo knew that every minute was critical.

Making matters worse, Tomonaga's planes returning from their attack on Midway were arriving. They were low on fuel and badly damaged. A strike against the American ships could not be launched until the Midway strike force had been recovered. The aircraft being rearmed on the flight decks were lowered to hangers below decks, and the Midway strike planes began landing.

Just off the horizon, 15 U.S. Navy Devastator torpedo bombers from the *Hornet* spotted smoke plumes in the distance. It was Lt. Cmdr. Waldron's ill-fated squadron. Following the plumes, they found Nagumo's ships.

At 9:30 A.M., the Devastators, each with a crew of three, flew through thick antiaircraft fire and a swarm of some 50 enemy fighters to get to Nagumo's flattops. Without fighter protection of their own, the slow-flying Devastators pressed the attack. Every plane, including Waldron's, was blown out of the sky. One pilot crashed in the sea and survived. Fourteen more from the *Enterprise* attacked. Three survived. The *Yorktown* sent 12 more. Ten were destroyed.

As the American torpedo bombers were being wiped out, Japanese sailors on their flight decks were busily preparing more than 100 planes for an attack against the American fleet. They had recovered all of the surviving planes from the Midway strike and raised the rearmed planes from the hangers back to the flight deck. But they had also lost a lot of time.

At 10:15 A.M., Nagumo ordered his air commanders to attack. Almost at once, 55 Douglas Dauntless dive bombers from the *Enterprise* and the *Yorktown* swept down from 14,000 feet. The Japanese, who were racing against the clock and scanning the horizon and just above it for another run by the torpedo bombers, were caught completely off-guard by the high-altitude, dive-bombing attack.

Known as "the fatal five minutes," the attack literally altered the course of the war. The *Akagi* was struck first, followed by attacks on the *Kaga* and the *Soryu*. The strike was devastating. Armed and fueled aircraft on the flight decks erupted in flames. Torpedoes in hangar decks exploded. Fires swept throughout the ships' lower spaces. All three carriers, completely incapacitated, would sink within hours. About 200 Japanese planes went to the bottom with them.

Forty-five minutes after the first dive bomber nosed down on the *Akagi*, the *Hiryu* launched a counterstrike with approximately 24 fighters and dive bombers led by Nagumo's trusted flight commander, Tomonaga.

Around noon, the Japanese planes were intercepted by American fighters which shot down all but seven of the enemy's dive bombers. The latter broke through the American fighter screen, which sealed the fate of the *Yorktown*. Swooping down on the American carrier, six of the enemy bombers were destroyed. Tomonaga himself was killed, but not before his planes had crippled the ship with four well-placed bombs.

The *Yorktown*'s sailors worked feverishly to extinguish fires, repair damage, and treat the wounded. By early afternoon, the slowed carrier was again operational, underway, and launching fighters. But a second striking force had been launched from the *Hiryu*. Around 2:30 P.M., ten Japanese torpedo bombers and six fighters penetrated the *Yorktown*'s air defenses and struck her amidships with two well-placed torpedoes. Dead in the water, the carrier began listing hard. Fearing that she was going to capsize, the crew was ordered to abandon ship.

Admiral Spruance then ordered 40 Dauntlesses, from the *Enterprise* and the *Hornet*, to hunt and kill the *Hiryu*. Just before 5 P.M., *Hiryu* was sighted. The lead Dauntlesses were intercepted by six enemy fighters, but the American planes that followed struck and mortally damaged the fourth Japanese carrier.

Conceding that his losses were far too great to continue the fight, Yamamoto ended his quest for Midway. In the wee hours of June 5, he ordered his remaining ships to withdraw from the region.

In midmorning, the burning hulk of the *Hiryu* was torpedoed by her own destroyer escort.

To ensure that he would go down with his ship, Rear Adm. Tamon Yamaguchi tied himself to the bridge. The ship's captain accompanied him.

The *Yorktown*, severely damaged and listing badly, was taken in tow to Pearl Harbor. The carrier was escorted by a screen of destroyers. But on June 6, a Japanese submarine was able to slip through, sinking one destroyer and launching two torpedoes into the *Yorktown*. Fortunately, her crew had been previously transferred to other vessels. On the morning of June 7, she rolled over and slipped beneath the surface.

Though the carrier actions were the main event, other lesser engagements took place during the battle, including the sinking of two Japanese heavy cruisers by Midway-based dive bombers and carrier-based bombers on the June 4.

The battle was not without its lighthearted and lucky moments. During the actions against the two Japanese cruisers, a group of 26 Army Air Corps B-17 bombers were dispatched from Midway Island to find the enemy. During the afternoon, several of the B-17s sighted a vessel they identified as a Japanese cruiser and bombed it. Returning to base, they proudly boasted that they had sunk an enemy cruiser in what must have been a record 15 seconds. Several days later, the American submarine *Grayling* eased into the harbor at Midway with an angry crew. The sailors inquired as to why they were bombed by B-17's and forced to crash dive at the exact location the "enemy cruiser" was "sunk."

Regarding the performance of American aviators at Midway, Nimitz said, "our pilots pressed it [the attack] home with resolution and matchless audacity." Indeed, in the early stages of the battle, entire squadrons of American warplanes were wiped out in what were deemed courageous albeit suicidal attacks. In future air attacks, American planes would fight as concentrated air groups.

CHAPTER 9

GUADALCANAL

(AUGUST 7, 1942–FEBRUARY 9, 1943)

On August 7, 1942, exactly eight months to the day after the Japanese attack on Pearl Harbor, America launched its first ground offensive of World War II. The offensive began in the southern Solomon Islands with the amphibious assault on—and subsequent battle for—Guadalcanal.

The Guadalcanal campaign included simultaneous landings on the nearby islets of Tulagi, Gavutu, Tanambogo, and Florida Island. The landings were also the first decisive ground actions aimed at eating away at the Japanese who had extended their lines deep into the western Pacific and threatened Australia.

Located in the southern Solomons some 600 miles southeast of the expansive Japanese base at Rabaul, the island of Guadalcanal—known in Marine vernacular as simply "the Canal"—was a formidable chunk of tropical terrain.

"If I were a king, the worst punishment I could inflict on my enemies would be to banish them to the Solomons," acclaimed novelist Jack London once wrote. And American marines, sailors, and soldiers would soon discover why.

"THE CANAL"

In early August 1942, most Americans had never heard of Guadalcanal. Those who had—primarily merchant seamen, naval officers, a handful of adventurers, and a few academics—viewed it as a remote dot on the far side of the world. To the Marines tasked with taking the island, it was a 92-mile long, 35-mile wide stretch of steaming, rain-forested mountains and dormant volcanoes. Some of the peaks were as high as 8,000 feet. At the lower elevations, the landscape was cut with steep gorges, deep streams, and dark, twisting jungle surrounded by fields of razor-sharp Kunai grass. The terrain, combined with the oppressive heat and humidity, created a virtual breeding ground for malaria- and dengue-carrying mosquitoes, leeches, poisonous snakes, rats, wild hogs, and man-eating crocodiles. And of course there were the Japanese, some 8,400 defenders— mostly Imperial Army units and a handful of men from the special naval landing forces (Marines)—under the command of Lt. General Harukichi Hyakutake.

Hardship and harsh environs were nothing new to the Japanese: The recruits were recent graduates of Japan's physically brutal military indoctri-nation camps. Their leaders had been fighting the Chinese for years. And nearly all were prepared to fight to the death.

It would be tough going for the Americans and they knew it. But the island had great strategic significance. If it was seized, American military forces would be able to use it as a staging area for future operations against Rabaul and destinations north. Additionally, future Japanese invasions of Australia and New Zealand might well be postponed or cancelled entirely if the Americans were in possession of Guadalcanal.

North of the island, across a channel some 20 miles wide, lay Florida Island. Just south of Florida Island was the two-mile-long atoll of Tulagi and two tiny islets, Gavutu and Tanambogo, which were connected by a narrow 500-yard causeway.

From an invasion standpoint, the Canal's coastline offered no natural harbors or inlets. Miles of surrounding coral reef made most of Guadal-canal's beaches inaccessible to any landing force. Only the northern central shoreline offered a suitable entry point for landing forces. The Japanese had landed on the narrow beach in July, and the Americans would be forced to land on the same sand the following month. The upside was that the island's Melanesian population was not supportive of the domineering Japanese invaders. They did, however, welcome the Americans, whom they viewed as liberators.

STRATEGY AND FORCES

The Guadalcanal landings were the brainchild of Adm. Ernest Joseph King, chief of naval operations. Code-named Watchtower, the landings would involve some 100 ships and 16,000 marines. The operation itself was overseen by Vice Adm. Robert Lee Ghormley, a pessimistic commander of the U.S. south Pacific forces. Disturbed by his lack of confidence, the Pacific fleet commander, Adm. Chester W. Nimitz, would replace Ghormley in October with Adm. William F. "Bull" Halsey. In the meantime, Ghormley was calling the shots.

Ghormley's tactical commander was Vice Adm. Frank Jack Fletcher, one of the heroes of the Battle of Midway. Fletcher commanded Task Force 61, the aircraft carrier element responsible for supporting the landings. Task Force 62, the overall troop-ferrying and amphibious element, was commanded by Rear Adm. Richmond Kelly Turner. Task Force 63, encompassing all Allied shore-based aircraft in the south Pacific, was under the command of Rear Adm. John S. McCain (father of American senator John McCain, who also had a distinguished naval career).

The U.S. force tasked with invading the island was the 1st Marine Division, under the command of Maj. Gen. Alexander Archer "Sunny Jim" Vandegrift. A future Marine Corps commandant, Vandegrift, 55, had earned the nickname "Sunny Jim" while fighting Caco bandits in Haiti prior to World War I. Vandegrift's Marines were mostly green recruits fresh from boot camp. They were led by hard-bitten cigar-chewing sergeants whose favorite pastimes were gambling, drinking, and barroom brawling.

The American invasion was to be composed of five landings. One force—led by Vandegrift himself, and composed of elements of the 1st and 5th Marine Regiments of the 1st Marine Division—would hit the beach three miles east of Lunga Point on Guadalcanal. There the Japanese had constructed an airfield that Vandegrift wanted. The second force, a Marine Raider battalion under the command of Lt. Col. Merritt Austen "Red Mike" Edson, would storm Tulagi's south beach. Seizing Gavutu and Tanambogo would be the task of the 1st Marine Parachute Battalion under the command of Maj. Robert H. Williams. The "chutes" battalion, as it was known, was the first airborne unit from any branch of service to see combat in World War II. However, they didn't jump into action. They hit the beach in traditional Marine fashion. (Though the modern Marine Corps still maintains paratroopers for special operations, independent Marine airborne units were disbanded after World War II.) Behind

Tulagi and Gavutu-Tanambogo, elements of the 2nd Marine Regiment were responsible for the south coast of Florida Island.

In New Zealand, where they had undergone a crash course in seizing islands, Vandegrift's marines boarded Turner's troop ships and set sail for Guadalcanal. On the evening of August 5, a Japanese propaganda radio broadcast asked "Where are the famous United States Marines hiding? The Marines are supposed to be the finest soldiers in the world, but no one has seen them yet." The following night, Task Force 62 eased undetected into Sealark Channel between Guadalcanal and Florida Island.

THE BATTLE

Just before 6:15 A.M. on August 7, Naval gunfire and carrier-based dive bombers began softening up the shorelines. Thirty-five minutes later, marines aboard the troop freighters began climbing down cargo nets into hundreds of Higgins landing boats. Soon they were making their way toward the smoking island, over four miles away. Vandegrift had previously assured his men that "God favors the bold and strong of heart." The statement proved to be providential.

Just after 9:10 A.M., the first waves—elements of the 5th Marine Regiment—hit the beach. Other Marine units followed.

The invaders were surprised to find little to no opposition upon landing. As they moved inland, the only sounds were the machetes of the lead elements slashing their way through the thick vegetation and strange birds calling and cackling from the tops of the huge trees. The Japanese were simply falling back deeper into the jungle.

By the afternoon of the second day, the Marines easily seized the airfield at Lunga Point.

The airfield was named Henderson Field in memory of American Marine major Lofton Henderson, a pilot killed during the Battle of Midway. As the airfield was taken and defenses set up, marines simultaneously captured the surrounding hills where the Japanese had positioned artillery.

Meanwhile, Hyakutake received a message from Tokyo ordering him to drive the Americans off Guadalcanal and promising support. The Japanese general was also given command of the 17th Army based on neighboring Rabaul.

Just after midnight, a force of Japanese cruisers and destroyers, under the command of Adm. Gunichi Mikawa, steamed south through a sea passage known as "the slot," an otherwise unnamed body of water running from Bougainville through the Solomons. Entering the region northwest of the Sealark Channel, the enemy completely surprised Fletcher's and Turner's task forces, which were supporting the follow-up landings of supplies for the marines. In the ensuing Battle of Savo Island, the U.S. Navy lost three heavy cruisers. An Australian cruiser was also sunk.

The Japanese suffered the loss of only one cruiser, hit by an American submarine as it returned to Rabaul. But the enemy missed an enormous opportunity to regain control of the island by not following up their victory and sinking the American transports. Feeling vulnerable, Mikawa instead chose to withdraw. It was a fatal decision for which he was severely reprimanded by the admiral of the Japanese fleet, Isoroku Yamamoto.

Still, it was a dark hour for the U.S. Navy and Marine Corps. Fletcher was forced to withdraw, and Vandegrift was temporarily on his own. For the time being, the Japanese had naval superiority in the Solomons. But in the months ahead, that supremacy would be wrested from the enemy during several naval engagements in "the slot." In fact, so many vessels on both sides were sunk in "the slot" that the Sealark Channel and the northern passage into it became known as "Iron Bottom Sound."

Soon after the Battle of Savo Island, Japanese aircraft began a night-and-day bombing campaign on the Marine positions. Though morale never wavered—the Marines knew their navy would return—disease, infection, and attacking Japanese began to sap their strength. For five weeks, the Americans were dangerously short of ammunition and medical supplies. And they were limited to half food rations, though occasionally supplementing their diets with sake (rice wine), canned crab, and rice captured from the Japanese. Still they held.

During that time, the Marines began to realize that though their foes were not invincible, they fought with a fanaticism unfamiliar to Western armies.

One of the more tragic episodes on the island occurred when Lt. Col. Frank Goettge, a division intelligence officer, led a group of Marines on an ill-fated mission to recover a pocket of isolated enemy soldiers near the Matanikau River, a few miles west of Lunga Point. Goettge had been convinced by captured Japanese soldiers that their comrades were starving, sick, and without leadership. The prisoners made the case that they, too, could be induced to surrender.

On the moonless night of August 12, Goettge took a team of 25 picked men out in 2 light motor boats. One of the Japanese prisoners accompanied the team. The Marines believed the prisoner was directing them along the coast toward the location of his fellow soldiers who were ready to call it quits. But it was a trap. As the Marines came ashore, they were ambushed. Goettge was killed. A dying sergeant blew the head off of the accompanying Japanese prisoner. Only three Marines escaped by swimming out to sea and then east along the coast, but not before witnessing maniacally screaming Japanese soldiers rush from their positions, pounce on the wounded and dying, and cut them apart with knives and swords.

The atrocities mounted. In one instance, a Marine patrol came upon an American body that had been bayoneted more than 30 times. As the final insult, the dead American had been castrated and his genitals stuffed in his mouth. Marines became enraged. In many future engagements, no quarter was given the enemy, even when he attempted to surrender. The white flag, in fact, was almost always perceived as a ruse to lure Americans into a trap.

"I've never heard or read of this kind of fighting," Vandegrift wrote in a letter to the Marine commandant's headquarters in Washington. "These people refuse to surrender. The wounded will wait till men come up to examine them and blow up themselves and the other fellow with a hand grenade."

After the ambush of Goettge's party, three companies of Marines were ordered to cut their way toward the Matanikau River. But the Japanese retreated deeper into the jungle. On the occasions the enemy did make a stand, he was defeated. By the end of the week, the companies had killed 65 Japanese. They had also lost four marines.

Meanwhile the Japanese were being reinforced from nearby Rabaul. Vandegrift's forces numbered some 10,000 on the Canal, another 6,000 on Tulagi. Fortunately, the Japanese had grossly underestimated his strength. They believed that there were only 2,000 marines on Guadalcanal. And after witnessing the withdrawal of the U.S. fleet, they also believed that Vandegrift had been permanently abandoned. Hyakutake decided that only 2,000 Japanese soldiers were needed to retake Guadalcanal. That force would be led by the ruthless Col. Kiyono Ichiki.

On August 18, Ichiki and 900 veteran Japanese soldiers from Rabaul landed at Guadalcanal's Taivu Point, approximately 20 miles east of the Ilu River (often mistakenly referred to as the Tenaru River because of the inaccuracy of the Marines' maps during the beginning of the Solomons campaign). At the same time, 500 men of the elite Japanese special naval landing forces came ashore west of the American positions. Once landed and grouped, Ichiki decided to attack rather than wait on the remainder of his force to arrive. Perhaps it was impatience or a fear that his force had been detected, but the Ichiki detachment pressed toward the Ilu.

Marines positioned on the river's west bank sent out patrols in front of their defenses. First blood was drawn on the morning of August 19 when an American patrol led by Capt. Charles Brush made contact with 35 of Ichiki's men who were laying telephone wire. An hour-long firefight ensued wherein 33 Japanese soldiers and 3 American Marines were killed. After defeating the enemy, Brush's Marines fell on the far side of the Ilu where they and their fellow leathernecks braced for the inevitable.

The following day, relief arrived in the form of two groups of U.S. warplanes—fighters and dive bombers—that landed on Henderson Field.

On the evening of August 20, Vandegrift received word that one his native island scouts, Jacob Vouza, had escaped from the Japanese after having been tortured by his captors. Vouza, a retired sergeant major with the British Solomons Constabulary, had been recruited as a scout by the Marines soon after the landings. His information regarding Japanese troops on the island had proven invaluable. However, shortly after the landing of Ichiki's men, Vouza was captured by the Japanese, tied to a tree, and interrogated. Refusing to divulge information about the Americans, he was beaten and bayoneted in the chest, and had his throat cut by a samurai sword. Left for dead, he was able chew through his bindings and make his way to the Americans. Staggering into the Marine lines, Vouza was rushed to an aid station, but not before warning Marine officers that the Japanese were coming and their force was at least 500 strong. (Vouza was subsequently awarded a Silver Star and the title honorary sergeant major of Marines.)

Just after 3 on the morning of August 21, the Japanese attacked along the Ilu River in what would become known as the Battle of the Tenaru River. The first wave consisted of some 200 screaming Japanese soldiers, their sword-wielding officers leading from the front. Despite devastating American artillery, mortar, and rifle fire, the Japanese pressed forward, dying in bunches, never retreating. The attack was momentarily slowed as the enemy struggled to get through the marines' barbed wire. There, American machine guns ripped into their ranks, but the Japanese showed

ALPHA BRAVO DELTA GUIDE TO DECISIVE 20TH-CENTURY AMERICAN BATTLES

no sign of withdrawing. At one point along the line, the enemy broke through and the fighting degraded into a fierce hand-to-hand struggle with swords, knives, machetes, rifle butts, and fists. An American company held in reserve was rushed forward. They counterattacked and drove the Japanese back across the Ilu.

The Japanese then attacked from the sea, near the mouth of the river. That attack was beaten back by machine guns and artillery fire. When the sun rose, the enemy dead littered the area in front of and just behind the Marine lines.

Vandegrift then ordered another reserve force to cross the Ilu upstream and flank the remnants of Ichiki's force. The marines hit and quickly encircled the Japanese. Some of the enemy panicked and tried to break for the sea. There they were destroyed by the newly arrived American fighters and dive bombers. Ichiki himself and a handful of Japanese soldiers escaped into the jungle and made their way toward Taivu Point. There, Ichiki burned his regimental colors, drew his pistol, and shot himself in the head.

Soon thereafter, fast convoys of Japanese troop freighters and warships, both loaded with infantry, began ferrying troops to Guadalcanal. The convoys, referred to by journalists as the Tokyo Express (American servicemen referred to the convoys as the Cactus Express) sailed from Rabaul through the "slot" and deposited troops at various points on Guadalcanal.

Meanwhile, American ships were again braving the waters around the islands, and Vandegrift ordered Marines from Tulagi to Guadalcanal. On a destroyer crossing the channel, the sailors gave the Marines bread and jelly. After weeks of nothing but captured rice on Tulagi, "you'd have thought it was a t-bone steak," said Lt. Eddie Bryan.

On September 7 and 8, the newly arrived Raiders from Red Mike's battalion attacked the enemy at Taivu Point and subsequently gleaned new intelligence about the enemy. They learned that a large enemy force under the command of Maj. Gen. Kiyotake Kawaguchi had landed and was preparing to attack and seize Henderson Field. The Japanese chose to attack the airfield from the south, believing it was not as well defended as the coastal perimeter. They were wrong. Dug in on a ridge overlooking Kawaguchi's approach were Red Mike's Raiders, reinforced by a Marine parachute battalion and backed by artillery.

On the nights of September 12 and 13, the Japanese attacked. The fighting was bitter, with both sides suffering heavy losses. The Marine line was bowed, but never broken. And on the morning of September 14,

Edson counted 40 dead and 103 wounded out of his force of 700 Marines. But an estimated 1,200 Japanese soldiers had been killed on the slopes, giving the battlefield its name, "Bloody Ridge." For his repulse of the enemy, Edson would receive the Congressional Medal of Honor.

The Japanese, unaccustomed to reverses and unnerved by the defeat of Ichiki and Kawaguchi, were determined to destroy the Americans and regain total control of the island.

In September and October, Japanese troops streamed onto the island near Cape Esperance some 25 miles from Henderson Field. Hyakutake's numbers increased to approximately 20,000.

Meanwhile, Vandegrift received some 6,000 reinforcements, increasing his effective strength to 23,000. The reinforcements included elements from the 7th Marine Regiment, the 3rd Infantry Regiment of the U.S. Army's 1st Infantry Division (the Big Red One), and eventually the 164th Infantry Regiment of the Americal Division (the only American division during the war to bear a name instead of a number).

On October 23, Hyakutake attacked with nearly 6,000 men along the Matanikau River. The force was beaten back by artillery fire. The following night, the Japanese again attacked and were badly mauled. On October 25, Hyakutake withdrew his force, leaving behind 3,500 dead Japanese soldiers.

In early November, Vandegrift's numbers increased as elements of the 2nd Marine Division linked with his force. Additionally, the 2nd Raider Battalion landed in Aola Bay, roughly 40 miles east of the Lunga, and began a 150-mile-long trek through some of the world's worst terrain. Lead by colorful Evans Fordyce Carlson, an author and former observer with the Chinese army, the 2nd Raiders fought numerous actions en route to Vandegrift's headquarters. By the time they arrived they had killed hundreds of Japanese while losing only 17 of their own.

While Carlson was battling his way through the interior, Vandegrift was also heavily engaged. On November 19, Vandegrift's men again battled Hyakutake for control of Henderson Field. The Japanese were repulsed with heavy losses.

On December 8, the Americal Division's 132nd Infantry Regiment arrived and Vandegrift relinquished his command of all ground forces on Guadalcanal to U.S. Army general Alexander M. Patch. That same day, the 5th Marines departed for Australia. Other Marine units followed. Vandegrift would later be awarded the Congressional Medal of Honor.

Not longer after, U.S. Army forces on Guadalcanal—designated the XIV Corps—were strengthened by the 25th Infantry Division. Patch's force then began a successful drive west of the Lunga River. They destroyed all comers in their path. The remaining Japanese in the interior endured a severe pummeling by American aircraft, naval gunfire, and land-based artillery. Conceding that Guadalcanal was a lost cause, Hyakutake began withdrawing his broken battalions.

On February 9, 1943, the American army reached Cape Esperance and Patch declared the end of all organized resistance. Six months of bitter fighting had resulted in a decisive American victory.

A long road and many islands lay ahead of the Marines and soldiers in the Pacific. But after Guadalcanal, the ability of the Japanese to launch a major offensive in the theater no longer existed. Beyond that, the mythical invincibility of the Japanese army had been dispelled. The Japanese soldier was certainly tough and wholly committed, but the American Marine and soldier proved to be every bit as formidable.

CHAPTER 10

EL GUETTAR

(MARCH 23, 1943)

American army forces under the command of Lt. Gen. George Smith Patton Jr. achieved their first major victory against elements of Germany's vaunted Afrika Korps near the oasis of El Guettar in Tunisia. Previously, inexperienced American troops at Kasserine Pass had fumbled on offense, and then rallied on defense. At El Guettar, the American soldier, who had been whipped into shape under the severe tutelage of Patton, literally outfought his German and Italian counterpart in the North African desert.

In late October 1942, the British 8th Army, under the command of Gen. Bernard Law Montgomery, defeated German and Italian forces under the command of German field marshal Erwin Rommel at El Alamein, Egypt. Rommel, affectionately known as the Desert Fox, had previously fought a series of brilliant actions in North Africa, earning him the admiration of his countrymen and the tempered respect of his enemies. But after a sound thrashing by Montgomery, the Fox was forced to retreat some 1,500 miles across Libya toward Tunisia. There, after having been reinforced, Rommel counterattacked in mid-February 1943. Driving hard through Kasserine Pass, Rommel's forces struck and defeated the U.S. Army's inexperienced II Corps before retiring toward a line of fortifications near the town of Mareth. Soon thereafter, Rommel assumed command of Army Group Africa, composed of all German and Italian forces.

For the Americans, Kasserine was nothing less than a disaster. Over an 8-day period, the Germans killed or wounded some 3,000 U.S. soldiers. Another 3,700 were taken prisoner. Two hundred tanks were destroyed, and fleeing American soldiers abandoned enormous stores of equipment. Two factors contributed to the defeat at Kasserine: The American II Corps was inexperienced, and its commander, Maj. Gen. Lloyd Ralston Fredendall, had mismanaged his force to the point of losing complete control of it in combat.

By the time of the defeat at Kasserine, the II Corps' division commanders had completely lost faith in the ability of Fredendall to fight, much less lead. Gen. Dwight David Eisenhower, commander in chief of Allied forces in North Africa, knew it. So did most of his staff, including one of his top advisers, Maj. Gen. Omar Nelson Bradley. The only man, the latter two believed, capable of whipping II Corps into fighting trim was a brash, uncompromising major general who was obsessed with his perceived destiny as a great warrior, George S. Patton Jr.

As the II Corps was struggling in Tunisia, Patton was busy organizing elements of what would become the U.S. 7th Army (the 7th would be activated at sea en route to Sicily in July). But Eisenhower felt the problems of the II Corps needed immediate attention: After all, unit morale—good or bad—was infectious, even more so at the corps level. Back home, the press was spreading alarm over the ill-directed American defeat at Kasserine. Rommel's Afrika Korps was still in the field. The British were planning to launch a big offensive in about two weeks and they needed the Americans (though they had little respect for them). Beyond that, the war was still up for grabs.

PATTON IS GIVEN COMMAND

On March 4, Patton was on horseback hunting wild boar in the Moroccan backcountry when he was flagged down by a motorcycling courier with a message from his boss. The message directed Patton to meet Eisenhower in Algiers. The following day, the two generals held a meeting over the hood of a car at an Algerian airstrip where Eisenhower ordered Patton to assume command of II Corps. The order was issued with a personal caveat: "You [Patton] must not retain for one instant any man in a responsible position where you have become doubtful of his ability to do his job ... I expect you to be perfectly cold-blooded about it."

Patton was the best choice to turn things around and score a big win for the team, and he enthusiastically accepted the order. He was even moved to tears when he began to discuss his virulent hatred of the Germans.

Bradley, as Eisenhower's representative, was to remain with Patton. Uncomfortable with a spy in his midst, Patton asked Eisenhower to make Bradley his II Corps deputy commander. Eisenhower agreed.

In the wee hours of March 7, Fredendall packed his bags, a picnic lunch, and a few bottles of French burgundy. Then he vacated his headquarters at the primary school in Le Kouif, Tunisia. Afraid of flying to Algiers, he left in a civilian automobile hoping he would not be strafed by patrolling German fighter planes.

Later that morning, Patton was spotted on the outskirts of Le Kouif in a grand procession of machine gun–bristling armored vehicles with sirens shrieking and flags flying. To hell with German fighter planes; Patton hoped they would attack just so he could take a shot at them, possibly with his ivory-handled pistols. "In the lead car Patton stood like a charioteer," Bradley would later write. "He was scowling into the wind and his jaw strained against the web strap of a two-starred steel helmet."

No one doubted Patton had arrived to command. And the Germans, who studied their opponents, were not too happy about it. They knew Patton liked to fight. Though his star would rise dramatically over the next two years, he would soon develop a reputation for being willing to employ tactics and attempt maneuvers others thought rash. This concerned his enemies, who were unable to predict how Patton might react in rapidly changing battlefield situations. What was known about Patton was that the bended knee had no place in his credo.

Within an hour of assuming command, Patton began the process of preparing his new organization for battle. The II Corps was composed of the 1st (the Big Red One), the 9th, and the 34th Infantry divisions; the 1st Armored Division; the 13th Field Artillery Brigade; the 213th Coast Artillery Regiment; the 19th Engineer Combat Regiment; elements of a tank destroyer group; and the tough 1st Ranger Battalion. The rangers were a newly formed American unit, trained by British commandos and grounded in the traditions of American rangers during the colonial wars and the American Revolution. At El Guettar, they would serve as the tip of Patton's spear.

Patton turned the II Corps into a crack combat unit, but his methods of reconstituting the organization were considered harsh and unforgiving. Under Patton's reign, all soldiers, even rear-echelon troops, were forced to wear neckties, leggings, and buckled-down helmets in the stifling African heat on a daily basis. Any soldier caught not doing so was subjected to stiff fines of between $25 and $50, a lot of money considering the Army pay rate in 1943. Proper salutes and reporting procedures were also demanded. Beyond the military courtesies, officers and men were ordered to be tough and aggressive. Private soldiers who did not measure up to Patton's standards were severely punished, and officers were fired. Officers were also ordered to wear rank insignia at all times, regardless of the fact that shiny bars, oak leaves, and eagles made them the choice target of enemy snipers. Patton's philosophy was simple: better to die as a visible leader in command than a cowering officer attempting to blend in with the rank and file.

The idea of digging in disgusted Patton. A victorious army, in his mind, was always on offense, never on defense. In one instance, Patton was touring the positions of the 1st Infantry Division when he came upon a series of slit trenches which had been dug around the division's command post. When he inquired as to the reason for the trenches, division commander Maj. Gen. Terry de la Mesa Allen replied, "as protection against air attack." Patton asked which trench belonged to Allen. When Allen pointed to it, Patton walked over, unzipped his fly, and urinated into the pit. "There," Patton said, zipping up his trousers. "Now try to use it."

On March 9, unbeknownst to the British and Americans, Rommel turned over command of Army Group Africa to 5th Panzer Army commander Col. Gen. Hans Jurgen von Arnim. The Desert Fox then flew to Berlin to meet with German leader Adolf Hitler. Officially, the meeting was to confer with Hitler regarding the hopelessness of the Axis situation in North Africa. In reality, Rommel had been recalled to Germany. There he was decorated and placed on sick leave. His request to return to Africa was denied. After two brief commands in Greece and Italy, Rommel would ultimately begin preparations for the defense of France.

On March 12, Patton received his third star, making him a lieutenant general. He wrote in his diary, "Now I want, and will get, four stars."

With the British about to kick-start an offensive against Axis forces in North Africa, Patton wanted to launch an all-out attack to drive the enemy into the sea. But the British leadership—specifically Montgomery's senior Allied ground forces commander, Gen. Harold Alexander—was wholly unimpressed with the Americans after the debacle at Kasserine Pass and unconvinced of the II Corps' supposed new combat prowess under Patton.

Alexander was not alone in his disregard for U.S. ground forces. In fact, many British army officers mockingly referred to their American allies as "our Italians." The insult was analogous to the German army's disappointment with the poor battlefield performance of their Italian comrades-in-arms.

The decision was made by Montgomery and Alexander that only limited American attacks in support of the British army would be authorized. The II Corps would be tasked with engaging Axis forces some 100 miles north-west of Mareth, thus drawing enemy reserves away from Montgomery's 8th Army. The II Corps was also responsible for seizing the various air-fields in the region, as well as capturing and holding the village of Gafsa. Both the airfields and Gafsa could be used to support Montgomery's forces as the latter attacked the Germans along the vital Mareth Line.

At Mareth, the Germans and Italians, under the overall command of von Arnim, were dug in behind a 22-mile-long series of fortifications stretching from the mountains in the south to the Mediterranean Sea in the northeast. Behind the Mareth Line in the east was the seemingly impenetrable *terrain chaotique* (translated into English, chaotic ground). It was in fact covered with desert salt lakes, and that is where Montgomery struck the enemy.

Patton wasn't enthusiastic about playing the proverbial second fiddle to the British army. But, ever the romantic, he considered his place in the upcoming battle as something akin to Confederate general Thomas J. "Stonewall" Jackson's role supporting Gen. James Longstreet in the Second Battle of Manassas during the American Civil War. Other than that, Patton was simply thrilled to have the opportunity to kill the enemy. He would later be disappointed to discover that the enemy was not led by Rommel himself.

On the night of March 16, Patton stood before his senior subordinate officers in his dank and dimly lit command post. Flashing his eyes about the room, searching for the slightest hint of fear, he issued an apocalyptic order. "Gentlemen, tomorrow we attack," he announced. "If we are not victorious, let no man come back alive." One can only imagine the combination of enthusiasm and knotted stomachs the officers must have felt as they returned to their respective units in the darkness.

OPENING SHOTS

Just after midnight, the entire 88,500-man II Corps began moving east in a torrential rain. Meeting little opposition along the way, U.S. major general Orlando Ward's 1st Armored Division and trucked elements of Terry Allen's Big Red One advanced 45 miles, reaching Gafsa well before sunrise. The defending Italian soldiers quickly withdrew, melting into the hills beyond the palm tree oasis of El Guettar.

In Gafsa, the Americans quickly secured the dwellings and began setting up defensive positions.

On March 18, the American force reached El Guettar, about 10 miles away. There, Patton received newly expanded orders from Alexander. The II Corps was to continue driving east from Gafsa toward Sened Station, some 40 miles away, move another 20 miles and seize Maknassy, then dispatch a small force toward Mezzouna where they would attack a Luftwaffe air base.

At El Guettar, Patton ordered Allen to take the heights surrounding the main highway. A daylight frontal assault was considered but quickly dismissed because it would be too costly in terms of lives and equipment. Instead, the 1st Ranger Battalion, under the command of Lt. Col. William Orlando Darby, moved into the hills during the night of March 20. With faces blackened and bayonets fixed, the rangers closed undetected with the Italian Centauro Division. Just after first light, a bugle sounded from the ranger ranks and the Americans attacked. Screaming Indian war cries, the rangers quickly panicked the Italians who in many cases dropped their rifles and ran. Some of the Centauros fought, only to be shot, blasted with grenades, or bayoneted by the American rangers. Rushing forward with his advance elements, Darby was heard shouting, "Give them some steel!"

Achieving complete surprise, the rangers routed the entire Italian division. Countless numbers were killed. More than 700 were taken prisoner. Follow-up attacks were launched by two regiments of the Big Red One.

Elsewhere, Patton was growing irritable over what he considered to be his own inactivity at the front. His separated forces, a risky undertaking in enemy territory, kept him in the rear and on the telephone. "I wish I could do more personally," he confided in his diary. He was also frustrated over the fact that heavy rains had turned the surrounding terrain into thick mud, temporarily slowing II Corps' advance from Gafsa. But on March 21, Ward's tanks rolled into Sened Station, seizing Patton's second main objective. Again, the opposition was light, and advance units spotted enemy soldiers fleeing in the distance.

On March 22, Axis soldiers attempted to make a stand in the hills just beyond Sened. Ward ordered the bulk of his force forward. Soon thereafter, Maknassy was also in American hands.

Meanwhile, Allen's infantry was still mopping up in El Guettar. In five days, the Americans had covered a great deal of inhospitable ground, crushing everything in their path, and suffering fewer than 60 killed or wounded. It was almost too good to be true, Allen thought.

Too good, indeed. On the early morning of March 23, the earth began to rumble. Almost immediately, gunfire could be heard echoing across the desert floor and forward observation posts began reporting huge numbers of tanks heading straight toward them. The tanks, the advance guard of the 10th Panzer (armor) Division, were rolling through the valley toward the American positions. The panzers—one German division, one Italian division—under the command of former Luftwaffe commander Field Marshal Albert Kesselring, were followed by mobile artillery pieces and mechanized infantry. As the German force closed the gap between the two armies, German fighters roared overhead, and screaming Stuka dive bombers descended from the clouds. A few American fighters entered the fray. They provided close air support and engaged the enemy planes. The German aircraft attacked the Big Red One's artillery positions, bombing and strafing targets dangerously close to Allen's command post. Allen, frantically messaging for reinforcements from Gafsa and supplies from posts more distant, could barely hear over the deafening enemy tank fire. An aide frantically appealed to Allen to move the 1st Division's command element further back. "I will like hell pull out," the general snapped back, adding, "I'll shoot the first bastard who does."

Two American tank destroyer battalions rushed forward to stem the tide. The tank destroyers were light, mobile, high-velocity field guns, which could be quickly brought to bear against advancing armor. They were successful at El Guettar, but at great cost to their own ranks. "It requires great nerve and training for antitank gunners to meet a tank charge," British war correspondent Alan Moorehead would later write. "You must hold your fire until, as a rule, you are yourself being shelled."

Before noon, the panzers broke off the attack to regroup. But the Stukas continued pummeling the American positions. German tanks resumed the attack hours later but were again beaten back by tanks, tank destroyers, and heavy artillery.

Cannon fire was devastating to the Germans caught in the open. Some of the enemy attempted to find cover behind small hills, but the guns blasting over and striking the reverse slopes forced them to bolt from their positions and seek better protection. There the big guns blasted their ranks mercilessly. "Our artillery crucified them," reported an American forward observation post. Patton, directing the repulse of the Germans from a nearby hilltop, remarked, "My God, it seems a crime to murder good infantry like that."

Several points along the II Corps lines faltered momentarily, but the points never broke. On the American left flank, rangers were hurried forward to reinforce wavering U.S. infantry. The flank held and the Germans were again beaten back.

The Americans fought courageously, even when close to being overrun. When two artillery battalions were directly assaulted by German infantry, they stayed with their guns as long as possible, firing as rapidly they could. Some of the gunners pitched buckets of water on the overheated barrels. Others loaded and fired. Still others jogged forward from the rear with 90-plus-pound shells on their shoulders. As the Germans closed with the cannoneers, the guns were lowered and fired directly into the faces of the enemy. The Germans pressed forward. Finally, the artillerymen, realizing they were about to be overrun, spiked the barrels of their cannon with live hand grenades. Refusing to surrender, the artillerymen withdrew to secondary positions, fighting with their rifles as infantry.

By the end of the day, Allen had halted the German advance. Tenth Panzer had been decimated. Nearly 40 German tanks were destroyed. Some were towed back to the enemy rear. Approximately 30, burning furiously, were scattered across the valley floor.

To the east of El Guettar, Ward's 1st Armored Division continued moving forward. Actions were fought at Maknassy and 1st Armored tanks struck Mezzouna, all supported by a variety of Army Air Force bombers and fighter bombers. But Ward's forces achieved limited success.

Reversing course, 1st Armored rejoined the main body of the II Corps by the end of March. On March 30, the Big Red One and the 9th Infantry Division, supported by 1st Armored, attempted unsuccessfully to drive the Germans and the Italians from the hills near El Guettar. But faced with stiff resistance, that battle was inconclusive.

THE AFTERMATH

Still, the first Battle of El Guettar was a stunning victory for the Allies. While the 10th Panzer Division was struggling unsuccessfully to defeat Patton's II Corp, Montgomery's British 8th Army was able to smash through the Mareth Line. The latter was a hard-fought win lasting four days. But it was the beginning of the end of Germany's trek across North Africa.

Bradley would later refer to El Guettar as "the first solid, indisputable defeat we inflicted on the German army in the war." Aside from soundly defeating the enemy in a pitched battle over open ground, Patton's victory restored the Allies' faith in the combat prowess of the American soldier. It also restored the American soldier's belief in himself—an important rite of passage after the demoralizing defeat at Kasserine.

CHAPTER 11

TARAWA

(NOVEMBER 20–23, 1943)

The Battle of Tarawa, which launched the Central Pacific Campaign of World War II, is considered to be the bloodiest battle of the war up to that point. The fighting lasted 76 hours and cost the lives of more than 1,000 Marines. Japanese casualties were far greater.

Tarawa was one of three objectives in the invasion—code-named Operation Galvanic—of the Gilbert Islands. The other two objectives were the islands of Makin and Apamama.

In the previous year, a Marine Raider battalion under the command of Col. Evans Fordyce Carlson, one of the heroes of Guadalcanal, had landed on Makin. In two days, the Raiders killed scores of Japanese defenders, burned equipment, destroyed a radio station, and captured several important documents before withdrawing. As a result, the Japanese reinforced their positions throughout the Gilberts, a chain that had to be broken in the American drive through the central Pacific.

STRATEGY

From the naval point of view, the key to success at Tarawa was speed. Adm. Chester W. Nimitz, commander in chief of the U.S. Pacific Fleet, ordered his Central Pacific Force commander,

Vice Adm. Raymond Ames Spruance, to "get in there, and get the hell out." Spruance, in turn, ordered the amphibious forces to seize their objectives with "lightning speed."

Spruance, considered to be Nimitz's right arm after the stunning victory at Midway the previous year, had a substantial flotilla at his disposal. The two primary task forces slated for the Gilberts was Task Force 52, under the command of Vice Adm. Richmond Kelly Turner, and Task Force 53, under the command of Rear Adm. Harry Hill. Task Force 52 was responsible for the landings on Makin; Task Force 53 would land the troops on Tarawa. The day after the Makin and Tarawa landings, the American submarine *Nautilus* would launch a Marine Reconnaissance Company, which would land on Apamama.

Tasked with capturing the three atolls was the V Amphibious Corps, under the command of Maj. Gen. Holland McTyeire "Howlin' Mad" Smith, a hard-bitten Alabaman who had won the French Croix de Guerre for his actions at Belleau Wood during World War I. Smith was nick-named "Howlin' Mad" because of his unforgiving approach to failure on the part of subordinates. Smith was also diabetic and, at 60, one of the old-est two-star generals in any of the services (he would ultimately become *the* oldest three-star). Overlooking his physical condition, President Franklin Delano Roosevelt arranged for Smith to command Marines in the Pacific. Smith knew how to fight and his Marines adored him, and that was enough for FDR.

Smith's V Amphibious Corps was composed of two divisions—one army, one Marine—both commanded by unrelated Smiths. The 27th Infantry Division (army), under the command of Maj. Gen. Ralph C. Smith, was responsible for capturing Makin. The 2nd Marine Division, under the com-mand of Maj. Gen. Julian C. Smith, was responsible for taking Tarawa.

Makin, defended by approximately 800 Japanese soldiers, was seized fairly quickly, as was Apamama. Tarawa was another matter entirely. Located some 1,250 miles from both Australia and Hawaii, the palm-covered isle was to become the scene of one of the Corps' most legendary fights.

Accurately described by Brig. Gen. Edwin H. Simmons as "an extended thumb and forefinger," Tarawa was an elongated, sharply curving chain of little islands with a heavily defended southwest tip—the "thumbnail" of the "extended thumb" —the island of Betio. Known to Marines as "bloody Betio," the islet was less than three miles long, a half-mile at its widest point, and relatively flat, no more than ten feet above sea level at any point. Stretching across most of the little isle were three overlapping airstrips. The remainder of Betio consisted of a series of bunkers and other defensive positions constructed of coconut logs, coral, and concrete. The fortifications were bristling with all manner of naval guns, coastal defense artillery pieces, mortars, and machine guns.

Behind those walls and guns were some 5,000 men from the Japanese special naval landing forces (Marines) and a handful of Korean laborers, all under the command of Rear Adm. Keiji Shibasaki. Having previously participated in landings along the China coast, Shibasaki was well-versed in the art of amphibious warfare. He appreciated the difficulties encountered by the landing elements in such operations. Consequently, Shibasaki created a nearly impregnable defense system along the southern shorelines—the most probable landing sites for any invading force (the Marines in fact attacked on the northern side). Beyond that, he had a knack for training and motivating the soldiers and sailors under his leadership.

Described as "young, experienced, and ruthless," Shibasaki was the consummate warrior. He loved his men and he loathed his enemies. Shibasaki boasted that "a million Americans could not take Tarawa in a hundred years." In fact, it was taken in three days with far fewer numbers. But it wasn't without appalling loss of life in a very short period of time.

THE LANDINGS

On the morning of November 20, Betio was subjected to a fierce air and naval gunfire bombardment that literally raked the island from one end to the other.

While the atoll was being softened up, Marines from the 2nd Marine Division were making last-minute preparations before going ashore: wiping down weapons, waterproofing field packs, and sharpening K-Bar fighting knives. Others were on the mess decks eating the traditional preinvasion breakfast of steak and eggs, a fact that concerned the Navy's medical officers and hospital corpsmen who correctly surmised they would be treating stomach wounds later in the day. Those anxious to get ashore and put the frightening wait behind them watched the bombardment from the decks of troop ships.

Just after 7:30 A.M., an ammunition dump on Betio was hit. It exploded with a terrific concussion followed by a thick plume of roiling black smoke. Not surprisingly, Marines and sailors offshore believed their enemy was being wiped out by preparatory fires. What they didn't know was that the banging and burning was creating more show than real damage to the enemy's works. And some of the navy's timed-fuse projectiles were either bouncing off the tops of Shibasaki's bunkers and falling harmlessly into the sea on the other side of Betio or overshooting the islet altogether.

The landings were slated to begin at 8:30 A.M., but were postponed until 9 because the Japanese shore batteries continued firing. The fact that the enemy's guns were still operational unnerved marine commanders. The Americans knew that if the guns were still firing after the pummeling they had received, the Japanese were deeply entrenched and virtually unaffected by preparatory fires.

Shibasaki's lookouts soon determined that the Americans were going to attempt a landing on the northern shore. They informed the admiral, and he quickly shifted his forces across the island from the south. A plus for Shibasaki was the fact that the landings would occur in low tide over rugged coral that stretched out some 800 to 1,200 yards from the beach.

The landing fight began when the 2nd Marine Division's assault waves struck at three predetermined points—Red Beaches 1, 2, and 3. The first wave, loaded onto amphibious tractors (amtracs), began churning toward a cove on Betio. They quickly struck coral and ground forward toward the beach. Once in the cove, the Marines found themselves under a murderous fire from three sides, worse than any of the invasion planners could have imagined. Some of the amtracs erupted into balls of fire, their unarmored fuel tanks hit. Others spun wildly out of control after their drivers were killed.

The second assault waves struck Red 2 and 3. The three assault waves, blasted by the enemy's coastal artillery and machine guns, were barely able to gain a foothold. They were followed by more Marines ferried in by landing craft. The craft ran aground on the reefs, and the leathernecks scrambled down the ramps and over the sides. Wading hundreds of yards across razor-sharp coral toward the burning shoreline, the Marine ranks were shot to pieces. Some of the men, weighted down with heavy equipment, stepped into deep holes and drowned. Of the first wave, only 30 percent made it to the beach. The second wave moved beneath a 500-foot-long pier. There they began suffering terrible losses. The third wave was nearly annihilated. The fourth and fifth waves were either beaten back or held off by enemy fire.

"Tarawa was a brawl, the nastiest kind of close quarter fighting between two dedicated, relentless, and ruthless forces," Professor Dirk A. Ballendorf of the University of Guam would later write. A brawl indeed: Those who survived the trek to the beach were often wounded, exhausted, and without their weapons. Sadly, plenty of extra weapons were lying around on the beach. Most of the men were separated from their squads and platoons. But officers quickly reorganized them into new, cohesive units.

Meanwhile, U.S. warplanes and offshore destroyers were pounding the enemy, providing as much covering fire as possible for the invading force. Flying over Tarawa, navy lieutenant commander Robert A. McPherson later recalled, "The water never seemed clear of tiny men, their rifles held over their heads, slowly wading beachward. I wanted to cry."

Col. David Monroe Shoup, a future Marine Corps commandant, was wounded early in the fighting and spent much of the morning in waist-deep water beneath the pier where he directed the attacks. By midday, Shoup was ashore, but only 15 feet inland and within a few yards of an enemy bunker.

The Marines inched forward, but their losses were appalling. By nightfall some 3,000 Marines had a tenuous foothold on the beach. A few of them had reached the edge of the airstrip. Another 1,500 were either dead or wounded.

It was feared that the Japanese would capitalize on the Marines' early difficulties in securing a beachhead and use the cover of darkness to launch one of their infamous banzai counterattacks. Such an attack was in the works. Fortunately for the weary leathernecks, Shibasaki and his entire staff were killed by supporting naval gunfire. The following day, the Marines broke out of their beachheads and moved inland.

The airfield was seized, landing parties linked with one another, and counterattacks were beaten back. Officers leading the way were specifically targeted and cut down by the withering fire. Some lived and became the stuff of legends.

Red-mustachioed Maj. Jim Crowe, swagger stick in hand, calmly strolled his embattled lines and exhorted his men to fight. "All right, Marines, try and pick out a target and squeeze off some rounds," he said, as bullets and hot shell fragments zinged past his head. "You better kill some of those bastards or they'll kill you. You don't want to die, do you? Come on, now, let's kill some of them!"

Shoup, who quickly consolidated his forces and directed them forward against pockets of fierce resistance, signaled his superiors, "Casualties: many. Percentage dead: unknown. Combat efficiency: we are winning."

Refusing to surrender, the Japanese literally had to be blasted out of their positions or burned to death with flamethrowers. In many instances Marines had to climb on top of enemy pillboxes and either shoot down into the position or toss in hand grenades or satchel charges.

On November 22, the Marines intercepted a radio signal from Betio to Tokyo, "Our weapons have been destroyed. From now on everyone is attempting a final charge. May Japan exist for ten thousand years!"

That night, the Japanese launched two suicidal charges against the Marines. The enemy screaming "Marines you die!" "Japanese drink Marine blood!" and *"Banzai!"* (translated into English, "10,000 years!") attacked along a wide front. In both attacks, the Japanese penetrated the American lines and the fighting went hand to hand. In both cases, the enemy was beaten back, with terrible losses on both sides.

The fighting raged on the following day, but resistance began to lessen by the early afternoon. At 1:30 P.M., on November 23, the island was declared secure.

THE AFTERMATH

Tarawa was a decisive victory for the Marines. The landings had been successful. The island and its strategically vital airstrip had been seized, and the defending force had been annihilated. Still, the losses were such that the Americans on the home front reacted as if the Marines had lost. Marine casualties (including sailors) numbered more than 1,020 killed and nearly 2,300 wounded. American newspapers published photographs of dead Marines on the beach and angry editorials calling for congressional inquiries into the so-called "Tarawa fiasco."

Military leaders like Nimitz and Holland Smith were faulted for supposedly rushing into a meat grinder that critics argued could have been bypassed. "You killed my son on Tarawa," a mother wrote Nimitz.

Japanese mothers could only weep: Of the 4,836 defenders on Tarawa, 4,690 were killed.

Of the U.S. Marine Corps, military historian S. L. A. Marshall would later write:

> The most important contribution of the United States Marine Corps to the history of modern warfare rests in their having perfected the doctrine and techniques of amphibious warfare to such a degree as to be able to cross and secure a very energetically defended beach.

CHAPTER 11: TARAWA

Nowhere was that perfection better exemplified than on the beaches of Betio. And lessons learned at Tarawa would ultimately save lives on other beaches, including the lives of untold thousands of Allied soldiers who would storm Fortress Europe in another seven months.

CHAPTER 12

LEYTE GULF

(OCTOBER 23–26, 1944)

The Battle of Leyte Gulf was the last great naval battle of the Pacific during World War II and a lopsided victory for the Americans. A four-part engagement fought in defense of the U.S. effort to retake the Philippines, the battle virtually ended the Japanese navy's ability to fight as a substantive fleet. And it was also history's last sea battle in which battleships engaged one another in combat.

By the fall of 1944, Japanese forces had suffered numerous set-backs and were fighting a defensive war. On October 20, American naval forces began bombarding the island of Leyte: It was the first stage of a campaign aimed at recapturing the Philippines (seized by the Japanese in the spring of 1942). Supported by the U.S. 7th Fleet, under the command of Vice Adm. Thomas C. Kinkaid, the U.S. 6th Army began landing troops on the island of Leyte. Two days later, the 6th Army's commander, Lt. Gen. Walter Krueger, waded ashore. He was accompanied by his boss, army general Douglas MacArthur, and Philippine president Sergio Osmena. On the beach, MacArthur announced, "People of the Philippines, I have returned! Rally to me! Let the indomitable spirit of Bataan and Corregidor lead on!"

Japanese military leaders realized that losing the Philippines would be disastrous: Aside from its strategic value, the Philippine island chain was one of Japan's last remaining sources of raw materials. To counter the American gains, the Japanese launched Operation Sho I (translated into English, "Victory 1") hoping to trap and destroy American admiral William F. "Bull" Halsey's 3rd Fleet.

THE COMMANDERS

Halsey's primary attack arm was Task Force 38, under the tactical command of Vice Adm. Marc Mitscher. Task Force 38 was composed of four task groups designated as TG38s. The first was TG38-1 commanded by Vice Adm. John S. McCain (father of the famous American senator, also a celebrated naval officer). TG38-2 was commanded by Rear Adm. Gerald S. Bogan. TG38-3 was commanded by Rear Adm. Frederick C. Sherman. TG38-4 was commanded by Rear Adm. Ralph E. Davison.

Though the entire task force was technically under the tactical command of Mitscher, Admiral Halsey exercised tactical authority during most of the battle. Commanders in other operations might have chafed under the yoke of such authority, but Halsey was greatly admired by his subordinates, and no one could argue over the results (though some would later question Halsey's tactics in the fight itself).

Between the two fleets—Kinkaid's 7th and Halsey's 3rd—the American force consisted of 32 aircraft carriers with more than 1,000 planes, 12 battleships, 29 cruisers, 104 destroyers, and an array of smaller combat vessels, submarines, oilers, and other supporting ships—a vast armada indeed.

JAPANESE STRATEGY

The enemy strategy was based upon a bold gamble: A Japanese naval decoy force composed of four light carriers, two battleships, three light cruisers, and six destroyers would steam south toward the primary Philippine island of Luzon. The force, under the command of Adm. Jisaburo Ozawa, would then reverse course and steam north. This action would theoretically lure Admiral Halsey's fleet away from the ongoing landings at Leyte. Two additional Japanese naval groups would then strike through the Philippines' San Bernardino Strait—between Luzon and Samar, and Surigao Strait—into Leyte Gulf.

The two groups were the Japanese Central Force under the command of Vice Adm. Takeo Kurita; and the Japanese Southern Force under the command of Vice Adm. Shoji Nishimura. Their targets were U.S. ships supporting the amphibious operations.

The combined forces of the Japanese included 4 carriers with just under 120 planes; 9 battleships, 2 of which were the huge new battlewagons *Yamato* and *Musashi;* 20 cruisers; 31 destroyers; and a number of support vessels.

To counter the U.S. Navy's numerical superiority in carrier-based war-planes, Japanese land-based aircraft would strike Halsey's carriers in the north and around Leyte, and *kamikaze* (translated into English, "divine wind") attacks would be launched against ships in Leyte Gulf. Trained to crash their explosive-laden airplanes onto the decks of American warships, kamikazes were suicide pilots of the Japanese Special Attack Corps.

The ruse worked. Halsey was tricked. But the Japanese ultimately lost.

THE BATTLE

The Battle of Leyte Gulf encompassed four separate engagements; this ultimately cost the Japanese because it enabled the U.S. Navy to engage Japanese forces piecemeal. The first action was fought in the Sibuyan Sea from October 23 through October 24. The second was fought in the Surigao Strait from October 24 through October 25. The third and primary engagement was fought off Samar on October 25. And the final engagement took place off Luzon's Cape Engano from October 25 through October 26.

Sibuyan Sea

The battle began on October 23 when two scouting American submarines, the USS *Darter* and the USS *Dace,* sighted the advance elements of Admiral Kurita's Central Force making their way north from Brunei through the Palawan Passage. The force was divided into two groups approaching the Philippines from either side of Palawan Island. The submarines attacked and sank two enemy cruisers, the *Atago* (Kurita's flagship) and the *Maya.* A third cruiser, the *Takao,* was badly damaged and forced to withdraw.

Halsey, who had been lured north by Ozawa's decoy force, ordered Admiral Mitscher's planes to attack two of the three groups spotted by the submarines. That order opened the Sibuyan Sea action which would ultimately cost the Japanese their giant battleship, *Musashi,* and the Americans, the carrier USS *Princeton.*

Halsey's force was coming under heavy air attack from land-based planes. To counter the attacks, the *Princeton* and her planes, under the command of Capt. William H. Buracker, were dispatched to take out the enemy's two airfields on Luzon.

On the morning of October 24, one of the *Princeton*'s lookout sailors spotted a lone Japanese fighter-bomber diving from the clouds. Sounding the alarm, antiaircraft gun crews began frantically pounding the skies around the attacking plane. But the aircraft slipped through the black puffs of flak, zeroed in on the carrier's main deck, and unleashed a 500-pound bomb. The great ship shuddered under the terrific impact. Within seconds, thick black smoke was roiling up from the vessel, and secondary explosions ripped through her lower spaces. Uncontrollable fires quickly spread, and the crew began to abandon ship. Nearby ships moved in and began plucking survivors from the sea.

Just before 3:30 P.M., the cruiser USS *Birmingham* was assisting in the recovery efforts when the *Princeton*'s reserve-bomb and torpedo magazines exploded. The blast sent a wall of hot steel fragments across the main deck of the *Birmingham* and killed or injured some 650 sailors. The casualties on the cruiser were in fact higher than those on the carrier.

By early evening, U.S. destroyers launched torpedoes into the burning *Princeton* and mercifully sent her to the bottom. More than 100 officers and men of the ship's complement had perished during the day. Miraculously, 1,361 survived.

As American seamen were struggling to save their brothers on the *Princeton*, others were engaging Kurita's main body sailing through the Sibuyan Sea. There, several enemy warships, including the great battle-wagon *Yamato*—to which Kurita had transferred his flag after the *Atago* was struck—and the *Yamato*'s sister ship, the *Musashi*, were met and struck by numerically superior U.S. forces under the command of Admiral Davison. Without benefit of air cover, Kurita's forces fought valiantly. But it was not much of a contest. The combined naval air groups from the carriers USS *Intrepid*, *Cabot*, *Lexington*, and *Essex* flew 259 sorties against the Japanese battle fleet. They pummeled the enemy for most of the day. When it was over, the *Musashi* was mortally wounded. The *Yamato* was hit. A heavy cruiser, the *Myoko*, was badly damaged and forced to withdraw. And practically every other Japanese vessel had been struck, many of which were either burning or sinking. Realizing that his badly mauled Central Force would be committing suicide by sailing toward Halsey's or Kinkaid's main elements, Kurita should have withdrawn. He did in fact retreat, but only temporarily.

Convinced that Kurita had permanently retired from the field, Halsey sailed farther north toward Ozawa's main body. However, when darkness fell, Kurita reversed course and steamed toward Kinkaid's 7th Fleet.

Surigao Strait

That same night, Admiral Nishimura's Southern Force steamed toward the waters of the Surigao Strait. As they entered the strait, Nishimura ordered his vessels to reform into a single column; in so doing, they would be able to easily navigate the narrow passage. But the maneuver sealed his fate as elements of Kinkaid's fleet were about to spring a trap.

Having been sent to intercept Nishimura, a sailing gun-support group under the command of Rear Adm. Jessie B. Oldendorf was lying in wait on both sides of the waterway.

In the wee hours of the morning, the Japanese line quietly churned toward the passage. Suddenly, the silent darkness was shattered by white flashes and riveting explosions. Nishimura's column was under attack by U.S. Navy patrol torpedo (PT) boats and destroyers. Nishimura continued to advance, but soon his vessels were being shelled mercilessly by the big guns of Oldendorf's battleships and cruisers. At the entrance to the strait, the American force passed back and forth in front of the advancing Japanese fleet, blasting away at the enemy's ships. In so doing, Oldendorf was employing the famous Nelson maneuver of crossing the T.

In naval warfare, "crossing the T" is a classic maneuver wherein a line of ships sails across the bow of an enemy fleet in order to bring all of its guns to bear while the enemy is only able to employ those that can fire forward. Royal Navy admiral Horatio Nelson perfected the maneuver, and successfully crossed the "T" of Adm. Pierre Charles Jean Baptiste Villanueva's Franco-Spanish navy off Cape Trafalgar in 1805. Nelson's maneuver essentially won for Great Britain supremacy on the high seas for the next century.

"In the unearthly silence that followed the roar of Oldendorf's 14 inch and 16 inch guns in Surigao Strait, one could imagine the ghosts of all great admirals, standing at attention to salute the passing of a kind of naval warfare they all understood," Rear Adm. Samuel Eliot Morison would later write. "For in the opening minutes of October 25, 1944, the Battle Line became as obsolete as the row-galley tactics of centuries before."

Only two Japanese ships survived the engagement. Not one of Oldendorf's vessels was sunk or seriously damaged. It was a textbook example of crossing the T, and it would be the last such maneuver in history.

Samar

As Oldendorf's victorious force regrouped, the battle's primary engagement was unfolding off the island of Samar. There, three of Kinkaid's carrier task groups, TG774-1, TG774-2, and TG774-3—known informally as Taffy One, Taffy Two, and Taffy Three—were stationed in support of the ground forces on Leyte.

Taffy One was under the command of Rear Adm. Thomas L. Sprague. Taffy Two was under the command of Rear Adm. Felix B. Stump. Taffy Three was under the command of Rear Adm. Clifton A. "Ziggy" Sprague (no relation to Thomas, but both were classmates at the U.S. Naval Academy in Annapolis).

Just before daybreak, Taffy Three, the northernmost group, began picking up radio transmissions in Japanese. The American sailors monitoring the radios initially believed the transmissions to be a joke. But around 6:45 A.M., a surface contact was picked up on radar by Ziggy Sprague's flagship, the USS *Fanshawe Bay*.

Minutes later, American navy ensign Hans Jenson, flying a Grumman Avenger torpedo bomber, sighted Kurita's Central Force and signaled Taffy Three: "Enemy surface force of four battleships, seven cruisers, and 11 destroyers sighted."

Not convinced, Ziggy Sprague directed Jenson to confirm his sighting. "Confirmed," the young pilot responded. "Ships have pagoda masts."

By 7 A.M., lookouts with the lead elements of the U.S. 7th Fleet spotted enemy masts just over the horizon. But the surprise had been complete. A jubilant Admiral Kurita radioed his own fleet headquarters. "By Heavensent opportunity, we are dashing to attack enemy carriers."

Alerting Admiral Kinkaid to the threat now facing the beachhead (supplies were still being unloaded and brought ashore for the ground forces), Ziggy Sprague launched what was nothing less than a courageous sacrifice of his own flotilla. With only six light carriers and seven destroyers, and the enemy within striking distance, he was clearly outgunned. Worse, his carrier planes were armed with ordnance for either antisubmarine patrols or for the support of infantry on the island. What was needed against battleships were armor-piercing bombs, and he had none. Nevertheless, Ziggy rushed his force toward the Japanese battle fleet. He hoped to buy enough time, before the arrival of planes from Taffy One and Taffy Two, to save the transports at the beach.

Closing with Ziggy's task force, the Japanese ships opened fire. Dismissing the enemy's shells, the American destroyers countercharged headlong into a line of four big Japanese cruisers. One of the destroyers was hit "like a puppy being smacked by a firetruck." Two others traded salvos with the enemy. The remaining destroyers rushed ahead. Though outgunned, Taffy Three fought an incredible running action, surging inside, outside, and around the enemy fleet. The carrier USS *Gambier Bay* was hit and lost, as were three destroyers. But in the two-hour shootout, through rain squalls and smoke, the Japanese ships had been forced into so many evasive maneuvers that Kurita's force had been drastically slowed and completely disorganized. On top of that, planes from Taffy One and Taffy Two arrived and wasted no time ripping into the isolated ships. Like Taffy Three's planes, they had no armor-piercing ordnance, and in many instances they made dry runs against the enemy's ships in order to divert fire and create confusion. Still, the American planes managed to sink three heavy cruisers and severely damage several smaller vessels.

Halsey also ordered Admiral McCain to dispatch elements of his own naval air arm to the effort to defeat Kurita's force.

Cape Engano and the Aftermath of Leyte

As the fight was raging off Samar, Admiral Mitscher's Task Force 38 was battling Ozawa's Northern Forces off Cape Engano. Just before 9 A.M., also on October 25, the first of four major U.S. air strikes was launched against Ozawa. By late evening, American planes had flown 527 sorties and broken the back of the Japanese fleet. Ozawa's flagship *Zuikaku* (the last of the carriers that had participated in the attacks against Pearl Harbor) was sunk, as were the carriers *Chitose*, *Chiyoda*, and *Zuiho*.

The Battle of Leyte was over. All total, 282 American and Japanese warships and 190,000 sailors on both sides were directly involved in the epic battle. By the time it was over, 4 Japanese carriers, 3 battleships, 6 cruisers, 14 destroyers, and nearly 10,000 sailors were sent to the bottom. The U.S. Navy suffered the loss of three carriers, three destroyers, and one submarine.

Although no one knew it at the time, Leyte Gulf marked the end of a centuries-old tradition of naval warfare—that of the great ships pummeling one another with big guns until one force is the victor.

CHAPTER 13

NORMANDY INVASION

(JUNE 6–AUGUST 22, 1944)

Often referred to as the 20th century's "Great Crusade," the American-led Normandy Invasion was—and still remains—the largest amphibious operation in world history. It was also the beginning of the relentless Allied thrust into the heart of German leader Adolf Hitler's Third Reich.

Code-named Overlord, the operation was conceived during the famous meeting between U.S. president Franklin Delano Roosevelt and British prime minister Winston Churchill at Casablanca in January 1943. An invasion of Hitler's "Fortress Europe" was discussed. But as resources were not available at the time, the idea was forwarded to the office of British lieutenant general Frederick Morgan. There, initial plans were developed for a full-scale Allied invasion of occupied France. The invasion was slated for May 1944.

COMMANDERS, CONCEPTION, AND EARLY RECONNAISSANCE

In January, American general Dwight David Eisenhower was appointed commanding general of Supreme Headquarters Allied Expeditionary Force (SHAEF). As such, he replaced Morgan's office and moved the date back to June, and the overall scope and tempo of the upcoming operation began to blossom.

As Supreme Allied Commander, Eisenhower oversaw a group of seven able deputies—five British and two American. Eisenhower's deputy supreme commander was British air chief marshal Arthur William Tedder. Chief of staff was American lieutenant general Walter Bedell Smith. Allied air forces were commanded by British air chief marshal Trafford Leigh-Mallory. Allied naval forces were commanded by British admiral Bertram Home Ramsay. Allied ground forces were organized into two armies under a single 21st Army Group commanded by British general Bernard Law Montgomery. The two Allied armies were the 1st U.S. Army, under the command of Lt. Gen. Omar Nelson Bradley, and the 2nd British Army, under the command of Lt. Gen. Miles Christopher Dempsey. SHAEF headquarters was based at Bushy Park near London. The invasion force was organized and developed at locations throughout the United Kingdom.

Prior to the invasion, extensive reconnaissance was made of the Normandy coastline, accomplished with low-flying American and British fighter planes equipped with cameras. Intelligence was also gleaned from commando units that slipped ashore under cover of darkness. Clandestine forces such as the U.S. Office of Strategic Services (OSS, the predecessor organization to the modern Central Intelligence Agency), the British Special Operations Executive (SOE), and the French resistance were also major sources of preinvasion intelligence.

Hitler appointed Field Marshal Erwin Rommel, Germany's celebrated Desert Fox of North Africa fame, as inspector of France's coastal defenses and then as commander of Army Group B. In both capacities, Rommel was responsible for shoring up the English Channel coastline defenses and then holding the proverbial fort against invasion. He did this by ordering the massive extension and reinforcement of the Atlantic Wall: This included coastal artillery batteries, machine-gun bunkers, mortar positions, and connecting works, all constructed by 500,000 laborers. At the surf line, all manner of obstacles from mines to steel tank traps were placed as a deterrent to landing craft and tracked vehicles. Rommel viewed his line of guns, fortifications, and the soldiers who manned them as Germany's only hope of survival. The war, he believed, would ultimately be won or lost on the beaches. "The first 24 hours of the invasion will be decisive," he told an aide. It was an opinion not held by his immediate superior, Field Marshal Gerd von Rundstedt, the western front commander in chief.

Von Rundstedt—who oversaw Rommel's Army Group B, Colonel General Johannes Blaskowitz's Army Group C, and General Geyr von

Schweppenburg's Panzer (armor) Group West—hoped to cut off and destroy the invading Allied forces as they moved into the interior.

The German high command, aware that an Allied invasion was inevitable, believed that the landings would occur somewhere along France's Pas de Calais coastline, some 20 miles across the Channel from Dover.

The landings were in fact destined to take place along a 50- to 60-mile front in the Bay of Seine between Caen and the Cherbourg peninsula. But through a series of effective ruses, code-named Fortitude, the Allies were able to deceive the enemy as to where, when, and in what strength the force would come ashore.

In one instance, an actor who closely resembled General Montgomery traveled to North Africa. This diverted the attention of Nazi intelligence forces away from Europe. Mock tanks, storage depots, airfields, and landing craft were positioned along England's southeastern coastline to deceive German aerial reconnaissance. Additionally, Lt. Gen. George Smith Patton Jr. was given command of the fictitious 1st U.S. Army Group, a ghost host which the deceived German leadership feared was preparing to land at Pas de Calais. Rumors, misinformation, and Allied bombing targets led the Germans to believe that the invasion might also occur in Holland or Norway. As a result the Germans, attempting to defend against all scenarios, found their lines dangerously extended and thin.

THE GREEN LIGHT

D day was set for June 6. (*D day* is military jargon used to designate the first day of a military operation—much like the term *H hour* is used to designate the first hour—thus, military planners and historians referring to successive days in a military operation might refer to those days as D+1 or D+2, for D day plus the first and second days. However, the size and scope of the invasion of Normandy was such that it is still loosely referred to by the general public as simply *D day* or the *D day invasion*.) But the weather was so poor—high wind, rain, a low cloud cover, and heavy seas—that the Germans believed there to be no immediate threat of an Allied invasion. On June 4, Rommel left the front and drove back to Germany in order to celebrate his wife's June 6 birthday.

Weather indeed was a factor for the invasion force. So was the need for low tides for landing and clear skies for flying—the most favorable landing tides accompanied by a full moon on June 5, 6, or 7. Meteorologists forecasted a brief clearing on June 6, followed by more bad weather.

On the morning of June 5, Eisenhower called a meeting of his senior subordinates. It was either go during the clear weather window of June 6 or face an indefinite delay. If the date was postponed, he surmised, it could affect the security of the enormous force, thus degrading the element of surprise. A delay could also affect troop morale.

"Okay, we'll go," Eisenhower said. Those three words launched the largest amphibious operation in history.

On the eve of battle, Eisenhower issued his battle message, which was read over loudspeakers to all American and British forces as their transporting ships cleared harbors all along the British coastline. The message read as follows:

> Soldiers, Sailors, and Airmen of the Allied Expeditionary Force!
>
> You are about to embark upon the Great Crusade toward which we have striven these many months. The eyes of the world are upon you. The hopes and prayers of liberty loving people everywhere march with you. In company with our brave Allies and brothers-in-arms on other fronts, you will bring about the destruction of the German war machine, the elimination of Nazi tyranny over the oppressed peoples of Europe, and security for ourselves in a free world. Your task will not be an easy one. Your enemy is well trained, well equipped and battle-hardened. He will fight savagely.
>
> But this is the year of 1944! Much has happened since the Nazi triumphs of 1940–41. The United Nations have inflicted upon the Germans great defeats, in open battle, man-to-man. Our air offensive has seriously reduced their strength in the air and their capacity to wage war on the ground. Our Home fronts have given us an overwhelming superiority in weapons and munitions of war, and placed at our disposal great reserves of trained fighting men. The tide has turned! The free men of the world are marching together to Victory!
>
> I have full confidence in your courage, devotion to duty and skill in battle. We will accept nothing less than full Victory!
>
> Good Luck! And let us all beseech the blessing of Almighty God upon this great and noble undertaking.

On the night of June 5 and 6, some 5,000 warships, freighters, and supporting vessels crossed the English Channel and moved into position off France. Overhead, Allied transport aircraft were ferrying three Allied airborne divisions toward the coast. Simultaneously, French underground operatives began conducting sabotage operations against German transportation and communications targets. The resistance forces had received the go-ahead to destroy the German targets by way of coded radio messages broadcasted by the famous British Broadcasting Corporation (BBC).

AIRBORNE!

Just after 2 on the morning of June 6, D day began. Paratroopers from the American 82nd and 101st Airborne and the British 6th Airborne led the invasion. They jumped into the darkness along both flanks of the invasion front and behind German lines. Antiaircraft tracers reached toward them as they and their ferrying planes filled the skies. Some were killed before they exited the doors of the aircraft. Others died swinging in their harnesses. On the ground, the surviving sky soldiers found themselves off target as much as 35 miles, dispersed throughout the countryside, or struggling to get through areas which had been deliberately flooded as a defense against airborne landings. In many cases paratroopers discovered that their units had been destroyed or their unit leaders killed. But airborne troops, being the world's most adaptable fighters, quickly regrouped and moved toward their objectives: seizing bridges, roads, and other inland routes of egress for the primary landing forces that would soon be hitting the beaches. They were also tasked with confusing the enemy, diverting his forces, and protecting the seaborne force's all-important flanks.

The British 6th Airborne quickly secured the flanks of Sword Beach on the Allies' extreme left, and seized bridges over the Caen Canal and the Orne River.

The American 82nd and 101st did not fare quite as well. Tasked with securing Utah Beach on the Allied right, they encountered stiff resistance near Sainte Mère-Eglise and Carentan, and spent much of the first day either fending off attacks or regrouping their scattered numbers.

Jumping with the paratroopers were dummy parachutists, large dolls wired with popping firecrackers that misled the Germans deep in their interior, diverting attention away from the real sky soldiers.

A second component of the airborne assaults were glider-borne troops. As quiet as rushing wind, thousands of gliders whisked undetected over treetops and crash-landed into predetermined fields. As soon as the gliders slid to a stop, American and British infantrymen poured out of the exit doors and quickly linked up with their parachuting brothers. Like the paratrooper transport planes, some of the gliders were destroyed by German antiaircraft fire. In some cases, glider pilots misjudged their landing fields in the darkness and crashed too hard, killing themselves and their occupants. Other planes had their bellies ripped open by preplanted wooden poles known as "Rommel's asparagus," also with disastrous results.

STRIKING FROM THE SEA

Offshore, Allied soldiers and sailors made last-minute preparations before embarking on the mission they all knew would define the rest of their lives.

Prior to moving onto the landing craft, unit commanders gave pep talks to their nervous and seasick soldiers. "This is it men, pick it up and put it on, you've only got a one-way ticket and this is the end of the line," one announced. Another said, "This is probably going to be the biggest party you boys will ever go to, so let's all get out on the floor and dance."

As the first light of dawn broke, German soldiers peering from their bunkers spotted a seemingly endless flotilla of ships coming toward them. Frantically, they began screaming "Invasion!" into their field telephones.

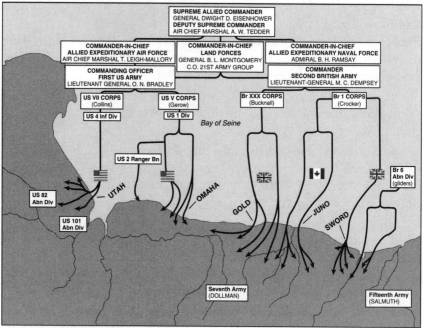

The Normandy Invasion.

At 5:50 A.M. naval gunfire, from ships six miles offshore, began ripping into the German defenses on the beach. Enemy coastal batteries returned fire. As the in- and outbound shells shrieked over the heads of the invasion force, American and British soldiers watched the explosions and black smoke on the distant coastline, each man hoping, most praying, that the beach would be nothing more than a smoldering wasteland when they reached it. The veterans knew better.

With engines running at full throttle, the flat-bottomed landing craft bounced hard in the rough seas. Anxious, seasick men crowded together in the boats began vomiting, causing others to do the same. Some of the craft took direct hits from the shore batteries, killing everyone aboard.

At 6:30, the first seaborne assault waves of the initial 175,000-man Allied force began storming the beaches of Normandy at France's Bay of Seine. From the Allied left to its right flanks, the beaches were divided into five primary areas of responsibility: Sword was assaulted by the British I Corps under General Dempsey's 2nd Army. Juno was assaulted by a Canadian force under the umbrella of the British I Corps. Gold was assaulted by the XXX Corps, also under the British 2nd Army. Omaha was assaulted by the U.S. V Corps. Utah was assaulted by the U.S. VII Corps. Both corps fell beneath the umbrella of General Bradley's 1st Army.

The landings were hotly contested, but wholly successful on Dempsey's British and Canadian beachheads—Gold, Juno, and Sword—on the Allied left. On the far right at Utah Beach, the assault was also going well for Bradley's Americans. Omaha Beach, where the Americans encountered an unexpected veteran German infantry division, was altogether different. The Germans were occupying bunkers and other reinforced positions atop high bluffs. When the first waves of Americans came ashore, they were badly mauled by withering enemy machine gun and mortar fire. Casualties among the initial elements have been referred to as "ghastly," with some companies suffering 90 percent losses within minutes of landing. Bradley briefly considered abandoning the landings at Omaha, but changed his mind after his infantry began making slow gains.

Exposed and disorganized, members of the U.S. Army's V Corps quickly realized that they had two options: Move forward and seize the seemingly impenetrable bluffs, or die on the beach. They chose the former and with tremendous personal courage on the part of individual soldiers, they fought their way up the bluffs and killed or captured the defenders.

RANGERS LEAD THE WAY

Four miles west of Omaha Beach and seven miles east of Utah Beach, 225 men of the independently operating U.S. 2nd Ranger Battalion were given the dangerous task of scaling the rugged 100-foot cliffs of Pointe du Hoc. There Allied intelligence had determined were five 155-millimeter guns emplaced in reinforced concrete bunkers. As such, the position encompassed "the most dangerous battery in France," and it had to be knocked out to protect the landings.

Like the other seaborne forces, the Rangers endured heavy seas and withering enemy fire. One of their landing craft was sunk. Other boats pressed on, their occupants bailing water, vomiting, and trying to avoid enemy bullets. At one point, the enemy fire was so heavy from the heights that a destroyer moved forward and with her naval guns pummeled the tops of the cliffs. This action drove the defenders back temporarily, allowing the Rangers to get a toehold on the beach.

Securing the base of the cliffs at the surfline, the Rangers encountered German infantry and a firefight ensued. The Rangers simultaneously aimed and fired rocket-propelled grapnel hooks up and over the ridge tops. The hooks gripped deep into the earth. Fixed to the hooks were thin cablelike ropes and rope ladders which the Rangers, weighted down with equipment, then climbed to the summit. Within minutes, the first man was up. He was quickly followed by the second and so on. Once the heights had been negotiated, the Rangers grouped into small teams and fought their way to the bunkers. There they discovered that the artillery had been moved. The Rangers then cut the highway behind the guns' original position and found the artillery pieces nearly 600 yards behind the lines. Killing the defenders, the Rangers destroyed the guns with thermite grenades.

The question has often been raised as to why American Marines did not participate in the landings. After all, the Marine Corps' specialty has always been amphibious operations, and some Normandy-bound army units were in fact instructed by Marines prior to the invasion. The reasoning for the Corps' nonparticipation had origins stretching back to World War I. Following the 1918 Battle of Belleau Wood in France, in which Marines played a leading role, newspaper headlines in the United States credited much of the American Expeditionary Force's success to the Marines. This occurred at the expense of deserving army units even when referring to actions in which Marines did not participate. Incensed army commanders refused to be upstaged by the leathernecks again. Thus, Marines were deliberately excluded from the European theater of World War II. However, when the Rangers at Pointe du Hoc began suffering heavy losses, it was briefly considered that Marines from one of the offshore ships' detachments might go ashore and reinforce them. At the last minute, however, word was passed down through the army chain of command that no Marines would be allowed to go ashore, not even riding shotgun on landing craft ferrying army troops or supplies. Rumors quickly spread that the army leadership feared a repeat of the media gaffes in 1918. They did not want to see headlines that read *Marines save Rangers at Normandy.*

THE BATTLE

Normandy at ground zero was a fight in its purest form: No feinting. Very little maneuver. Just two huge armies slugging it out toe-to-toe. The Americans had to attack straight-on to survive and win. The Germans had to stand fast and repel the attack or die, lose the battle, and ultimately the war.

From the outset, the German army was plagued with problems, not the least of which was a lack of air cover. The Allies had and maintained air superiority over the battlefield and far in advance of the front, a fact that German commanders would later attribute to their own defeat.

The invasion force was supported by more than 13,000 Allied aircraft, including the paratrooper transports, but also fighters and heavy bombers. Germany's *Luftwaffe* (translated into English, "air force"), on the other hand, was only able to muster some 400 planes on the first day. Eisenhower knew that aircraft would be critical to the overall success of Overlord. For two months prior to the invasion, approximately 11,000 Allied planes flew 200,000 sorties against French railroad hubs, highways, and river bridges that were vital to the German ground forces. The aircraft also attacked enemy airfields, barracks, radar sites, and gun positions along the Atlantic Wall. The Allies lost 2,000 planes in the preliminary raids, but they were able to cut off the Normandy invasion area from the rest of France.

Another problem the Germans faced was an inability to reinforce their embattled troops on the front lines. Rommel and other commanders were in fact away from the front when the landings began. Insufficient transportation prevented reserve forces of infantry being moved up to reinforce embattled German units on the line. Stunned German leaders, still not convinced where the primary landings would occur, were never able to come to a consensus as to where the only reserve panzer division in the region should be positioned. And three panzer divisions in the rear were never moved forward. Hitler had placed those three divisions under his own direct command. Unfortunately for the defenders, der Führer was sleeping hard after a dose of barbiturates when the Allied landings commenced. No one was willing to awaken him, inform him of the invasion, and ask his permission to unleash the panzers.

By the end of the day, approximately 150,000 Allied troops were ashore, and some 80 square miles of occupied France had been seized. Rommel's wall had been breached. Unfortunately, 6,500 Americans (including 2,500 men at Omaha Beach and 2,500 among the ranks of the American para-troopers) and 4,000 British and Canadians were dead or wounded. Still, the casualties were substantially lighter than preinvasion estimates. Fearing that Hitler might respond with poison gas, Eisenhower had ordered his senior medical officers, major generals Albert W. Kenner and Paul R. Hawley, to prepare for at least 12,000 killed and wounded in the U.S. 1st Army, alone.

The only sizeable German counterattack on D day was against the British in the Sword Beach sector. But it was quickly repulsed.

Hedgerow Country

On the second day of Overlord, D+1, Allied soldiers began pushing inland through the unaccommodating walls of hedgerows, which crisscrossed the French countryside. "No terrain in the world was better suited for defen-sive action with the weapons of the fourth decade of the twentieth century than the Norman hedgerows," historian Stephen Ambrose would later write. "Only the lava and coral, caves and tunnels of Iwo Jima and Oki-nawa were as favorable."

Indeed. The hedgerows, great earthen berms used to mark boundaries and corral livestock, had existed for centuries. On top of the berms were tight walls of high shrubs and trees. Hedgerows lined either side of many of the sunken roads throughout Normandy. They provided excellent cover and concealment for defending or retreating German soldiers. And they presented formidable—often dangerous—obstacles to attacking Allied infantry and armored forces.

As the American units pressed forward, they often found themselves lost in the maze of hedgerows where they became isolated or cut off from other units. In fact, it was nearly impossible to launch a company-size (roughly 200 men) attack in hedgerow country.

Platoon and squad-size units moving through fields surrounded by hedgerows were often subjected to unseen mortar, machine gun, and sniper attacks.

Tanks also found hedgerow country to be nearly impassable. A few Allied tanks attempted to crash their way through the earthen berms, but were unable to break through the cementlike base. Whenever tracked vehicles tried to climb over the berms, the unarmored bellies of the machines were dangerously exposed to German antitank weapons. A breakout from the hedgerows was desperately needed.

The Mulberries

As the invasion force pressed inland, the first of some 70 decommissioned ships was sunk off the American and British beaches. The sunken ships were to form "breakwaters" around areas slated for two prefabricated harbors, which were later towed across the English Channel from British ports. Code-named Mulberry, the harbors had been constructed in Great Britain and were brought in sections to the Normandy coast. There they would handle the endless stream of cargo needed to support the invasion and the drive inland. One of the harbors was slated for St. Laurent off Omaha Beach. The other was slated for Arromanches off Gold Beach. Once operational, the Arromanches harbor was able to handle approximately 12,000 tons of supplies and 2,500 vehicles per day. The harbor towed to St. Laurent was destroyed in a storm.

Hitler Retaliates and the German Defense Collapses

On June 13, with the Allies still struggling in hedgerow country, Hitler began launching his *Vergeltungswaffen* (translated into English, "retaliation weapons") or V-1 rockets. The V-1s were flying bombs designed to be launched from sites behind German lines on the continent and hurtle over the channel to England where they would run out of fuel and drop on population centers. The precursors to modern intercontinental ballistic missiles, some 2,000 V-1s were launched against civilian targets in Great Britain. Hitler believed that punitive rocket attacks would demoralize his enemies. But the V-1 terror tactics only strengthened the Allies' resolve.

On June 18, the Americans gained control of the Cotentin Peninsula on the Allied far-right flank, thus isolating the fortified port at Cherbourg.

By the end of June, Cherbourg itself had been captured. One million Allied soldiers supported by 600,000 tons of supplies and some 200,000 vehicles were ashore and taking the fight to the enemy. And Allied reinforcements were pouring in daily.

In early July, American and British soldiers began breaking out of the hedgerows.

On July 9, Dempsey's Britons seized Caen. Several days later, Bradley's forces captured St. Lô and within weeks launched a series of well-coordinated air/ground attacks that stunned the Germans and created a vast gap in the lines through which the Americans were able to drive in force.

Von Rundstedt and Rommel practically begged Hitler to allow their forces to withdraw to the Seine River. Hitler refused, characteristically demanding his generals hold "at all costs." This infuriated Von Rundstedt, who argued that the only "sensible" thing German forces in Normandy could do was negotiate a peace settlement. Hitler, equally enraged, replaced his western front commander with Field Marshal Guenther von Kluge.

Things deteriorated further within the German high command. On June 17, Rommel's car was strafed by a British fighter. The field marshal, suffering a serious head wound, returned to his home in Germany to recover. Two days after the strafing incident, several German officers attempted a coup d'état. One of them, Count Claus von Stauffenberg, planted a bomb which detonated beneath a table at the headquarters where Hitler was holding a strategy meeting in Rastenburg, East Prussia. Hitler was wounded but survived. Von Stauffenberg was captured several hours later and shot.

In the reprisals that followed, Rommel was implicated and ordered to commit suicide or face a humiliating public trial, execution, and the punishment of his family. Choosing suicide, Rommel took poison given him by two German generals. His death was declared to be a result of his wounds. He was given a state funeral with full military honors. Von Kluge was also implicated in the assassination attempt and relieved of command. He, too, committed suicide.

On August 1, the newly arrived U.S. 3rd Army, under the command of General Patton, led the overall breakout from Normandy. Within two weeks he surrounded and captured over 100,000 Germans at the Falaise-Argentan Gap.

On August 19, Parisians revolted en masse. The Germans who were able to escape fled. Three days later, Normandy and Brittany were in total Allied control. And by the end of August, Paris had been liberated and Patton was threatening the German defenses along the Saar River.

The German army, or what remained of it, was on the run. But the war was far from over. Eight months of some of the toughest fighting lay ahead as the Allies advanced toward Germany's heartland, and Hitler grudgingly gave up ground. Moreover, the Allies were destined to suffer their most unsettling setback of the entire war on the edge of the Ardennes Forest in Belgium.

CHAPTER 14

BATTLE OF THE BULGE

(DECEMBER 16, 1944–JANUARY 28, 1945)

In late 1944, the American and British armies were in Belgium poised to strike the industrial heartland of Germany. The fast-moving Allied armies had been stalled on the German border west of the Rhine in September. The following month, the U.S. 9th, 1st, and 3rd Armies had resumed the offensive, slugging it out with retreating Nazi forces and seizing the city of Aachen—the ancient capital of Charlemagne and the first captured German city of World War II. The advance again bogged down, and took the form of a fight of attrition with the Germans on the losing end.

The German army had been all but defeated, or so it seemed. A bitter winter had set in. The weather was poor. And Gen. Dwight David Eisenhower, the supreme Allied commander, was regrouping his forces for an upcoming campaign that would surely open in spring.

No one believed the Germans would attack. That fact alone convinced Hitler that he had one last hope of winning the war. As a result, he ordered a surprise attack against American forces in Belgium and northern Luxembourg that penetrated deep into Allied territory, quickly surrounded an American airborne division, and threatened the entire western front. American and Allied forces counterattacked, ultimately forcing the Germans to withdraw.

Officially known as the Battle of the Ardennes, the action is more commonly referred to as the Battle of the Bulge because of the 70-mile wide, 50-mile deep salient (or bulge) the German thrust created in the lines.

PLAN OF ATTACK

Hitler's strategy was simple: He would launch a surprise winter attack from the forest, slice through the thinly manned American positions in the Ardennes, cross the Meuse River, and capture the city of Antwerp. In so doing, the German armies would be able to encircle Allied armies west of the Meuse.

Hitler's plan to split the allied forces.

The Ardennes was deemed the perfect location for the German offensive. Strategically, the dense forest provided excellent cover and concealment for both the buildup of forces and the initial thrust. From a morale standpoint, it was also the point from which Germany had launched its successful invasion of France in 1940, and thus the spirit of earlier victories would embolden German soldiers.

Hitler believed that by launching a surprise attack against the Allies, the initial shock would lead to disputes and infighting among the Allied leaders. He believed the alliance was unstable and could be weakened further in a time of crisis. This in turn would buy Germany more time to develop secret weapons, rebuild their armies, and, at a minimum, remove the immediate threat to the Ruhr, the vital German industrial area east of the Rhine. Hitler also believed that if he could inflict a major defeat on his Western enemies, he could negotiate a peace with them. This would enable him to turn his full attention to the eastern front where the Third Reich's greatest threat—the Soviet army—was crushing everything in its path.

The plan was originally named *Wacht am Rhein* (translated into English, "Watch on the Rhine"). Hitler believed that with such a code name, he could trick Allied intelligence operatives getting wind of the plan into believing it to be nothing more than a defensive operation. He changed the name to *Herbstnebel* (translated into English, "Autumn Fog") after becoming frustrated with several senior German generals who tried to convince him that an all-out attack to recapture Antwerp would fail. He also changed the launch date. The generals—including Chief of Staff Col. Gen. Alfred Jodl, western front Commander in Chief Field Marshal Gerd von Rundstedt, and Army Group B Commander Field Marshal Walter Model—proposed a smaller operation that would simply weaken Allied military forces in the area, thus prolonging the war. Hitler rejected the idea. He wanted to follow his original plan because it was bold.

By late 1944, Hitler's mental and emotional stability had degraded to a point of complete irrationality. He refused to heed the advice of his senior military commanders. He was prone to fits of rage in front of them. He trusted almost no one after the assassination attempt on his life in July 1944. And his lack of strategic grasp was evident in the fact that he hoped to retake Antwerp with little to no air support.

Hitler's plan, however, was effective in that it surprised the Allies and the initial ground achieved by the German army was substantial. He kept the operation secret by forbidding any radio or telephone transmission regarding it. Corps and division commanders were not told of the plan until a week before the attack, and soldiers did not learn of what they were about to do until the night before they were to advance.

"Soldiers of the West Front! Your great hour has arrived," announced von Rundstedt on the evening of December 15. "Large attacking armies have started against the Anglo-Americans. I do not have to tell you anything more than that. You feel it yourselves. We gamble everything! You carry with you the sacred obligation to give everything to achieve things beyond human possibilities for our Fatherland and our Fuehrer."

THE OFFENSIVE BEGINS

The surprise was complete. On the morning of the December 16, an intelligence summary published by Supreme Headquarters Allied Expeditionary Force (SHAEF) stated that the Germans were involved in a defensive campaign on all fronts. According to the report, "his [the enemy's] situation is such that he cannot stage major offensive operations." At 5 A.M., however, German artillery opened fire on six divisions of the U.S. 1st Army, under the command of Lt. Gen. Courtney H. Hodges. Simultaneously, three German armies—eight armored divisions and thirteen infantry divisions—burst through the snow-covered Ardennes Forest and smashed headlong into the weakest stretch of the Allied front lines. The German armies, some 250,000 crack troops and nearly 1,000 tanks under the command of Model, were composed of SS Panzer (SS armored units), *Volksgrenadier* (infantry), *Panzergrenadier* (armored infantry), and a division of *Fallschirm-jäger* (paratroopers). Attacking along a 70-mile front—from the German town of Monschau in the north to the Luxembourg town of Echternach in the south—the enemy made early gains.

In the north, the 6th SS Panzer Army, under the command of Col. Gen. Joseph "Sepp" Dietrich, had the misfortune of striking two divisions of the U.S. V Corps, under the command of Lt. Gen. Leonard T. Gerow. The V Corps was the only concentrated American force in the region. But the Germans were still able to advance.

On the night of December 17, German armor had pushed to within eight miles of 1st Army headquarters. Worse, the enemy was less than one mile from a major American supply depot which stored some three million gallons of gasoline, and the German army was suffering from a shortage of fuel. If the depot had been captured, it could have resulted in a major setback for the Allies. Fortunately, American resistance stiffened.

The Germans' only real success in the north was when Lt. Col. Joachim Peiper's SS Panzer Division broke through a thin screen of U.S. cavalry connecting the American 99th and 106th divisions and captured some of the units' vital gasoline stores. The following day, Peiper's forces took 140 American soldiers prisoner at Baugnez near Malmedy. The Americans were marched into a field and summarily shot with rifles and machine guns. The Germans then strolled among the dead and wounded, shooting with pistols anyone who moved. More than 40, feigning death, escaped to tell the story. As rumor spread of the Malmedy Massacre, enraged U.S. soldiers began fighting with greater resolve. The incident also resulted in American soldiers thinking twice before surrendering and SS soldiers being shot when they did.

During the same period, U.S. intelligence uncovered a special mission by German parachute commandos who—dressed in American uniforms, driving American vehicles, and speaking English—attempted to seize bridges over the Meuse River and spread misinformation and confusion. Code-named *Greif* (translated into English, "Seize"), the operation was orchestrated by SS colonel Otto Skorzeny, the scar-faced commando leader whose glider-borne troops had rescued Italian leader Benito Mussolini after the latter was overthrown in 1943.

Fortunately, Greif failed. Eighteen Nazi commandos were captured and shot as spies, but not before they and their at-large comrades had penetrated the American lines and created a wave of hysteria. Everyone was suspect. One captured German officer confessed that a principle goal of the mission had been to penetrate SHAEF and assassinate Eisenhower. But SHAEF's senior commander was not nearly as concerned with the threat of assassination squads as he was with the desperate situation of his army. At this stage of the war, Eisenhower was supposed to be working out the details of the upcoming push into Germany. Instead the chain-smoking general found himself piecing together shattered units and rushing fresh ones forward to plug gaps in the line.

As desperate as the situation was along the northern portion of the lines, circumstances were worse in the south and the center.

In the south, the German 7th Army, under the command of Lt. Gen. Erich Brandenberger, struck a thinly spread American 4th Division and one regiment of the 28th, and was able to move between and isolate them.

In the center, the 5th Panzer Army, under the command of Lt. Gen. Hasso-Eccard von Manteuffel, struck elements of the U.S. VIII Corps and ultimately reached the town of Celles, just six miles from the Meuse. The VIII Corps, under the command of Maj. Gen. Troy Middleton, included the 106th Division and two regiments of the 28th. The men of the 28th were crack troops. But many of the soldiers in the 106th were green replacements, many of whom were 18-year-old draftees who had seen little if any combat. Though no American unit left the field without fighting, elements of the 106th quickly folded or were encircled near St. Vith, a vital road junction in the *Schnee Eifel* (translated into English, "Snow Mountain") region some 12 miles behind the front lines. Bradley ordered the 7th Armored Division up to support the inexperienced 106th. They, too, were pummeled and many of the 7th's units began falling back to the safety of the rear in near panic.

The front's center collapsed, Eisenhower's forces were split, and St. Vith was completely surrounded.

American units throughout western Europe were rushed forward, including the 82nd and 101st Airborne Divisions of Maj. Gen. Matthew B. Ridgeway's vaunted XVIII Airborne (parachute) Corps. Both divisions were being rested and refitted in France after the recent invasion of Holland. But when the German offensive was launched, they were hurriedly trucked toward the salient.

The 82nd, under the command of Maj. Gen. James Maurice Gavin, was the lead division on the road north. The unit was tasked with blunting the enemy's advance along the Salm River, west of St. Vith. En route, the advancing Germans passed between the 82nd and the 101st, separating the two.

RACE TO BASTOGNE

The 101st, under the acting-command of Brig. Gen. Anthony McAuliffe (the 101st's commanding general, Maxwell D. Taylor, was in the United States on War Department business), was about to make history. The division was rushed toward Bastogne, another vital crossroads town just south of St. Vith.

Bastogne was critical: The allies believed that by holding the town, they could regroup their forces and launch a counterattack. The Germans also realized the value of Bastogne: It served as a major highway junction in the Ardennes and a potentially important hub for mechanized forces.

Control of the roads was vital: The surrounding terrain was rugged and not particularly vehicle-friendly. Thus the Germans and the 101st raced to the city. On the road to Bastogne the 101st's paratroopers were shocked to see frightened, fleeing American soldiers. Always underequipped, the paratroops demanded ammunition from their retreating brethren. The latter happily complied.

The Americans arrived first on December 18, and set up defensive positions. The Germans arrived the following day, quickly surrounded the 101st and laid siege to Bastogne. At that point, 18,000 Americans at Bastogne were facing 45,000 Germans. Worse, the weather was so bad that Allied aircraft were not able to provide close air support for Allied forces on the ground. Nor were they able to make resupply drops for besieged forces like the 101st.

Nicknamed the "screaming eagles," the 101st had been in the vanguard of every major western European fight since Normandy. Both the Americans and the Germans knew from the outset that if any force in the U.S. Army was capable of holding out against impossible odds, it was the 101st.

On December 19, Eisenhower called a meeting of his senior chiefs in the town of Verdun, the name itself ominous as the point where hundreds of thousands of men were slaughtered in the previous world war.

"The present situation is to be regarded as an opportunity for us and not of disaster," Eisenhower said, trying to set a positive tone. "There will only be cheerful faces at this conference table."

Lt. Gen. George Smith Patton Jr. agreed, adding, "Hell, let's have the guts to let the sons of bitches go all the way to Paris. Then we'll really cut 'em off and chew 'em up."

Patton's brassy suggestion was not an option. Eisenhower's immediate concern was Bastogne. He asked Patton when he and his 3rd Army would be able to attack. Patton responded, "the morning of December 21." An impossible boast in Eisenhower's mind, he gave Patton an additional two days.

Eisenhower then reorganized his forces. He placed the U.S. 1st and 9th Armies, previously under Gen. Omar Nelson Bradley's 12th Army Group, under British Field Marshall Bernard Law Montgomery's 21st Army Group. This rankled a number of senior American officers, but the move was done for practical reasons: The Germans had flooded the area between Bradley's and Hodges's headquarters, splitting the Allied force in two and creating a dangerous communications problem. Montgomery was simply in a better position to direct Hodges's 1st Army and the 9th Army under Lt. Gen. William Hood Simpson. Patton's 3rd Army was placed under Bradley's 12th Army Group. Two U.S. Tactical Air Commands were also placed under Royal Air Force control.

On December 21, besieged St. Vith fell to the Germans. Five hundred American soldiers had been killed and 1,200 were wounded. And, in the most serious American reverse in the European theater, 9,000 American troops were taken prisoner.

Poised to strike the Germans along the Saar River in Luxembourg, Patton then initiated one of the boldest feats of the war. He extricated his forces in the face of the enemy, wheeled his east-facing 3rd Army 90 degrees toward Bastogne in the north, and attacked. Racing nonstop up 150 miles of ice and snow-covered roads, without air cover and often in night blackout conditions, he knifed into the German southern flank and pressed toward the objective. On Christmas Eve, Patton liberated the town of Ettelbruck, and continued north.

"NUTS!"

On December 22, German officers under a flag of truce delivered a rather long-winded message from Lt. Gen. Heinrich von Luttwitz to General McAuliffe. The message, which demanded the surrender of Bastogne, appealed to the "well-known American humanity" to save the citizens of Bastogne from further suffering. The Americans were given two hours to reply.

McAuliffe, who had no intention of surrendering, was initially at a loss for words. One of his aides remarked that the general's first comment upon receiving the surrender demand might be wholly appropriate. McAuliffe agreed and penned his now-famous response to the Germans. It read "NUTS."

This message was then delivered by American colonel Joseph Harper to a group of German officers waiting in nearby woods. Harper handed the note to one of the German officers who read it and then looked at Harper in confusion.

"What does that mean?" the German asked. "Is this affirmative or negative?"

Harper responded, "It means you can all go to hell."

The following day, skies were clear and aircraft were up. Fighters provided close air support for attacking allied infantry and armored forces, and transports airdropped much-needed supplies to the 101st.

On Christmas Eve, with the exception of a German air raid, things were relatively quiet at Bastogne. General McAuliffe visited German prisoners of war and wished them well. He also shared with his men the story about his response to the surrender demand. And he presented a Christmas message to the 101st Airborne, a portion of which read: "What's merry about all this, you ask? We're fighting. It's cold. We aren't home. All true. But what has the proud Eagle Division accomplished with its worthy comrades ...? Just this: We have stopped cold everything that has been thrown at us from the north, east, south and west. We have identifications from four German panzer divisions, two German infantry divisions and one German parachute division. These units, spearheading the last desperate German lunge, were heading straight west for key points when the Eagle Division was hurriedly ordered to stem the advance. How effectively this was done will be written in history; not alone in our Division's glorious history but in world history. The Germans actually did surround us, their radios blared our doom. Allied troops are counterattacking in force. We continue to hold Bastogne. By holding Bastogne we assure the success of the Allied armies."

Out on the perimeter, cold, hungry soldiers shook hands with one another and said good-byes. Despite McAuliffe's words, the situation was looking bleak for the paratroopers of the 101st, and they knew it. They were running perilously short of food and ammunition. Frostbite and pneumonia casualties were thinning their ranks almost hourly. And there was a numerically superior enemy force surrounding them in the darkness.

Elsewhere, the "bulge" was beginning to shrink. Fighting was heavy throughout much of the region, and the German high command, with the exception of Hitler, could see the writing on the wall. The operation was doomed. Von Rundstedt appealed to Hitler to allow his forces to disengage. But his words fell on deaf ears. By Christmas Day, von Manteuffel's army was being mauled by counterattacking American forces.

On December 26, Patton's 3rd Army punched through to Bastogne. The following day, Hitler consented to a limited withdrawal from certain sectors.

On New Year's Eve, soldiers on both sides allowed a momentary sense of optimism to rush through their ranks. Despite the terrible fighting that lay ahead, most believed that 1945 would be the last year of the war.

"Just before midnight the shooting stopped almost entirely," recalled Cpl. Paul-Arthur Zeihe, a panzer soldier on the front lines near the German border town of Trier. "As the clock struck twelve, the Americans began with their fireworks, sending illuminated rockets into the air. Suddenly, by the light of their rockets, we saw the Americans getting out of their holes, clutching their rifles and pistols, jumping, skipping around, shooting their weapons and lighting up the whole valley. I can still see them before me today, caught against the light of their rockets, prancing around on a background of fresh snow. It did not take long before we were doing the same thing, firing off illuminated rockets, shooting our weapons."

HITLER'S LAST GASP

On the morning of January 1, Hitler launched an ambitious air attack against Allied aircraft and air bases in Belgium, Holland, and Northern France. The objective was to gain air superiority, deny the Allies any ability to provide air support to their ground forces in the Ardennes region, and, again, shock the Allies. Hitler hoped the latter would further erode what he believed was a fragile alliance. Code-named *der Grosse Schlag* (translated into English, "the Great Blow"), the operation consisted of 3,700 German fighters. Two hours after German pilots took to the air, several Allied bases had been severely damaged and 206 Allied planes were destroyed. But the cost to the Luftwaffe—300 planes and 253 aviators—was irrecoverable.

South of the primary front, in France's Alsace-Lorraine region, the Germans launched a secondary ground offensive code-named *Nordwind* (translated into English, "North Wind"). The attack, often referred to as the Second Battle of the Bulge, struck the U.S. 7th Army. The attack was beaten back within a few weeks, but not before U.S. forces had suffered some 16,000 casualties.

On January 8, the Germans began withdrawing from the farthest point on the bulge. A new Soviet offensive had been launched in the east and that posed a far greater threat to the heart of Germany.

On January 21, Allied forces reestablished the line that had been broken in mid-December. The following day, the final German order came to fall back. Six days later, it was over. By January 31, the Germans had been driven back to a point beyond their original jumping-off positions at the start of the offensive.

THE AFTERMATH

The Battle of the Bulge, which lasted from December 16, 1944, to January 28, 1945, was the largest land battle of World War II in which Americans forces participated. All total, over one million men fought during the battle, including some 500,000 Americans, 55,000 British, and 600,000 Germans. When the battle ended, some 19,000 American soldiers were dead (of 81,000 total U.S. casualties). Two hundred British soldiers had been killed (of 14,000 British casualties), and more than 1,000 thousand Germans soldiers had been killed, wounded, or captured. Additionally, Hitler had lost 800 irreplaceable tanks and 1,000 planes. American troops and equipment, however, continued pouring onto the continent.

The noose began closing tighter on the Third Reich. While the German army was falling back in the west, three million German soldiers in the east were being mauled by six million Soviet soldiers supported by overwhelming numbers of aircraft and tanks. For all intent and purpose, Hitler's Germany was finished.

CHAPTER 15

IWO JIMA

(FEBRUARY 19–MARCH 17, 1945)

The Battle for Iwo Jima (translated into English, "Sulfur Island") was a decisive victory for the U.S. Marines, but a terrible slugfest which historians have since described as "throwing human flesh against reinforced concrete."

By early 1945, U.S. forces had systematically defeated Japanese forces on land, sea, and air, but at tremendous cost. The Japanese, beaten back to their final defenses, were trying to postpone the inevitable—an invasion of their homeland. And Iwo Jima was the last line of defense.

Iwo Jima was a flyspeck on a map: a tiny, 8-square-mile chunk of volcanic rock jutting out of the sea between Saipan (an island in the Marianas chain some 700 miles south, which U.S. forces had captured in June 1944) and Tokyo (about 700 miles north-northwest). Five miles long and two miles wide, the pork chop–shape atoll was anchored at its southern point by a 550-foot high dormant volcano, Mount Suribachi. At the northern end was a rise that encompassed the Japanese underground command post. Between the two points was a rugged, treeless stretch of real estate topped with two functional airstrips and a third under construction. It was a craggy, barren no man's land, smelling of rotten eggs from sulfur fumes. But it was strategically vital to both the United States and Japan.

To the United States, Iwo Jima would provide an emergency air base for B-29 bombers flying back and forth between Saipan and mainland Japan. It would also serve as a refueling stop for escorting fighters, which had a shorter range than the bombers. To the Japanese, the island was a radar station and a base for fighter interceptors. Beyond that, the loss of the island would bring the Americans perilously close to the Japanese mainland and it would seriously wound the Japanese psyche.

THE COMMANDERS

Handpicked by Emperor Hirohito to command Japanese forces on Iwo Jima was Lt. Gen. Tadamichi Kuribayashi, a 53-year-old samurai warrior and a former Imperial Cavalry chief. Sworn to defend his island fortress to the death, Kuribayashi had posted his "Courageous Battle Vows" at every bunker and gun emplacement. The vows ordered each man to kill 10 of the enemy before dying. "Each man should think of his defense position as his graveyard," wrote Kuribayashi. "Fight until the last and inflict much damage to the enemy."

Kuribayashi knew the invaders were coming and that the defenders would be outnumbered. But he wanted his men to be heartened by their sense of duty to their families, their homes, and their emperor. He appealed to his men to force their assailants to come to them and pay for every inch of ground with blood, regardless of their own imminent deaths. There was to be no surrender. The reasoning—though incomprehensible by Western standards—was simple: Iwo Jima was Japanese soil, and no foreign military force had stepped foot on Japanese soil in 5,000 years. That was about to change.

On February 16, the American 5th Fleet under the command of Adm. Raymond Ames Spruance steamed into the area around the island. Many of the flotilla's ships were carrying members of the V Marine Amphibious Corps—consisting of the 4th and 5th Marine Divisions (with the 3rd Marine Division in reserve)—under the command of Maj. Gen. Harry "the Dutchman" Schmidt, the senior shore commander. Schmidt's division commanders—also major generals—were Keller E. "the Great Stone Face" Rockey of the 5th, Clifton Bledsoe Cates of the 4th, and Graves B. "the Big E" Erskine of the 3rd.

The overall "Expeditionary Troops" commander was Lt. Gen. Holland McTyeire Smith, nicknamed "Howlin' Mad" because of his unforgiving approach to failure on the part of subordinates. He had, in fact, fired two subordinate U.S. Army generals for lack of aggressiveness. At 62, he was the oldest three-star in any of the services. But President Franklin Roosevelt arranged for him to be ranking Marine commander in the Pacific. Back home, the American newspapers were often critical of Smith, accusing the general of needlessly wasting lives. But he was loved by his men.

OPENING SHOTS

Prior to the landings, Iwo Jima was subjected to the longest sustained aerial bombardment of the Pacific war. It wasn't as much as the Marines wanted or needed, but it was enough to turn the already eerie-looking and strange-smelling atoll into something akin to a "lunar landscape."

With the exception of its defending garrison, no one lived on Iwo Jima. Yet on the morning of February 19, it became one of the most densely populated places on Earth. It would also become the place with the lowest life expectancy.

Just before 2 A.M., naval gunfire opened up on Iwo, pounding the island for one hour. The shelling stopped momentarily as more than 100 bombers dove on the smoking atoll to deliver their preparatory payload. When the aircraft had finished their attack, the ships' big guns again opened up. Surprisingly, neither the air bombardment nor the naval gunfire had much of an effect on the island's deeply burrowed underground fortresses or its 21,000 armed inhabitants—a fact that would prove costly to the leathernecks tasked with taking Iwo.

Offshore, Marines sweating it out in the holds of troop transport ships made final preparations: They checked their equipment, cleaned weapons, wrote required letters home, and nervously ate the traditional preinvasion breakfast of steak and eggs.

At 8:30 A.M., the order was issued to begin ferrying the Marines ashore. Just after 9 A.M., the first waves were scrambling out of the landing craft and onto the island's southeastern beaches. Initial opposition was minor. To the men hitting the beach, it seemed as if the preparatory fires had been effective. The immediate problem was terrain. Much of the ground was nothing more than rock, volcanic ash, and deep black sand, difficult for infantry to move through—the Marines were sinking in up to their ankles—and often impassable for amphibious tractors, tanks, and other vehicles.

Deeply entrenched in a 16-mile labyrinth of tunnels and reinforced caves, Kuribayashi's men waited. In previous battles, the Japanese had resorted to terrifying banzai charges, suicidal attacks led by sword-wielding officers. But such "bamboo spear tactics" proved too costly. There were some suicidal Japanese counterattacks on Iwo Jima, but Kuribayashi's primary strategy was a defense-in-depth—fortifying an area, and then garrisoning each connected position point-to-point.

Once ashore, the Marines launched two attacks along a 4,000-yard front: The 5th moved against Mt. Suribachi, Iwo Jima's dominant feature, and the 4th pressed toward the island's largest airstrip, located about a half-mile inland.

The patient Japanese waited for the largest possible concentration of Marines to enter their previously sighted fields of fire. Then they opened up. According to one Marine, "You could've held up a cigarette and lit it on the stuff going by."

Kuribayashi had predicted that the massive fires and subsequent high casualties would cause the Marines to lose heart. He misjudged his enemy.

Gunnery Sgt. John Basilone, already famous as the first Marine to win the Congressional Medal of Honor in World War II, single-handedly wiped out an enemy blockhouse and then charged up the beach. Having recently returned from a stateside war bond tour where he was kissed by Hollywood starlets, he now found himself under fire and looking for a position where he could place a machine gun. Basilone turned to his men and urged them forward. At that instant, an enemy shell exploded, killing Basilone and four other Marines.

"They waited until we got on the beach, then they unloaded on us," said Cpl. Robert W. Hughes, a Marine who landed in the second wave and was later carried off the island with two shattered legs. "The dead and wounded were everywhere. We were all scared, but we had a job to do and we did it."

By early evening, Mt. Suribachi had been isolated from the rest of the island, and the Marines had reached the edge of the air strip which was quickly captured. But the price was high. The Americans suffered some 2,500 casualties on the first day.

Pilots and war correspondents flying above the battle reported "surprise" at what appeared to them to be thousands of Marines on one side of the island fighting against a solid wall of stone. It wasn't an inaccurate description. Without cover, the Americans were exposed to constant fire and counterattack. Fighting yard by yard, were it not for the tenacity of the individual Marine, Iwo Jima might have proven to be impregnable.

The fighting was merciless: Marines were having to clear caves, tunnels, and blockhouses. Believing they had destroyed one position, the Marines would move to the next only to discover the previous position suddenly burst to life again behind them. In such close quarters, the combat was almost primal, often becoming hand-to-hand. Many Marines were hacked to death, one man losing both arms at the shoulder to a samurai sword.

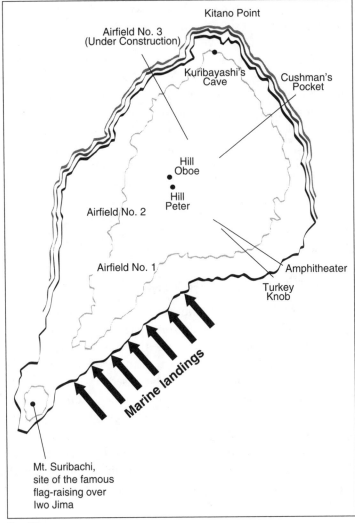

Iwo Jima.

Victory was the result of men like 19-year-old Pfc. Douglas Jacobsen, who single-handedly killed 75 Japanese soldiers and captured 16 gun positions. Sgt. Billy Harrell, losing his left hand in a savage night attack, continued fighting until an explosion severed his right hand. And handsome 1st Lt. Jack Lummus—a defensive lineman with the New York Giants and former All-American at Baylor University—who charged an enemy bunker, was hit by a grenade blast, but continued to fight. A second grenade shattered his shoulder. Still he attacked, ultimately destroying the enemy position. Then leading his men in a wild charge against another Japanese position, both of his legs were blown off when he stepped on a mine. Lummus continued shouting commands, "Keep moving! You can't stop now!" At first, Lummus's Marines thought their lieutenant was standing in a hole. They quickly realized he was upright on two bloody stumps. Several men, weeping, ran to him. For a moment they considered shooting him to put him out of his misery. But Lummus kept urging them forward. "Their tears turned to rage," according to the official report. "They swept an incredible 300 yards over impossible ground ... There was no question that the dirty, tired men, cursing and crying and fighting, had done it for Jack Lummus." Lieutenant Lummus died later in a field hospital and was subsequently awarded the Congressional Medal of Honor.

> At night the exhausted Marines attempted to sleep on unfamiliar ground the Japanese had previously practiced crawling over in the dark.

THE FAMOUS FLAG ON SURIBACHI

On the morning of February 23, after several days of savage fighting, elements of the 5th Marine Division captured the summit of Mt. Suribachi. Just after 10:30 A.M., a small flag was raised on Mt. Suribachi, the first time the Stars and Stripes had ever flown over Japanese territory. But a Marine officer ordered that a larger flag be raised so that it could be seen from the far end of the island. A large flag was then found on a beached landing craft and brought back to the top. Ironically, the flag had been salvaged from Pearl Harbor, Hawaii.

Then, in what would become one of the most dramatic scenes of the war, five Marines and one navy hospital corpsman raised the American flag over Iwo Jima. (Three of the five Marines would later be killed in action, and the sailor would be wounded.) Joe Rosenthal, a veteran photographer with the Associated Press, captured the moment on film. It was a picture for which he would win the Pulitzer Prize and on which the famous Marine Corps War Memorial in Arlington, Virginia, would be based.

The Stars and Stripes fluttered hard in the Pacific wind. Marines cheered across the island. From the main deck of the command ship *Eldorado*, a beaming Secretary of the Navy James Forrestal turned to General Smith and exclaimed, "Holland, the raising of that flag on Suribachi means a Marine Corps for the next 500 years." But the fighting was far from over.

The day after the flag-raising, the 3rd Division came ashore and linked with the 4th and 5th. The three divisions then wheeled north and began moving toward two more airfields and a rise on the northern end of Iwo Jima where Kuribayashi's command post was located. Casualties were appalling. Many replacements, fresh from boot camp, were killed during their first day in combat. The survivors were tasked with rooting out the Japanese at points on the island with names like Hill Peter, Hill Oboe, Charlie/Dog Ridge, Turkey Knob, Tachiiwa Point, the Amphitheater, Kita, the Meatgrinder, Cushman's Pocket, and Kuribayashi's Cave. But the Marines' spirits were renewed when "The Big E" Erskine led a successful night attack against the enemy's final defenses on March 7. The leathernecks caught the Japanese asleep and destroyed them in their holes.

Another group of Marines, also operating in the north, didn't fare as well: Surrounding a 30-foot knoll, pitted with firing slits and honeycombed with tunnels, the Marines were exchanging fire with the Japanese defenders when, almost at once, the enemy's firing ceased. The silence was broken only when a cave entrance was detonated by American demolition experts. Meanwhile, a handful of Japanese soldiers emerged from a rear entrance and were quickly gunned down by waiting Marines. The lull continued as approximately 40 Marines gathered on top of the knoll. Then, according to official reports, "the unbelievable occurred: ... the whole hill shuddered and the top blew out with a roar heard all over the island. Men were thrown into the air, and those nearby were stunned by the concussion. Dozens of Marines disappeared in the blast crater, and their comrades ran to dig for them. Strong men vomited at the sight of charred bodies, and others walked from the area crying." The Japanese inside had blown up their entire position, killing themselves, and killing or wounding more than 40 Marines.

The following night, the Japanese launched a ferocious counterattack. A few of the enemy actually charged past Marine positions and into an American command post. The Marines, hunkered down in foxholes and shell craters, blasted away at the Japanese, many of whom were rushing forward with land mines strapped to their chests. Those who were unable to penetrate Marine lines blew themselves up with grenades. When dawn broke, nearly 800 Japanese bodies were lying in and around the Marine positions.

Other Japanese soldiers, still fighting from their underground positions and refusing to surrender, were either blasted out with dynamite and bazookas or burned out with flamethrowers.

THE AFTERMATH

Within 10 days nearly all organized resistance was quashed. On March 16, the island was declared secure. Pockets of surviving Japanese were still burrowed in their holes, and most were fighting to the death, but the battle had been clearly decided. U.S. Army units moved in to mop up the remaining resistance and relieve the shattered Marine units. And Naval Construction Battalions, known as *Seabees*, had repaired the bomb-pocked primary airstrip in the south.

On March 17, the first B-29 made an emergency landing on Iwo Jima. That same day, the commander in chief of the Pacific fleet, Adm. Chester William Nimitz, issued an official communiqué announcing the end of the battle. "Among the Americans who served on Iwo island, uncommon valor was a common virtue," he said.

On March 21, Kuribayashi sent the following message to Tokyo: "We have not eaten or drunk for five days, but our fighting spirit is still high." Hirohito promoted him to full general, and Japanese newspapers praised his unwavering defense. Three days later, the Japanese commander sent his final transmission, "… farewell." His body was never recovered.

By March 26, Japanese resistance had been virtually eliminated: Of the 21,000 defenders, some 20,800 had been killed. But almost 7,000 Americans were dead, and 26,000 wounded. Aside from Marine losses, a handful of casualties on Iwo Jima were suffered among the ranks of the U.S. Army, Navy, and Coast Guard.

"It is fortunate that less seasoned or less resolute troops were not committed," said Spruance. General Smith agreed, but added it was "the most savage and costly battle in Marine Corps history."

The most poignant reaction was that of President Roosevelt. Upon learning of the casualties, the infirm president was said to have gasped in horror. He himself would be dead in less than three weeks.

The numbers of lives saved will never be known. But by war's end, nearly 25,000 Army Air Corps crewmembers breathed sighs of relief when their damaged planes were able to make emergency landings on Iwo.

CHAPTER 16

OKINAWA

(APRIL 1–JUNE 21, 1945)

The last major campaign in World War II, the Battle of Okinawa, was the largest and the bloodiest amphibious battle of the Pacific. The island itself would have served as the primary launching pad for an invasion of the Japanese heartland. But the war ended suddenly as American air, sea, and ground forces were preparing for the great final thrust.

Located in the center of the Ryukyu Islands chain, Okinawa was about 500 miles northeast of Formosa (Taiwan) and nearly 400 miles south of Kyushu. It was also the final point where Adm. Chester W. Nimitz's push across the central Pacific intersected with Gen. Douglas MacArthur's drive north from the southwest Pacific. Okinawa was, in fact, the last stop before the mainland.

Roughly 60 miles long and between 2 and 18 miles wide, Okinawa was a rugged stretch of green island characterized by mountains, steep ridges, and bamboo forests in the north; and rolling hills and fields in the south. The south also had the largest concentration of civilian inhabitants on the island. Naha, the capital city, was in the south. Shuri, an ancient castle, was in the center. In the west were three airfields. And the east coast was defined by two excellent natural harbors.

COMMANDERS AND FORCES

Code-named Operation Iceberg, the Battle for Okinawa was under the overall charge of U.S. 5th Fleet commander Adm. Raymond Ames Spruance, best known as the hero of Midway. Spruance's fleet—the largest naval force ever marshaled in the history of armed conflict—included some 1,500 warships. The Joint Expeditionary Force command was under Vice Adm. Richmond Kelly Turner, who would be promoted to full admiral during the battle for Okinawa. Turner's Task Force 51, the primary invasion fleet, was composed of approximately 300 warships and 1,000 transports and supporting vessels. Turner's fleet was also supported by Vice Adm. Marc Mitscher's Task Force 58, Vice Adm. William Blandy's Task Force 52, and Royal Navy Vice Adm. Bernard Rawlings's Task Force 57.

Slated to go ashore was U.S. Army Lt. Gen. Simon Bolivar Buckner Jr. and his 10th Army. Buckner, the son of a Confederate Army general of the same name, had spent most of the war commanding defense forces in Alaska and the Aleutian Islands. At Okinawa, he commanded a hybrid Army-Marine force comprised of the III Marine Amphibious Corps and the XXIV Army Corps. The Marines' III Corps, under the command of Maj. Gen. Roy Geiger, included the 1st and 6th Marine Divisions as the primary assault force, and the 2nd Marine Division as the primary demonstration (feinting) force. The army's XXIV Corps, under the command of Maj. Gen. John R. Hodge, included the 7th, the 77th, and the 96th Infantry Divisions with the 27th Infantry Division in reserve.

Defending the island were 70,000 soldiers of Japan's 32nd Army and some 9,000 sailors all under the command of army lieutenant general Mitsuru Ushijima. Also under Ushijima's command were some 39,000 locals who were employed as both combatants and laborers.

PRELIMINARIES

In mid-March, a series of devastating air and naval gunfire attacks were launched against Okinawa aimed at softening up the enemy's positions, which would surely be fanatically defended. Included in those strikes were a number of B-29 "Superfortress" bombers under the command of Maj. Gen. Curtis Emerson LeMay, destined to become the architect of the U.S. Air Force's post-war Strategic Air Command.

Preinvasion strikes were also conducted on the ground. The nearby Kerama Retto Islands were raided by elements of the 77th Infantry Division in an attempt to gather intelligence and gain a forward base.

The 77th quickly overwhelmed the defenders. They also made a grisly discovery: About 150 Japanese civilians—many women and children—had killed themselves by holding grenades to their stomachs. They were given the grenades by Japanese soldiers after the latter had told them they would be tortured and raped by the invading Americans. The 77th also located and seized more than 200 enemy suicide boats packed with high-explosive materials which were to be used against U.S. ships. The capture of the enemy boats no doubt saved lives over the next few months. But, as the Americans had discovered in previous battles, the Japanese were also adept at launching suicide attacks on land (banzai charges) and in the air (kamikaze attacks). Okinawa would be no exception.

The landing points were initially the subject of a minor interservice tiff. The Navy wanted the landings to take place on the eastern shore so that the harbors could be quickly captured. The Army and the Marine Corps wanted to land in the west, closer to the airfields. The Army and Marines won the argument.

On March 31, the Marines and soldiers made final preparations. Their conversations ran the gamut from "home" to "why Okinawa" to discussions about the island's deadly Habu snake whose bite supposedly killed within seconds. The men also enjoyed a turkey dinner with all the trimmings. "Fattening us up for the kill," some of them joked.

THE LANDINGS

In the predawn hours of Easter Sunday, April 1, American soldiers and marines crowded into landing craft and began a four-and-a-half-hour run toward the island's western shoreline.

At 8:27 A.M., the 1st elements of the American amphibious force landed unopposed on Hagushi Beach. "The greatest April Fool's Day joke of all time," author William Manchester would later write. According to Manchester, a rifleman in the 1st wave of Marines, he and his fellow marines "walked inland standing up and took Yontan (now Yometan) and Kadena airfields before noon." As the main body moved inland, the diversionary force was landed on the southeastern coastline. They, too, were unopposed. By early evening, some 60,000 Americans were ashore. They had secured a beachhead on the western coast, 8 miles wide and 3 miles deep, suffering only 159 casualties (28 killed, 27 missing, and 104 wounded). It all seemed too good to be true.

Too good, indeed: U.S. intelligence forces soon discovered that the bulk of the Japanese force was waiting patiently, deeply entrenched in a series of connected caves and underground bunkers in the south.

While the 1st Marine Division was mopping up along the landing front, Buckner ordered the 6th Marine Division north. The Army's 77th Infantry Division was ordered to seize the nearby island of Ie Shima and its airfield. And Hodge's 7th and 96th Divisions were sent south against the known enemy positions.

On April 2, Geiger's leathernecks made contact in the north and a stinging firefight ensued. Several Marines and navy hospital corpsmen were killed, but the enemy positions were quickly knocked out. The fighting was not without a brief respite: The day after their 1st contact in the north, the Marines holding the line found time to hit the beach in a fun way. They "swam, roasted pigs and chickens, and 'liberated' horses to carry their mortars and ammunition." Over the next two weeks, the Marines swept the northern countryside, encountering stiff opposition, but ultimately achieving all of their objectives.

While the Marines were enjoying the crystal blue waters off Okinawa, the army's XXIV Corps was making its initial contact in the south. There, Hodge's divisions encountered fierce opposition. The Japanese pounded the Americans with massed artillery, presighted mortars, and interlocking machine-gun fire. The enemy also launched a determined counterattack, but the assault was beaten back with severe losses to the enemy.

On April 6, the Japanese launched the 1st in a series of costly bombing and kamikaze attacks on both Spruance's fleet and Buckner's western beachhead. The following day, the *Yamato*, the Japanese navy's enormous 70,000-ton battleship, and her escorts steamed into the region. The ships, with just enough fuel to reach Okinawa, were on a one-way suicide voyage aimed at destroying all comers. However, before making contact with the American ships, the enemy fleet was struck hard by an enormous force of dive and torpedo bombers from Admiral Mitscher's Task Force 58. The great ship *Yamato* was sunk, along with one cruiser and four destroyers. The remaining Japanese ships reversed course and sailed for home.

On April 10, the 27th Infantry Division, which had been held in reserve, began landing on Okinawa. Soon thereafter, the number of U.S. forces on the island had swelled to about 160,000 men.

On April 12, Buckner's command post received a gut-wrenching message: America's infirm President Franklin Delano Roosevelt had passed away in Warm Springs, Georgia. Soldiers, sailors, and Marines reportedly wept upon hearing the news. That same day, the enemy launched a two-day series of ferocious banzai attacks against Hodge's weary lines. Amazingly, the Americans held, repelling every attack without a major breach in the XXIV Corps' positions.

Meanwhile, the 77th Infantry Division was involved in a slugfest on Ie Shima.

> On Ie Shima, the famous war correspondent Ernie Pyle was killed in an ambush. Prior to landing on the island, another correspondent had shouted, "Keep your head down, Ernie." Pyle, a hard-bitten recipient of the Pulitzer Prize whose pro-soldier columns had earned him the unofficial title the "GI's friend," shouted back, "Listen you bastards, I'll take a drink over every one of your graves."

The soldiers were able to raise the American colors over Ie Shima by April 21, but not before a terrific fight in which the enemy's 2,000-man garrison was all but wiped out.

> While the Americans were slugging it out for control of Shuri and points south, the German army was collapsing on the other side of the globe. On April 30, German leader Adolf Hitler committed suicide, and almost immediately the war effort focused on events in the Pacific.

MAY

By early May, Buckner was concentrating all of his forces on breaking the Japanese defenses around the strongholds in the south and at the Shuri citadel in the center. Ushijimi's command post was located near Shuri. There, soldiers and Marines suffered heavy losses on hills and along ridgelines with names like Chocolate Drop and Sugar Loaf. Opting for frontal attacks instead of "end run" flanking maneuvers, Buckner and his senior commanders were criticized by the press. It seemed to many civilians and a few tight-lipped Army and Marine brass types, that the senior American military leadership had learned nothing from the costly head-on matches which took place on Tarawa in November 1943. Others believed that when fighting the entrenched Japanese, everywhere was a front, and the best way to eliminate one front was to throw everything available at it.

On May 4, Ushijima launched a fierce counterattack. The attack was timed to coordinate with a massive kamikaze attack that inflicted terrible losses on the Americans both on the island and at sea. Within two weeks, however, the Japanese defenses had been beaten back to a point that their lines tightly encircled Shuri. Ushijimi then conducted a fighting withdrawal south toward new positions. He ordered his rear guard to remain at Shuri and hold until May 31.

For several days in late May, heavy rains lashed the island, turning the battlefield into rolling plains of mud, difficult for infantry and nearly impassable for vehicles. Worse, American planes had been grounded. But by May 28, the rains had subsided. And with Ushijimi and his main body retreating south from Shuri, the Americans were able to capture the stronghold on May 29, two days before the defending force had been permitted to fall back.

JUNE

Regrouping his own, Buckner sent his army-Marine force south to destroy Ushijima and the remaining holdouts. Simultaneously, a force of Marines launched a shore-to-shore amphibious assault aimed at pressing the Japanese into a tight pocket. Knowing full well they were doomed, the Japanese fought tenaciously for another two weeks.

On June 17, Ushijimi received a hand-written appeal for surrender from General Buckner. "The forces under your command have fought bravely and well," the note said. "Your infantry tactics have merited the respect of your opponents …. Like myself, you are an infantry general long schooled and practiced in infantry warfare …. I believe, therefore, that you understand as clearly as I, that the destruction of all Japanese resistance on the island is merely a matter of days …." Ushijima found the letter to be both humorous and insulting. He was a samurai warrior, and samurai never surrender.

The following day, Buckner was watching his troops advance from a high point on the battlefield when several enemy shells exploded around his position. Buckner was struck in the chest by steel fragments and chunks of coral. He died within minutes, and command was passed to General Geiger.

On June 21, Geiger announced the cessation of all organized resistance. The following dawn, Ushijima, in full dress uniform, uttered his final words, "I'll take along my fan since it is getting warm." Then he, and his chief of staff, Lt. Gen. Isamu Cho, stepped out onto a ledge overlooking the sea. American soldiers could be heard advancing nearby. The two Japanese generals bowed toward the east, sat together on a clean white sheet, and thrust ceremonial daggers into their bared bellies. Their adjutant then raised his sword and severed their heads.

THE AFTERMATH

Nearly 108,000 Japanese and Okinawans were dead. Another 7,400 were prisoners, a remarkable phenomenon because Japanese combatants were not known for surrendering. Of the Americans, more than 68,000 were killed or wounded. Those numbers included 4,900 sailors and coast guardsmen, 3,000 Marines, and 7,700 soldiers killed in action. In terms of equipment, the Japanese lost 7,830 aircraft. The Americans lost 36 ships and 768 planes.

In the words of acclaimed military historian Robert Leckie, the battle for Okinawa was "indeed decisive." The Japanese had been soundly defeated in the greatest battle of the Pacific war. Had they won, the prowar arm of the Japanese leadership would have been so strengthened that Emperor Hirohito himself would not have been able to persuade Japan's Imperial Council to agree to any Allied surrender terms.

Once seized, Okinawa was prepared as an advance "springboard" for the upcoming invasion of the Japanese home islands. But the invasion was not to be. On August 6, the first-ever atomic bomb was dropped on the city of Hiroshima. On August 9, a second bomb was dropped on Nagasaki. The Japanese were devastated. They surrendered on August 15, 1945, though the official ceremony actually took place aboard the battleship USS *Missouri* on September 2. The war was over.

PART 3

THE KOREAN
CONFLICT

CHAPTER 17

INTRODUCTION TO THE KOREAN CONFLICT

The Korean conflict was one of the bloodiest struggles of the 20th century. The outbreak of hostilities in June 1950 followed close on the heels of World War II; and the conflict's cease-fire agreement, less than three years later, was soon overshadowed by the debacle in Vietnam. Thus, the Korean conflict has often been referred to as the Forgotten War.

If World War II was a political/military extension of the First World War, it can certainly be argued that the Korean conflict was in many ways an extension of World War II. During the latter war, Japan considered Korea to be nothing more than the Japanese emperor's personal "rice bowl." The 85,049-square-mile peninsula had been ruled by Japan since the end of the Russo-Japanese War in 1905. By the time World War II erupted, the Korean people had been reduced to little more than slaves, and their language and culture had been all but eradicated. Korean men were impressed into Japanese service as laborers. Often they were ordered to take up arms against Japan's enemies. And the nation's natural resources were used to support the Japanese war effort.

THE END OF WWII AND THE BEGINNING OF THE COLD WAR

On August 8, 1945, two days after the Americans dropped the atomic bomb on Hiroshima, the Union of Soviet Socialist Republics—then an ally of the United States—invaded Manchuria and Korea. In less than a month, the Soviets occupied all of the major cities in what would become North Korea. They stopped short of the 38th parallel.

In 1945, much of the world—particularly the previously embattled regions—was drawn up into spheres of influence controlled by the three senior Allied powers. Those powers included the United States, the United Kingdom, and the Soviet Union.

In November 1947, a United Nations (UN) resolution was passed calling for the removal of foreign troops from Korea after its national elections were held.

On February 8, 1948, the North Korean People's Army (NKPA) was officially activated. Exactly two months later, U.S. president Harry Truman ordered the measured withdrawal of all American troops from Korea. In the Republic of (South) Korea, a popularly elected legislature was created in May. And in August, the legislature elected Syngman Rhee president. The following month, the Soviet Union installed a Communist government in North Korea. The new Democratic People's Republic of (North) Korea, under Premier Kim Il Sung, claimed jurisdiction over the entire nation.

Tensions increased, and the North Korean government began supporting an insurgency effort in the South aimed at toppling the legitimate government of Rhee. The South was also guilty of fanning the flames. In May of 1949, the South Korean army crossed the 38th parallel (the line of latitude which approximately demarcates the two nations) and raided villages nearly three miles inside North Korean territory.

The United States, however, remained true to its word and continued to withdraw its forces from the peninsula. By late June 1949, all American troops—with the exception of a 200-man Korean Military Advisory Group (KMAG)—had left South Korea.

After nearly two years of sharp rhetoric and a fizzling guerilla movement in the South, the North Korean government—at the urging of both the Soviet Union and Communist China—decided to take direct action. The North gambled that the United States would not intervene. It was wrong.

OPENING SHOTS

On the night of June 24, 1950, North Korean ground forces crossed the 38th parallel and attacked in great strength. By 4:00 A.M. on June 25, seven enemy divisions and five brigades were supported by some 100 to 150 Soviet-built Ilyushin and Yakovlev fighters (the propeller-driven enemy planes were outclassed by the new American fighters like the F-80 Shooting Star). The Republic of Korea Army (ROK Army) defenses were quickly overrun. Attacking in three thrusts, the NKPA pressed south along the western third of the peninsula toward the South Korean capital of Seoul, approximately 35 miles below the 38th parallel.

Thrusts in the center and on the east side of the peninsula advanced at the same pace as the western thrust toward Seoul. On June 28, NKPA forces entered the city. The shock and speed of the attack forced the South Koreans, as well as U.S. Army forces stationed in Korea, to fall back. Desperate to stem the tide, ROK forces destroyed the bridges spanning the Han River south of Seoul. But in their haste to do so, they failed to bring their own supplies and equipment across first. The route was complete. The NKPA regrouped in Seoul, allowed their own supply lines to catch up, and then crossed the Han.

Within days, the ROK Army had been nearly destroyed, and the American 8th Army found itself forced into a pocket, its back to the sea around the southeastern port city of Pusan. The free world was stunned.

The UN Security Council immediately convened and passed a resolution demanding "an immediate cessation of hostilities and a withdrawal of North Korean forces to the 38th parallel." The demand fell on deaf ears. The war was on.

America's first shots were fired from the air as U.S. warplanes struck enemy formations advancing in the South and strategic enemy targets like rail hubs and supply depots in North Korea. President Truman then directed U.S. Army general Douglas MacArthur, the 70-year-old commander in chief of America's Far East forces, to provide war-fighting equipment to the ROK Army from quartermaster depots based in Japan. Moreover, American ground forces were ordered to attack the NKPA below the 38th parallel.

North Korea's invasion of the South marked the beginning of one of the 20th century's great events. In the eyes of Koreans on both sides of the parallel, it was the beginning of a violent civil war that would last for 3 years, yet not be decided 50 years later when the century closed. To the world, the attack marked the first time hot fighting broke out in the new Cold War between the Western powers and the Eastern Bloc nations.

By the close of hostilities in 1953, some 21 countries under the United Nations banner would have allied themselves with the United States and South Korea, directly participating in the effort either on the ground or at sea. Those nations included the United Kingdom, Australia, New Zealand, Canada, South Africa, Turkey, Thailand, the Philippines, Belgium, Columbia, Ethiopia, France, Greece, the Netherlands, Luxembourg, Denmark, India, Italy, Norway, Sweden, and even the Japanese.

The North Koreans were numerous and formidable. But within months of the conflict's opening salvos, hundreds of thousands of tough Chinese soldiers would enter the fight. And for the first time in history, two huge armies, whose leaders both possessed nuclear weapons, engaged one another in open combat.

To the Americans—particularly the tens of thousands of U.S. soldiers, sailors, airmen, and Marines who had to slug it out with both the North Koreans and the Chinese—North Korea's invasion of the south marked the beginning of a grim period wherein 54,229 American GIs would die. Another 103,248 would be wounded and 8,142 would be listed as missing in action.

When the war began in the summer of 1950, American troops were ill-prepared to fight it. There had been a large, across-the-board downsizing of the U.S. military after World War II. And much of the lower-echelon ranks of the Far East–stationed American armed forces were made up of inexperienced youths on Japanese occupation duty. With the exception of those men who served in crack airborne or Marine units or career officers and noncommissioned officers who had served during the previous war, most of the rank-and-file riflemen had never heard a shot fired in anger. Many of them were "typewriter jockeys out of Tokyo," said Dr. Richard Walker, a former U.S. ambassador to South Korea.

Combat training, whenever it was conducted, was marginal at best. Making matters worse, MacArthur had issued a 1949 directive that had relaxed the stern policing and martial law duties of the occupying forces in Japan. This warmed the Japanese populace to its conquerors, and simultaneously softened the character of the American soldier who often found himself hanging around town with nothing to do. The general mindset after World War II was that "war" was over. When war did erupt on the Korean peninsula, the green Americans who were hurried to the front believed themselves to be invincible and their enemy weak. They would simply sort things out and return to the "good life" on occupation duty. But, according to author-historian Clay Blair, the "languorous, travel poster Army life in Japan had come to an abrupt end."

WEATHER AND TERRAIN

U.S. ground forces found the Korean backcountry a miserable place to fight. It was terribly cold and snowing in winter, and it was often unseasonably cold and wet in the summer.

Aside from the weather, the terrain was extremely rugged. It was characterized by long, windswept bluffs, sparsely forested hills, and steep mountains. In such an environment, the enemy was able to hastily construct reverse slope positions. From those positions he was able to easily strike advancing American-led UN forces before they knew what hit them. And following an attack, the enemy could just as easily fall back into a defensive posture. The roads were poor in Korea, particularly above the 38th parallel. They were primarily narrow mountain passes, or trails and causeways connecting rice paddies and little farming villages.

THE CHARACTER OF THE WAR

With the exception of climate and terrain—which more closely resembled the harsh mountainous environs of northern Europe—ground combat in Korea was not unlike that experienced by American soldiers and Marines who had fought in the western Pacific campaigns during World War II. The Communist Chinese and North Korean soldiers fought much like the Japanese had 5 to 10 years earlier. With virtually no regard for their own losses, they often launched suicidal charges in massed human waves against the American and Allied positions. Additionally, the enemy had little respect for surrendering foes: American prisoners were savaged by their Korean captors, much like they had been at the hands of the Japanese during the previous war.

Tactically, the war was far different than the Pacific campaigns of World War II. The Americans marched and fought over great distances, particularly during the first year of the conflict. But by late 1951, much of the fighting on the peninsula had become static. The front, in fact, was not unlike that experienced by American doughboys in western Europe some 33 years earlier. The American front in Korea was composed of two linear elements: The most forward element was a string of observation and listening outposts, which served a twofold purpose. On the one hand, the outpost line was a tripwire, which would alert rear areas of any approaching enemy. On the other hand, it would theoretically serve as a combat line that would repel or slow the enemy's advance. In reality, the outpost line was so thinly manned that any attacking force would likely wipe out the defenders, but not before the latter had alerted the main body.

The line directly behind the string of outposts was known as the Main Line of Resistance (MLR). This line was interconnected by strong points that would absorb the shock of any enemy forces that got past the outposts and defeat them. The MLR was comprised of bunkers reinforced with logs and sandbags. The bunkers were joined by a network of trench works and tunnels. Barbed wire and minefields were directly in front of the MLR.

> The MLR was the direct predecessor to the 21st-century defensive positions now seen on Korea's dividing line at the 38th parallel.

Beyond the MLR, in the area where the outposts were located, was a half-mile wide stretch of border country known as "No Man's Land." There, both friendly and enemy forces routinely patrolled and often clashed. The Americans who ventured out into "No Man's Land" often found it littered with trash, burned-out vehicles, discarded weapons, equipment, and rotting corpses.

"We often came across the bloated bodies of dead enemy soldiers," recalled retired U.S. Army major Charles P. Andrews. "Their faces were blown up to the size of a basketball. There were only slits where their eyes used to be."

Occasionally, patrolling units came across downed fighter planes.

The Korean conflict was the stage for the first jet air war. The Communist prop-driven Ilyushin and Yakovlev warplanes, which had seen action during the summer of 1950, were soon replaced with the Mikoyan and Gurevich MIG-15 jet fighters. The latter, for a time, outperformed the older American jets like the F-80 Shooting Star. But when the new U.S. Air Force F-86 Sabre jet fighter debuted in December, Communist pilots found they had their hands full. The F-86s could not climb like the MIG-15s, but they could outmaneuver and outdive anything thrown at them. Additionally, a number of "old hands" from World War II were at the controls of American fighter planes.

Several future astronauts such as John Glenn (the first man to orbit the Earth), Neil Armstrong (the first man to walk on the moon), Edwin "Buzz" Aldren, Walter Marty "Wally" Schirra Jr., Virgil Ivan "Gus" Grissom, and others piloted U.S. jet fighters over the Korean peninsula during the war.

At sea, the navy's ships played a supporting role to the ground and air forces roaming across the peninsula. But sailors—particularly landing craft operators, medical corpsmen and chaplains attached to the Marines, and naval aviators—often found themselves in direct fire combat with the enemy.

CHAPTER 18

THE INCHON LANDING AND THE CAPTURE OF SEOUL

(SEPTEMBER 15–29, 1950)

Code-named Operation Chromite, the American landing at Inchon, South Korea, was considered to be a masterstroke of military strategy and arguably the greatest success of U.S. Army general Douglas MacArthur's storied career.

MacArthur, commander in chief of U.S. Forces Far East, was a fighting five-star general of the old school. In *Victory at High Tide*, author Robert Debs Heinl Jr. wrote, "To find a parallel to MacArthur—in seniority, in professional virtuosity, and in autocracy, egotism and personal style, too—would take us back to Winfield Scott." But the great general faced a most difficult task in the summer of 1950.

On June 24, the North Korean People's Army (NKPA) smashed through South Korean defenses all along the North-South border at the 38th parallel. They then drove hard south, captured the South Korean capital of Seoul, and overwhelmed their opposition at every defensive position before completely encircling the American 8th Army and elements of the South Korean army around the southeastern port city of Pusan.

South Korea, the United States, and the latter's Western allies were stunned. As American military commanders struggled with their options, MacArthur began putting together a bold plan. He would not rush troops into Pusan, fight a frontal defensive action, and then try to break free from the pocket. Instead, he would land somewhere north of Pusan, strike the enemy at a point on his exposed flanks, and cut off his supply lines. At a meeting of his subordinate commanders in late August, MacArthur said, "I can almost hear the ticking of the second hand of destiny. We must act now or we will die."

MACARTHUR'S PLAN

Located on the Korean peninsula's Yellow Sea coastline, the port city Inchon was considered an ideal landing point. It was only 25 miles west of Seoul, and as such, the nation's primary highway and railroad lines were either connected near or passed through Inchon. A master strategist, MacArthur knew that the deeper the NKPA pushed into the South, the more vulnerable they would be to an amphibious attack. He also realized that Inchon was a key transportation and communications hub for NKPA forces. Once ashore, American forces would only have to advance a few miles before severing the enemy's supply routes and isolating its army in the south. Once that was accomplished, the enemy's primary combatant force could be destroyed. "We shall land at Inchon, and I shall crush them," MacArthur boasted.

Although strategically Inchon was a perfect point on the map from which to land and strike east, at the tactical level the operation was fraught with danger. First, the attacking forces would have a number of shoreline obstacles to overcome, including a narrow channel, a high seawall, huge stretches of wide mudflats (a difficult obstacle experienced by American Marines and sailors during a limited expedition on the Korean peninsula nearly 80 years earlier), and tides that fluctuated some 20 to 30 feet twice daily. The landings would have to be conducted during high tides so that the men would be able to climb over the seawall. Additionally, the landing zone was surrounded by fortified islets, which would have to be neutralized.

Disembarking U.S. troops would be subjected to presighted defensive fires from machine guns, mortars, and cannons. Once ashore, the Americans would have to battle their way inland. And much of that fighting would be house-to-house. For those reasons alone, the North Korean leadership never suspected to be hit when and where they were.

COMMANDERS AND FORCES

Tasked with making the landing was MacArthur's newly created X Corps, a hybrid Marine-Army force made up of the 1st Marine Division and 7th Infantry Division. MacArthur awarded command of the X Corps to his former chief of staff, U.S. Army major general Edward Mallory Almond. The 1st Marine Division, considered the most experienced division at the time, was under the command of Maj. Gen. Oliver P. Smith. The 1st became famous during the Battle for Guadalcanal in World War II. On the Korean peninsula, the division would earn more laurels.

The 7th Infantry Division, under the command of Maj. Gen. David Goodwin Barr, had also distinguished itself during the Pacific campaigns of World War II. But following the war, the 7th had been cannibalized to strengthen the 1st Cavalry and 25th Infantry Divisions (in July, MacArthur had moved both the 1st and 25th Divisions from Japan to Korea and placed them under the 8th Army). Before it could join Almond's X Corps, the 7th had to be rebuilt.

At Pusan, the American 8th Army was positioned behind a 140-mile long defensive barrier running north and west of the city. The army's back was to the sea. The 8th was under the command of Lt. Gen. Walton H. "Bulldog" Walker, a native Texan who led the vanguard of Gen. George Smith Patton Jr.'s 3rd Army during World War II. As such, Walker was just the man MacArthur needed at Pusan in the fall of 1950.

The 8th Army's position at Pusan was vital. It was America's only "toehold" in Korea. If Walker's lines were breached by the enemy it would be the death of his army. For several weeks, Walker's Americans fought a series of brilliant defensive actions along the entire Pusan front. The upside for Walker was that his tight geographic position gave him the advantage of short interior lines. This afforded him excellent communications and tremendous mobility. Consequently, the general was able to easily manage the forces at his disposal and hurry forces forward to plug gaps in the line at critical moments. "The craft would come in pulling a unit out of a quiet sector and efficiently plugging it into a threatened one," wrote historian Donald Knox in *The Korean War: Pusan to Chosin.* "The art would be in knowing when to make the switch and with what size force."

The downside was that the marginal size of Walker's position afforded him no room for error. If he miscalculated in any facet of his fluid defense, at any time, the enemy could pierce his lines and overwhelm the entire 8th Army.

American and Allied naval forces at Inchon were under the overall command of Vice Adm. Arthur Struble, commander of the U.S. 7th Fleet. Designated senior task force commander, Struble directed seven subordinate task forces, all ultimately responsible for supporting the landings. Tasked with getting MacArthur's force ashore was Struble's second-in-command, Rear Adm. James H. Doyle.

THE BATTLE

On September 13, U.S. naval forces began a massive preparatory bombardment of the landing beaches and the nearby island of Wolmi-do. Connected to Inchon by a causeway, Wolmi-do served as a natural sentinel. It commanded the sea approaches to the city and the surrounding coastline, and no vessel could pass into the harbor without being subjected to direct fire from the isle's artillery. Described as an "unsinkable battleship," Wolmi-do had to be either seized or reduced to a lifeless chunk of smoking rock.

As the ships' big guns and aircraft pounded the enemy's defenses, Marines and soldiers made final preparations. Marine lieutenant Frank Muetzel spent the eve of the invasion checking and rechecking gear, and sharing two cases of smuggled beer with a couple of navy counterparts who would also be going ashore the next day.

"A *Life* correspondent named Fred Vidar was there with a fifth of bourbon," recalled Muetzel in Knox's *The Korean War.* "We helped him kill that and showed him how to load and unload his pistol." According to Muetzel, the correspondent was complaining that he and his fellow reporters would be landing in the same boat and that he wanted to go ashore in an earlier boat. "I offered to take him in mine, but he declined when he found out it was in the first wave."

At 6:30 A.M. on September 15, the first elements of Smith's Marines began landing on Wolmi-do. Opposition was stiff at certain points, but in less than an hour the isle was in American hands. Fighting continued over the next few hours as pockets of resistance were rooted out. Then the Marines began digging in.

That afternoon, the tides rolled in. So did the X Corps' initial landing force. With guts, ladders, ropes, and grappling hooks, the Marines and soldiers began scrambling over the seawall and into the open just after 5:30 P.M. Passing the wall, they fanned out across the flats like "angry ants." With the exception of a few NKPA strong-points, initial resistance was light and the first inland objectives were quickly secured. The enemy was shocked and wholly unprepared. They believed Inchon to be an impossible landing point. They underestimated both MacArthur's determination and the marines' toughness.

In less than two hours, the Americans seized the immediate high ground at nearby "Cemetery Hill." The North Koreans began to fall back toward Seoul. By midnight, all objectives around the town of Inchon had been seized.

From the deck of his flagship, the USS *Mount McKinley*, a beaming General MacArthur exclaimed, "the Navy and Marine Corps have never shone brighter."

The following day, Walker's 8th Army counterattacked from the South, breaking out of the Pusan pocket and driving the enemy north. Meanwhile, supplies streamed ashore at Inchon.

On the evening of September 17, American forces captured Seoul's primary airport at Kimpo, as resistance temporarily stiffened on the outskirts of the city.

On September 27, U.S. forces pushing south from Seoul made contact with their brothers advancing north from Pusan. Two days later, after nearly two weeks of tough street fighting, Seoul was recaptured. It was the zenith of MacArthur's storied career. Predisposed to histrionics, pomp, and ceremony, the general then arranged for a ceremony wherein he formally returned the capital city to South Korean president Syngman Rhee.

By October 1, the few NKPA soldiers who managed to escape MacArthur's trap were on the northern side of the 38th parallel. The combined victory over the North Korean forces at Inchon, Seoul, and Pusan had been decisive. The American army had recovered face after initial losses in June, and South Korea had been saved. But the win also whetted MacArthur's appetite for the entire peninsula. Soon thereafter, he would drive his forces north across the parallel into North Korea and press toward the Yalu River, the border with China and the Soviet Union.

At the Yalu, the Americans were confronted by a new, unexpected enemy and the possible annihilation of U.S. Army and Marine forces in Korea.

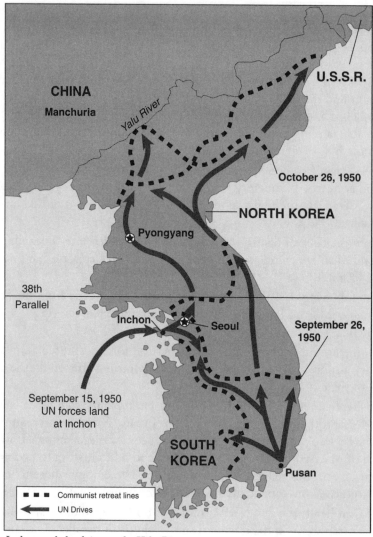

Inchon and the drive to the Yalu River.

CHAPTER 19

ATTACK ALONG THE YALU RIVER AND THE CHOSIN RESERVOIR

(NOVEMBER 25–DECEMBER 9, 1950)

The famous Chinese attack along the Yalu River and the subsequent American breakout from the Chosin Reservoir was a decisive victory in the sense that the Chinese were denied the opportunity to annihilate the 1st Marine Division and elements of the army's 7th Infantry Division. The Marines and soldiers conducted their famous "fighting withdrawal" in subfreezing temperatures over some of the world's most rugged terrain.

The campaign began in late September 1950, after U.S. president Harry Truman authorized an attack en masse across the north-south dividing line at the 38th parallel. Once the line was crossed, U.S. Army general Douglas MacArthur, commanding all American and United Nations (UN) forces in Korea, was to press north toward the Yalu River. (The Yalu River, which separates North Korea from Manchuria and to a lesser degree the Soviet Union, begins at the western border of Korea, near the 40th parallel, and proceeds northeast to the Sea of Japan.) Yet his drive was to be launched only if there were no major Chinese or Soviet army incursion into North Korea or a threat or an announcement of such by either of the Communist superpowers.

U.S. intelligence cables had begun to indicate that large numbers of Chinese forces were massing across the Yalu River. But the U.S. intelligence community, specifically the Central Intelligence Agency (CIA), did not believe the Chinese would attack. After all, in doing so it would threaten to expand the conflict into a general war with the nuclear-armed United States.

In early November, the United Nations gave tacit approval to MacArthur's drive north by agreeing to a resolution calling for the restoration of peace and security throughout the Korean peninsula. It was to be a "police action," in the words of President Truman, aimed at cleaning up the peninsula. That is exactly what MacArthur intended to do.

THE COMMANDERS

MacArthur felt he had the right army at the right time. Flush with success from their stunning victories at Inchon, Seoul, and Pusan, the American soldiers and Marines were self-seemingly invincible. And MacArthur had every confidence in his senior subordinate commanders.

MacArthur's force was composed of the U.S. 8th Army and an independent X Corps. The 8th, commanded by Lt. Gen. Walton H. "Bulldog" Walker, encompassed the U.S. I Corps and the IX Corps, as well as a South Korean army corps. The U.S. X Corps was under the command of U.S. Army major general Edward Mallory Almond. A hybrid Marine-Army force, the X Corps was made up of the 1st Marine Division and the 7th (Army) Infantry Division.

The 1st Marine Division, considered the most experienced division at the time, was under the command of Maj. Gen. Oliver P. Smith. The First became famous during World War II. Its actions at the Chosin Reservoir would become legendary.

The 7th Infantry Division, primarily occupation troops pieced together from Japan, was under the command of Maj. Gen. David Goodwin Barr. Like the 1st Marine Division, the Army's 7th had distinguished itself in combat during World War II. But most of the division's experienced officers and noncommissioned officers had been sent to other units prior to the Korean Conflict. At Chosin, elements of the 7th would be all but destroyed. But they would hold off two Chinese divisions, thus permitting the Marines to escape a similar fate.

MOVEMENT TO BATTLE

Despite the intelligence suggesting possible Chinese intervention, Mac-Arthur ordered Walker's 8th Army to push north-northwest, seize the Communist capital at Pyongyang, and then drive north toward the Yalu. In the east, the independent X Corps was to conduct an amphibious landing at Wonson. As a political and military buffer, MacArthur was to use only Republic of Korea (ROK) forces in the extreme northern territories along the Yalu.

Once ashore, the X Corps was to push toward the Chosin (also known as Changjin) Reservoir, a large body of water serving a vital hydroelectric plant near the North Korean town of Yudam-ni. The reservoir, fed by the Yalu River, was located in a remote region of North Korea, approximately 50 miles from the Chinese border at the Yalu.

By October 20, the vanguard elements of a massive Chinese force were moving toward and crossing the river.

Having seized and secured Pyongyang, the U.S. 8th Army began pushing north. On October 25, South Korean forces and elements of Walker's army met and clashed with the Chinese. After several days of fighting, the ROK and American forces had to fall back. Still, the American leadership dismissed the Chinese forces as being little more than 50,000 to 70,000 men total.

"They would have been utterly appalled to know that there were now six Chinese armies, eighteen divisions, between them and the Yalu River and the end of the war," said historian James L. Stokesbury. Making matters worse, the enemy force was growing.

On November 10, the 175th birthday of the U.S. Marine Corps, Almond ordered Smith to divide his forces at Hagaru-ri near the base of the Chosin Reservoir. There, where a road forked off to the northeast, Smith was to send one regiment to capture a second reservoir at Fusen. Such a maneuver over unfamiliar ground was dangerous. Smith persuaded Almond to rescind the order, arguing that his force was already spread too thin along the narrow road from Chin Hung-ni in the south. Almond agreed.

Instead, Smith was able to wait until the 1st Marine Regiment, under the command of Colonel Lewis Burwell "Chesty" Puller, could move up and place fresh American battalions—with a handful of Royal Marines—along the road at Hagaru-ri and further south at Koto-ri.

Smith then sent his 7th Marine Regiment north on the west side of the reservoir to Yudam-ni, while the 5th was sent along the east side. The goal was to eventually link up at the Yalu. It was not to be.

Almond ordered elements of the Army's 7th Infantry Division, specifically the 31st and 32nd Infantry Regiments (designated the 31st Regimental Combat Team), to relieve the 5th Marine Regiment east of the reservoir. The Marines then rejoined their fellow leathernecks on the west side.

The terrain surrounding the Chosin Reservoir was rugged. The banks on either side of the reservoir were dominated by steep mountains cut with only a few narrow, dirt roads capable of handling ox carts and wagons. Difficult indeed, but the weather was even more unforgiving—snow, ice, and mercilessly cold temperatures which often plummeted to 30 to 40 degrees below zero. Long, black nights and lashing winds of up to 40 and 50 miles an hour dropped the temperatures even further. The reservoir surface was a great sheet of ice, and everything else froze: the ground, the moving parts on weapons, vehicle motor oil, morphine and other medicines, blood plasma, even hands and feet. Soldiers touching the steel of their weapons often lost skin. Both the Americans and their enemies were bundled up as best they could be, but it was never enough. Making matters worse, the heavy clothes made the soldiers sweat whenever they exerted themselves. If they stood still for any length of time, the sweat turned to ice. Severe frostbite and other cold-related injuries were staggering.

On November 23, Thanksgiving Day, the Americans attempted to celebrate the holiday regardless of the unnerving situation developing around them. "We were served turkey and all the things that go with it on tin trays," said U.S. Navy hospital corpsman William Davis. "You had to eat fast because everything was turning cold. The gravy and then the mashed potatoes froze first. The inside of the turkey was still warm. Boy, you ate fast. And all the time the snipers were shooting at us."

As the Chinese continued to advance across the Yalu, thousands of copies of propaganda leaflets were circulated among the Chinese soldiers that referred to MacArthur as a "Wall Street house dog" and the U.S. Marine Corps as a "pack of despoilers." The leaflets also suggested that the Marines were specially trained to wage an "unprecedentedly brutal and inhuman, predatory war against the freedom-loving heroic Korean people."

THE CHINESE ATTACK

On November 25 and 26, the Chinese 9th Army Group, composed of four Communist armies under the command of Gen. Song Shilun, attacked in force. (Estimates have since varied as to how many Chinese soldiers actually crossed the Yalu. But it has been widely held that of one million Chinese soldiers massed on the border, some 300,000 attacked across the river into North Korea.)

In the face of overwhelming numbers, Walker's 8th Army began pulling back, avoiding major contact, and ultimately abandoning Pyongyang in early December. Soon thereafter, his force was on the south side of the 38th parallel and preparing a coast-to-coast defense.

Almond's X Corps was not nearly as fortunate.

The Chinese 9th Army Group had special orders. Chairman Mao Tse-tung, the Communist leader of the People's Republic of China, issued specific instructions to General Song stating that the U.S. 1st Marine Division was to be targeted for annihilation. "The American Marine First Division has the highest combat effectiveness in the American armed forces," wrote Mao to General Song. "It seems not enough for our four divisions to surround and annihilate its two regiments. You should have one or two more divisions as a reserve force." Moreover, all other American and Allied forces were to be eliminated to the last man.

The following night, the American Marines and soldiers, along with their UN allies, were struck by General Song's enormous force on both the eastern and western banks of the reservoir. The attacking Chinese forces numbered some 120,000 troops, whereas the combined strength of the Marines, army, and Allied troops was around 16,000.

On the west side of the reservoir the northernmost advance 5th and 7th Marine Regiments were cut off at Yudam-ni. The Chinese, rushing forward in massed human waves, attacked the American positions, screaming and blowing horns and whistles.

"It was enough to make your hair stand on end," said Marine corporal Arthur Koch in Martin Russ's *Breakout: The Chosin Reservoir Campaign*. "When the bugles died away we heard a voice through a megaphone and then the blast of a police whistle. I was plenty scared, but who wasn't? I couldn't believe my eyes when I saw them in the moonlight. It was like the snow was coming to life ... they came in a rush, like a pack of mad dogs."

Farther south, in the center at Toktong Pass, an isolated company was struck. Amazingly, the Chinese were unable to dislodge them. Two battalions each, of the 1st Marine Regiment, at Hagaru-ri (division head-quarters) and Koto-ri were also struck. Upon discovering that his force was completely surrounded by Chinese forces, Colonel Puller responded, "Those poor bastards. They've got us just where we want them. We can shoot in every direction now."

On the east side of the reservoir, the U.S. Army's 31st Regimental Combat Team was also hit and encircled.

"All hell broke lose," said U.S. Army private first class James Ransone Jr. whose position was struck hard on the night of November 27. "Some of my buddies, who were in an outpost line on the upward slope of a hill were being overrun. In the light of the flares that exploded overhead, I saw Chinese soldiers jumping in the holes with the GIs. There was panic in the area." According to Ransone, everyone was firing wildly, not knowing who they were firing at. "An awful lot of people on both sides got killed," he said.

The Chinese proved to be far more formidable on the attack than their North Korean allies. The latter would retreat when driven off of a position. Not so with the Chinese who would make a determined stand in every instance. There were, however, flaws in Chinese tactics: They repeatedly attacked impregnable positions regardless of their own losses. They failed to take advantage of their opponents whenever they broke through a point along the line or whenever the latter fell back from a position. And they needlessly exposed themselves to enemy fire during lulls in the fighting.

The Americans held on both sides of the reservoir, but the situation worsened by the hour. On the east side, the army's 31st Regimental Combat Team was slowing the Chinese advance to Hagaru-ri. But they were being cut to pieces in the process. His troops surrounded, literally freezing to death, and running out of ammunition, Lt. Col. Donald Carlos Faith Jr. sent his last radio transmission to 1st Marine Division headquarters at Hagaru-ri. "Unless someone can help us, I don't have much hope that anybody's going to get out of this," Faith said.

He was told that there was nothing beyond air support that could be sent in terms of assistance. There simply were not enough warm bodies with weapons to relieve the embattled 31st.

"I understand," Faith said. It was the last message he would ever send. Personally leading several counterattacks against an overwhelming number of Chinese, Faith was killed. He was subsequently awarded the Congressional Medal of Honor.

Almost immediately, Almond blamed the Marines for not stationing enough men at Hagaru-ri to send a relief force to rescue the soldiers in the east. But Smith's forces were perilously thin, and they, too, were catching hell. In fact, everyone from cooks to truck mechanics had been placed on the Marine line as riflemen. A minor attempt was made to reach retreating army forces in the east, but the effort was abandoned in the face of fierce enemy opposition. Most of the soldiers who did escape did so individually. To survive in the east required a superhuman summoning of strength. But those who did were physically and emotionally wrecked by the time they reached the Marines. The loss of his men was more than General Barr could emotionally bear. Mercifully, he was soon relieved of command.

On December 1, Almond ordered the most advanced elements of X Corps to begin falling back. The Marines, farthest north at Yudam-ni, loaded everything—field guns, equipment, badly shattered men, and frozen corpses—onto trucks and began their epic 78-mile fighting withdrawal toward the coast. Smith was determined to leave with all of his dead and wounded, and his withdrawal was to be an orderly breakout. Like a "contracting telescope," according to Stokesbury, each unit would close with and consequently reinforce the next. But the Chinese were trying to break the telescope at every joint. As the Marines pulled back along the narrow, windswept road, the enemy attacked again and again. The American column moved at a snail's pace, stopping long enough to counterattack at turns in the road, retrieve their dead and wounded, and continue to march. The column's flanks were constantly harassed, and many men were jumped by bayonet-wielding Chinese soldiers. When the men needed to relieve themselves, they did so on the road. To stray from the column was nothing less than suicide.

Three days after pulling out of their positions at Yudam-ni, the embattled Americans reached the outskirts of Hagaru-ri. When Smith reached division headquarters, he was met by several war correspondents. Eager to report positive news for the folks back home, the correspondents were thrilled with Smith's defiant words. "Gentlemen, we are not retreating," the general said. "We are merely attacking in another direction."

Fed, regrouped, and burning what they didn't need, the Americans left Hagaru-ri for Koto-ri on December 6. The Chinese continued launching savage attacks along the route.

At Koto-ri, several Marine officers expressed concern that their force might not survive the final trek to the coast. Colonel Puller, whose actions at Chosin would win him the Congressional Medal of Honor, snapped back, "There aren't enough [Chinese] in the world to stop a Marine regiment going where it wants to go! Christ in His mercy will see us through."

Puller's words rang true. By December 10, the column had passed through the safety of X Corps lines at Chinhung-ni, and reached the coast at Hamnung.

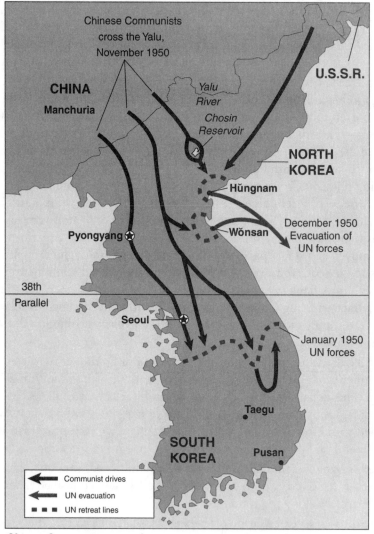

Chinese Communists enter the war.

THE AFTERMATH

In mid-December, the soldiers and Marines of Walker's 8th Army began boarding ships for points south. By Christmas Eve, all American forces had pulled out of northeast Korea, leaving the smoking port of Hamnung resembling something out of Dante's *Inferno*. (Everything that was not taken off the beach was burned or detonated, including unstable, frozen dynamite and several hundred bombs and hundreds of drums of gasoline.) On December 23, Walker was killed in a jeep accident while visiting troops. He was replaced by Lt. Gen. Matthew Ridgeway, the tomahawk-tough former commander of paratroops. As tragic as Walker's death was, Ridgeway's assumption of 8th Army command was just what the weary soldiers and Marines needed. In the coming weeks, he would whip his army back into fighting trim.

The fighting withdrawal at Chosin Reservoir will forever be regarded as one of the most remarkable breakout actions in history. The Americans suffered some 3,000 killed, another 6,000 wounded, and thousands of severe frostbite casualties. But they killed approximately 28,000 enemy soldiers and wounded another 12,500.

Seventeen Congressional Medals of Honor were awarded to combatants who participated in the campaign, and another 70 received Navy Crosses—the most ever awarded for a single battle in American military history.

For their magnificent performance, the 1st Marine Division was awarded a Presidential Unit Citation, a portion of which read:

> Battling desperately night and day in the face of almost insurmountable odds throughout a period of two weeks of intense and sustained combat, the First Marine Division, Reinforced, emerged from its ordeal as a fighting unit with its wounded, with its guns and equipment and with its prisoners, decisively defeating seven enemy divisions, together with elements of three others, and inflicting major losses which seriously impaired the military effectiveness of the hostile forces for a considerable period of time.

The Army's 7th Infantry Division would justifiably be included in the citation. But unfortunately, the inclusion was overlooked for nearly a half-century. In fact, had the 31st Regimental Combat Team not tied the Chinese up on the east side of the Chosin Reservoir, the enemy would have been able to cut off the main American body at Hagaru-ri. The Marines would have then been cut off from the coast and probably destroyed.

PART 4

THE VIETNAM WAR

CHAPTER 20

INTRODUCTION TO THE VIETNAM WAR

Whereas the Korean conflict was never decisively concluded, the Vietnam War—also known as the Second Indochina War—was the first war in American military history that the United States lost.

America's initial involvement in Vietnam was essentially the result of France's inability to overcome nationalist aggression in the French colony of Indochina after World War II. The nationalists—or Vietminh—led by Communist revolutionary leader Ho Chi Minh, waged a successful guerrilla war against their French colonial masters. The United States provided a tremendous amount of financial support to France in hopes the French would regain control in Indochina. But the French, after enduring four years of Nazi occupation during World War II and then struggling to recover their lost colonial possessions throughout the world, were more concerned with problems back home.

> Indochina included the colony of Cochin China and the protectorates of Tonkin, Annam, Laos, and Cambodia. Cochin China, Tonkin, and Annam were later united to form Vietnam.

In May 1954, French army forces, under the command of Lt. Gen. Henri Navarre, suffered a stunning defeat by the Vietminh, under the command of Gen. Vo Nguyen Giap, at the Battle of

Dien Bien Phu. Two months later, the Geneva Accords ended French control. France and the Communists agreed to a cessation of hostilities. France withdrew from Southeast Asia. Vietnam was temporarily divided into North and South Vietnam at the 17th parallel. And free elections in the new Republic of South Vietnam were slated for 1956. The Vietminh meanwhile established a Communist government in the northern city of Hanoi.

A power struggle soon developed in the South, and Ngo Dinh Diem, a Roman Catholic with a noble mandarin blood line, emerged as South Vietnam's premier. Diem quickly set up an authoritarian government run by members of his family. He cancelled the upcoming elections. He openly exhibited favoritism toward those loyal to him during his rise to power. And he favored the Roman Catholic community over the Buddhists. Consequently, he had a number of opponents. The latter and their followers fled to the backcountry, many of them ultimately forming the nucleus of what would become the National Liberation Front (the Communist Party in South Vietnam), also known as the Vietcong movement.

With France gone, American foreign service personnel and a handful of U.S. military advisers moved in to fill the vacuum and to make good on the preceding years of American financial support in Vietnam. Beyond that, there was a strong desire in Washington to contain the spread of communism. By 1960, roughly 700 American military advisers were in South Vietnam.

Several attempts were made by Diem's opponents to overthrow his regime. In 1963, U.S. president John Fitzgerald Kennedy—disturbed by the increasing opposition to Diem and the South Vietnamese leader's own inability to cooperate with the Americans—gave tacit approval to a planned coup d'état aimed at Diem's removal. In early November, Diem was overthrown. He and his brother were subsequently executed. Ironically, Kennedy himself was assassinated three weeks later.

A succession of coups led by South Vietnamese military officers followed Diem's ouster.

On June 20, 1964, U.S. Army general William Childs Westmoreland, a rising star whose rugged, rock-jawed presence suggested he had been tagged for leadership in central casting, became commanding general of the U.S. Military Assistance Command Vietnam (MACV). As chief of MACV, Westmoreland was the senior commander of all American forces in Vietnam. (Westmoreland would serve in that capacity until he was replaced by U.S. Army general Creighton Abrams in 1968. Though officially promoted to chief of staff, Westmoreland was said to have been "kicked upstairs," suggesting that his promotion was in fact a demotion from Vietnam.)

GULF OF TONKIN INCIDENT

On August 2, North Vietnamese torpedo boats attacked the USS *Maddox*, an American destroyer operating in North Vietnam's Gulf of Tonkin. The *Maddox* returned fire. American jets from the aircraft carrier *Ticonderoga* also engaged, and one enemy boat was sunk. The North Vietnamese claimed that the destroyer had been supporting South Vietnamese amphibious raiders operating on nearby islands the previous night. On August 4, the *Maddox* and the *C. Turner Joy*, another destroyer, returned to the Gulf. Both ships reported that they were again under attack. But the legitimacy of the second attack has since been subject of debate.

Nevertheless, in the summer of 1964, the Gulf of Tonkin incident was enough for U.S. president Lyndon Baines Johnson to strike back. He ordered carrier-based warplanes to strike targets in North Vietnam, and he asked Congress to pass legislation granting him the freedom to attack in the future if needed.

Less than a week later, Congress passed the Gulf of Tonkin Resolution. The act stipulated that the president of the United States, as commander in chief of the armed forces, could "take all necessary measures to repel any armed attack against the forces of the United States and to prevent further aggression." The resolution was essentially a mandate for offensive action in Vietnam.

In 1965, Nguyen Van Thieu, Duong Van Minh, and Nguyen Cao Ky assumed the reigns of the South Vietnamese government.

Political instability in the South coupled with an increase in Communist activity convinced Johnson that a more aggressive approach was needed. Thus, American financial support and military assistance were increased.

The initial strategy seemed simple: The United States would provide military support to the Republic of (South) Vietnam. In so doing, the Army of the Republic of (North) Vietnam—ARVN—would be able to theoretically prevail over the Communist Vietcong operating in the South. Moreover, North Vietnam, which was supporting the Communists in the South, would be subjected to massive aerial bombardments. American strategists believed that by bombing North Vietnam, the North Vietnamese would realize that the price in lives and property the Communists were paying for their support of the Vietcong was far too costly.

The problem in both instances was that the U.S. military was operating under restraints that prevented it from destroying the enemy in his sanctuaries. U.S. policymakers, justifiably fearful of opening a general war with the nuclear-armed Communist nations of China and the Soviet Union, restricted the American armed forces in terms of only allowing American soldiers to engage the enemy on specific ground within Vietnam. Laos and Cambodia, border countries where the Communists were able to move freely, were initially deemed off-limits. North Vietnam, off-limits to ground forces, was at times considered to be fair game for American warplanes, but only within limited sectors.

In the relatively new Cold War environment, the superpowers found themselves fighting one another through surrogate armies, thus avoiding direct armed conflict and possibly a nuclear exchange. For a superpower to directly involve its own army was to put that army in a situation wherein it would be restricted in its movements and it would not be able to employ all of the weapons in its arsenal (including nuclear weapons). Thus, proxy armies were the preferred method of waging war. It was an odd strategy, unfamiliar to both sides. But the U.S. government believed its army to be invincible even with that army's hands tied behind its back. The war was simply unwinnable from the start.

"Could more military pressure have been applied, in the sense of more bombing of the North? No," former U.S. Secretary of Defense Robert McNamara would tell CNN in a 1998 interview. "We dropped two or three times as much bombs in North and South Vietnam as were dropped by all Allied forces throughout World War II against all enemies. It was a tremendous air effort. But there are certain things bombing can't accomplish. They can't break the will of people under certain circumstances. They didn't break the will of the North Vietnamese. And it cannot stop the movement of the small quantities of supplies that were necessary to support the Vietcong and the North Vietnamese forces in the South. They didn't, and it couldn't; and no additional amount of money or bombing could have."

South Vietnam was divided into four primary tactical zones. Each zone was commanded by a South Vietnamese general, but American generals who commanded their own forces also had independent responsibilities within those zones. The I Corps Tactical Zone in the North bordered the Demilitarized Zone in the extreme north, Laos to the west, and the South China Sea to the east. I Corps was the primary responsibility of the U.S. Marine Corps. Below I Corps was II Corps, or the Central Highlands region, which bordered both Laos and Cambodia to the west and the coastline east. III Corps Tactical Zone, the most populated of the four zones, bordered Cambodia to the west and the sea to the east. Both II Corps and III Corps were the primary responsibilities of the U.S. Army. IV Corps Tactical Zone was located in the far south. The latter zone encompassed the storied Mekong River region. The area around Saigon, between III Corps and IV Corps, was considered a separate administrative Special Capital Zone.

By the end of 1964, the U.S. military presence in South Vietnam had increased to almost 24,000 personnel. By the summer of 1965, it was clear that America's involvement in Vietnam had evolved from an advisory capacity to a full-fledged combat role. Roughly 51,000 U.S. troops were "in country" (that number would eventually swell to 500,000), and Westmoreland was given the authority to commit American forces to battle whenever it was deemed necessary.

INTRODUCTION OF AMERICAN COMBAT FORCES

In early 1965, U.S. Marines landed in Vietnam. They were soon followed by U.S. Army airborne and cavalry forces. In August, dismayed Americans back home watched a televised CBS news report showing a Marine burning down a Vietnamese hut with a cigarette lighter. And newspapers around the country began publishing stories that described a "dirty little war" wherein GIs were killing Vietnamese civilians and torching their homes. American opposition to the war would continue to mount, ultimately dividing much of the nation, demoralizing already-stymied U.S. troops, and inspiring the enemy. But American troops, in the words of Marine Corps commandant general Wallace M. Greene Jr., were there to "kill Vietcong."

Fighting in Vietnam was a nasty affair. Unlike previous wars where soldiers marched across newly captured ground toward their military objective, victory, and home, the combat soldier in Vietnam was tasked with searching unfamiliar ground for an elusive, culturally alien enemy and killing him. Period. A high body count was the order of the day.

This strategy violated previous battle doctrine which had held for centuries. Frederick the Great, an 18th-century Prussian military strategist, once wrote, "It is the ground gained and not the number of enemy dead that gives you victory." In Vietnam, however, success was measured in terms of numbers killed, not ground gained.

"THE POOR BLOODY INFANTRY"

To accomplish this, soldiers and Marines were trucked, marched, or helicopter-lifted deep into the backcountry. There, young American GIs, carrying 50 to 100 pounds of equipment, plodded through flooded rice paddies and machete-cut their way through steaming jungles inhabited by poisonous snakes, all manner of insects, wild hogs, the occasional tiger, and an enemy who was often indistinguishable from the local civilian population. The Americans also waded across snake-infested rivers in order to avoid the heavily mined and booby trapped roads and causeways. The heat and humidity were stifling. Rain was often endless, and the soldiers were always soaking wet. Whenever the troops stopped, they picked leeches out of their boots and burned them off their skin with cigarettes.

By day, the American soldiers and Marines moved throughout the countryside munching on salt tablets and trying to shield the exposed metal parts of their weapons from the sun. The metal not only became blistering hot to the touch, but reflected light for miles around.

At night, the troops slept in the mud, stared at the stars and dreamed of home, or positioned themselves to ambush enemy patrols. "At their worst, at night, the mosquitoes would just about carry you away," 1st Lt. John Temple Ligon, an artillery forward observer with the 173rd Airborne Brigade, recalled years later. "You couldn't sleep with the buzzing in the ear, and when the buzzing stopped it was like a V-1 in WWII London. You knew you were about to lose blood."

Ligon added, "Mosquito repellent was okay as long as it was relatively fresh, maybe no more than three hours since the last application. Empty sandbags as head hoods worked but you couldn't see very well." It was a miserable environment.

When enemy contact was made, combat leaders attempted to quickly isolate their foes from support, shut down their ability to maneuver, and crush them with overwhelming firepower.

Firefights between opposing forces were often brief, violent clashes lasting approximately 15 minutes. If the enemy force was small, the fighting might last three to five minutes. If the force was large or well-entrenched, supporting jets, helicopter gunships, tanks, or artillery would be called in, thus extending the fight to an hour or more. Occasionally, huge enemy forces were encountered which were reinforced and resupplied through an extensive network of underground rooms and tunnels. Those clashes sometimes lasted for more than 24 hours.

CHAPTER 20: INTRODUCTION TO THE VIETNAM WAR

Enemy forces operating in South Vietnam were supplied with weapons and ammunition from North Vietnam via the Ho Chi Minh Trail. The trial extended southwest from North Vietnam into Laos, and then south along the eastern edge of Laos into Cambodia. The trail then turned east at various points along the Laotian and Cambodian borders into South Vietnam.

In the air, there was virtually no contest. American pilots ruled the skies. Still, many aircrew members were killed, wounded, or captured, their planes or helicopters having been hit or brought down by enemy small arms fire in South Vietnam and enemy antiaircraft artillery, surface to air missiles, or the occasional Soviet-made MIG fighter over North Vietnam.

In nearly all cases, American troops carried the day on the battlefield—a result and a foreshadowing of the overwhelming technological edge American forces would wield over their adversaries during the remainder of the 20th century.

But the war, mismanaged in Washington and unpopular throughout the heart of America, was a lost cause. In late January 1973, U.S. president Richard M. Nixon announced an internationally supervised cease-fire, the withdrawal of all American forces from South Vietnam, and promises from North Vietnam for both the imminent release of all American prisoners of war and the "fullest possible accounting" of those missing in action.

Nixon assured the South Vietnamese government that they would not be abandoned, and that the U.S. would respond militarily if North Vietnam violated the cease-fire agreement. The reality was that America permanently withdrew its military forces, excepting a few military advisers and Marine guards. Nixon, under threat of impeachment after the Watergate debacle, resigned the following year. The Communists continued to fight. And the South Vietnamese armed forces, without the support of the American military, continued to lose ground.

On April 25, 1975, an American military delegation met with North Vietnamese officials in Hanoi to discuss matters related to the status of American combatants still listed as missing in action. During the meeting, U.S. Army colonel Harry G. Summers Jr. turned to his North Vietnamese counterpart and said, "You know, you never beat us on the battlefield." The North Vietnamese officer pondered the statement for a moment and then responded. "That may be so," he said. "But it is also irrelevant."

Five days later, the last Marine at the U.S. Embassy in Saigon boarded a helicopter bound for the South China Sea and beyond. The war was over. Fifty-eight thousand Americans had been killed, and another three hundred thousand wounded.

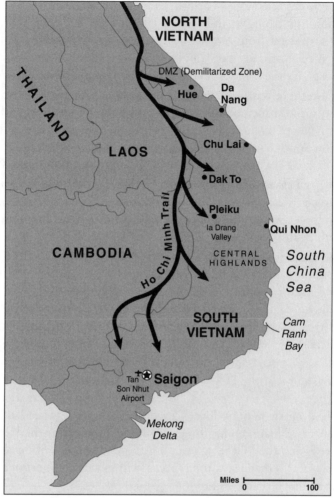

The Ho Chi Minh Trail and battle sites.

"Every soldier, sailor, airman, and Marine can look back upon their service in Vietnam with great pride," Westmoreland said years later, echoing Summers's comment. "And they can be sure that despite the final failure of the South Vietnamese, the record of the American military forces, of never having lost a war, is still intact. I have no doubt about this and no regrets."

CHU LAI

(AUGUST 17–24, 1965)

The 1965 Battle for Chu Lai—also known as the Battle of Van Tuong—was the first campaign in Vietnam in which U.S. troops engaged the enemy in a regimental-size pitched battle over open ground. The fighting lasted less than a week and ended in a decisive American victory.

Seeds for the battle, code-named Operation Starlite, were sown when, on August 15, a Vietcong deserter was apprehended by South Vietnamese forces under Brig. Gen. Nguyen Chanh Thi, who commanded the I Corps Tactical Zone. Interrogated at Thi's headquarters, the deserter revealed that the First Vietcong (VC) Regiment was massing for an attack against the isolated U.S. Marine base at Chu Lai. Located 55 miles south of Da Nang in I Corps, Chu Lai was a coastal installation that had a large airfield capable of handling both helicopters and jets. And the VC Regiment was hoping to knock it out of operation. According to the deserter, the 2,000-man enemy force was located in the village of Van Tuong, 12 miles southeast of Chu Lai.

General Thi deemed the information so sensitive he kept it from his subordinate officers, and directly informed Maj. Gen. Lewis William Walt, commanding general of both the III Marine

Amphibious Force and the 3rd Marine Division. Walt was also chief of Naval Forces Vietnam. Known to his men as "Uncle Lew," Walt was all-Marine and ready for a brawl.

Maj. Gen. Lewis William Walt grew up a Kansas farm boy and worked his way through Colorado State University were he was a standout lineman on the football team. During World War II, he distinguished himself as a Marines "Raider" in the south Pacific. More than two decades later, at age 52, he found himself responsible for defending three enclaves in South Vietnam's I Corps: Da Nang, Phu Bai, and Chu Lai.

Having his own intelligence sources corroborate the deserter's story, Walt immediately relayed the intelligence to his boss—U.S. Army general William Childs Westmoreland, commander of American forces in Vietnam—and requested permission to launch a preemptive attack against the enemy regiment and destroy it. Westmoreland agreed. Walt's leathernecks were to stage a classic land-sea-air assault, attacking the enemy stronghold at Van Tuong from two directions at once while blocking the enemy's escape routes. The operation, though directed by Walt, was to be led at the tactical level by Col. Oscar Franklin Peatross, a North Carolina native who also served as a Raider in World War II.

Starlite kicked off after a sunrise breakfast on August 17. At 10 A.M., a single company from the 3rd Marine Regiment was trucked a few miles south of Chu Lai. The Americans then disembarked and marched four miles to a position just north of Van Tuong and camped overnight. The terrain surrounding Van Tuong was open, pleasant-looking country: sandy flats laced with meandering streams and small forested hills. Tiny hamlets were scattered across the flats. The hamlets were surrounded by rice paddies and dry crop fields.

Encountering token resistance on the march, the Marines aroused no suspicion. The enemy believed the American company to be nothing more than one of many patrols often sighted in the area.

Just before dawn on August 18, the remainder of the company's battalion began rushing ashore on a nearby beach.

THE MARINES ATTACK

At 6:15 A.M., artillery and jets began pummeling three preselected helicopter landing zones (LZs) along a north-south line west of Van Tuong.

CHAPTER 21: CHU LAI

The landing zones were known as LZ Red (on the north end of the line), LZ White (in the center), and LZ Blue (on the southernmost point).

At 6:30, the seaborne Marine battalion moved inland. At 6:45, elements of the 4th Marine Regiment began flying into the landing zones by helicopter. Marines landing at LZ Red and LZ White encountered light opposition, whereas Marines at LZ Blue landed right on top of a VC battalion.

The enemy, lying low, allowed the first few helicopters to land and the Marines to disembark before revealing themselves. Once there was a substantial concentration of helicopters and Marines in the LZ, the VC opened up on them with machine guns, mortars, and rocket-propelled grenades.

The fighting was sharp and within minutes of the first shots, the Marines found themselves surrounded. Worse, the Americans were caught in the open and the bulk of the enemy force was occupying a nearby hill with good cover and concealment. Casualties mounted on both sides. Marine radios crackled with frantic requests for fire support. Soon, a few U.S. tanks rolled in and began blasting the enemy positions. Overhead, three U.S. Army helicopter gunships, thundering to the rescue, began rocketing the hill mercilessly. The Marine infantry counterattacked, captured the smoking heights, and wiped out what remained of the enemy battalion. The Americans then regrouped and pressed toward Van Tuong.

While the fight was raging at LZ Blue, the seaborne force attacked Van Tuong from the south. The helicopter-borne forces from LZ Red and LZ White attacked from the west. One company loaded in amphibious tractors (amtracs) made a river crossing north of Van Tuong and positioned itself to block any retreat of enemy forces in that direction. A handful of U.S. Navy warships prevented the enemy from escaping east along the coast or by boats in the South China Sea. Over the course of the battle, the ships would sink seven small sampans loaded with fleeing enemy soldiers. Naval gunfire would also pin down over 100 VC attempting to slip away from the beach.

As the attacking force closed in on Van Tuong, the enemy resisted stubbornly. Opposition was fierce at the village of An Cuong, a few miles south of Van Tuong, and a couple of miles northeast of the burning hill at LZ Blue.

The VC regiment was quickly surrounded by Peatross's leathernecks. The enemy soldiers, their backs to the sea, fought hard. But their weapons were unable to match the overwhelming firepower of the Americans.

By August 19, all organized VC resistance had ceased and what was left of the enemy regiment was on the run. The main body of the force had been broken up into several pieces, and the VC were trying to retreat the best way they knew how. Rear-guard elements covering the retreat continued shooting into the American ranks. Enemy snipers were also used to cover the retreat. But they were quickly silenced.

"The Viet Cong were disabused of any illusion that they could defeat the Marines in a stand-up battle," Brig. Gen. Edwin H. Simmons would later write.

For the next several days, the Marines, with the support of Army of the Republic of Vietnam (ARVN) troops, conducted a series of sweeps throughout the surrounding countryside. As the Americans moved into nearby villages, small clashes erupted from hiding enemy soldiers.

By August 24, nearly 600 VC soldiers were confirmed dead, and another 115 were estimated to have been killed. The Marines suffered the loss of 46 killed (including two who would posthumously receive the Congressional Medal of Honor) and another 204 wounded.

THE AFTERMATH

Starlite was a smashing success. Beyond the victory, it demonstrated the effectiveness of a single effort when land, sea, and air elements were brought under one roof. In Walt's mind, close air was key. The supporting aircraft flew "within 200 feet of our pinned down troops and was a very important factor in our winning the battle," he said. "I have never seen a finer example of close air support."

Minor tactical lessons were also learned during Starlite: The plan called for two gallons of fresh drinking water per Marine for the duration of the mission. But the stifling heat combined with the physical exertions required of each man proved that more water was needed. Additionally, the semi-automatic M-14 infantry rifle proved to be too heavy and unwieldy for fast-moving troops being transported in confined-space vehicles like amtracs and helicopters.

A new, lighter assault rifle was needed. It would debut in force with the U.S. 7th Cavalry in the storied Ia Drang Valley.

CHAPTER 22

IA DRANG VALLEY

(NOVEMBER 14–20, 1965)

The Battle for the Ia Drang Valley was the first large-scale battle between U.S. and North Vietnamese Army forces. Part of a larger campaign code-named Operation Silver (Shiny) Bayonet, the battle lasted for six days, involved troopers from the famous 7th U.S. Cavalry, and resulted in an American win. But its significance to both the overall war and future conflicts extended far beyond the victory in the valley. In his best-selling book, *We Were Soldiers Once ... and Young*, Lt. Gen. Harold Gregory "Hal" Moore Jr. referred to Ia Drang as something of a "dress rehearsal" for the new highly mobile form of warfare that would characterize the fighting in Southeast Asia. New weapons and techniques were tested which literally changed the face of modern American infantry combat. But it wasn't without great cost.

THE SITUATION

The Ia (translated into English, "river") Drang Valley was a desolate place. It was located near Pleiku in the II Corps Tactical Zone some 10 miles east of one of the points where the infamous Ho Chi Minh Trail crossed the Cambodian border and entered South

Vietnam. The landscape was characterized by flat to lightly rolling terrain covered with tall elephant grass, tangles of scrub brush, termite and ant mounds, and small scraggly trees. The ground itself was cut with dry gullies and creek beds, all surrounded by rolling, densely forested hills and a rugged mountainous mass known as the Chu Pong massif. There were in fact endless places for the enemy to conceal himself.

On October 19, North Vietnamese Army (NVA) forces attacked a South Vietnamese Civilian Irregular Defense Group (CIDG)/U.S. Special Forces camp at Plei Me in an opening act aimed at seizing South Vietnam's Central Highlands.

Intelligence reports indicated that three enemy regiments—the 32nd, the 33rd, and the 66th, under the command of NVA brigadier general Chu Huy Man—were planning to wipe out three such camps in the area, seize the city of Pleiku, and ultimately split South Vietnam in two.

The enemy's 33rd Regiment was at Plei Me. The 32nd Regiment was waiting along the expected route from Pleiku to Plei Me in hopes of ambushing any relief column. And soldiers of the 66th Regiment were organizing their forces in the remote Ia Drang Valley.

U.S. Army general William Childs Westmoreland, commander of all American forces in Vietnam, decided to send in the cavalry. His specific choice was U.S. Army major general Harry W. O. Kinnard's 1st Brigade of the 1st Cavalry Division.

The 1st Brigade became the supporting element of a larger Army of the Republic of (South) Vietnam (ARVN) force. Backed by heavy artillery and close air support, the allied force skirted the ambush sites along the Pleiku–Plei Me route by simply flying over them in helicopters or attacking them on the ground with overwhelming firepower and a few tanks. The allies then overwhelmed the enemy with massed fires and forced him to withdraw from Plei Me.

As the enemy force pulled back it was constantly attacked by roving bands of helicopter gunships from Kinnard's air reconnaissance arm, the 1st Squadron, 9th Cavalry Regiment.

Having suffered heavy casualties, the stunned 33rd NVA Regiment joined the 66th in the Ia Drang. The 32nd, also having suffered losses, retreated farther west toward the Cambodian border.

In early November, the 1st Brigade was relieved by the 3rd and mopping-up operations continued. Meanwhile, fresh intelligence indicated that a large enemy force was planning to launch a second attack on Plei

Me from a base camp in the Ia Drang Valley. To confirm the intelligence and preempt any thrust from the valley, Westmoreland ordered Kinnard to attack.

Having previously traded their horses for helicopters, the 1st Cavalry Division was the first airmobile division in Army history. Riding helicopters into battle was still something of a novel concept in 1965. But Kinnard believed his troopers had perfected the art of air-assaulting (delivering by helicopter) a large armed force into a combat zone. At Ia Drang he would prove it.

For the operation, Kinnard chose the division's famed 7th Cavalry Regiment. His primary striking force would be the 1st Battalion of the 7th Cavalry under the command of Lt. Col. Hal Moore, a tall, blue-eyed, fighting Kentuckian of the first order. Moore would rise to the rank of lieutenant general and would write the previously mentioned best-seller.

The 450-man 1st Battalion would serve as the advance element of a larger force that would include the 2nd Battalion of the 7th Cavalry, under the command of Lt. Col. Robert McDade, and one attached company, Alpha, of the 2nd Battalion, 5th Cavalry, under the command of Capt. George Forrest.

"SADDLE UP"

On the morning of November 14, Moore's troopers boarded helicopters bound for the Ia Drang Valley. As they approached their predetermined landing zone (LZ), Moore's immediate concern was that the landings be properly coordinated with the preparatory artillery bombardment. If the artillery ceased firing too soon, any enemy force around the LZ would be up and ready when the helicopters arrived. If the artillery lingered too long, the choppers would be landing under their own shellfire. Timing was critical.

Two minutes out, the cavalry troopers saw smoke rising up from around a small clearing no larger than a football field. The clearing was their designated landing zone, LZ X-Ray. Escorting gunships raced ahead of the landing force and peppered the LZ with machine guns and rockets.

Just after 10:45 A.M., the first transport helicopter thundered in, flared its nose and landed. The cavalry troopers, led by Moore, leapt out and sprinted toward a grove of trees on the western edge of the clearing.

The landings were textbook: perfect air and artillery coordination and no immediate opposition. To Moore, it seemed too good to be true. But the cavalry commander was also concerned about the area's highest terrain feature, the Chu Pong massif. From there, he believed, his force was under constant observation.

Indeed, within minutes of landing, Moore's men captured a lone enemy soldier who revealed that there were three battalions of his fellow soldiers on the mountain who wanted "very much to kill Americans."

Approximately 2,000 NVA soldiers—elements of the 66th and 33rd Regiments—were scattered along the mountain's slopes and on other, smaller hills surrounding the LZ. Unbeknownst to Moore, his force was outnumbered by more than four to one.

In an attempt to locate the enemy, one of Moore's companies moved out in northwesterly direction. The remainder of the battalion secured the area around LZ X-Ray.

INITIAL CONTACT

Just after noon, the sound of gunfire rang out from the direction of the advancing company. At the landing zone, some of Moore's troopers had just opened a few C ration cans for lunch. "Eat fast," their sergeants said. "And get ready to move." The advancing company had found the enemy, but one American platoon was quickly pinned down and isolated.

Almost at once, the entire landing zone was attacked by large enemy forces from the massif's foothills, south and west. Fighting was fierce as the enemy forces were determined to make close contact with the Americans.

Battling fanatical human-wave attacks in 100-plus-degree heat, Moore's troopers stood their ground on the LZ. Meanwhile, helicopter pilots braved murderous ground fire to deliver water and ammunition and retrieve the wounded.

In the early afternoon, the enemy temporarily broke off the engagement and withdrew to regroup. They returned within an hour and the fighting became "red hot." Moore's men suffered more than 100 casualties the first day, but the NVA casualties were far higher.

The encircled platoon was holding, but they were running out of water and ammunition. Wounds were bandaged with T-shirts and toilet paper. Several times the platoon's troopers were nearly overrun. But each time, platoon commander staff sergeant Clyde E. Savage (senior officers and noncommissioned officers were either dead or wounded) called artillery fire on his own position and drove the enemy back.

Fighting was sporadic throughout the night but resumed in full the following day. At 6:30 A.M., the enemy launched a massive assault against the

American lines along the southern perimeter. The line was broken within one-half hour and Moore issued a "broken arrow" alert, which signaled that he was about to be overrun. He then radioed in air and artillery on his own position and ordered his men to take cover. The enemy was driven back, but fighting continued along Moore's front.

The Americans fought with a fanaticism that surprised their foes. The surviving members of Savage's isolated platoon made a pact that, no matter what happened, they would not surrender. "They continued to fight until the Viet Cong overran the position and bayoneted all the Americans they could find," wrote author Victor Hicken in *The American Fighting Man*. But the enemy did not get them all, and the platoon held.

By midmorning, several war correspondents had hitched rides on helicopters making ammunition and water runs to the Ia Drang. Touching down at X-Ray, they found a smoking battlefield, still under enemy fire, but under the total control of the U.S. Cavalry. Two of the reporters were greeted by a breathless, though exhilarated, Moore who had just beaten back a three-hour assault on his 300-yard perimeter. The fighting had been savage, "clinging to the belt" close as the North Vietnamese liked to say. In fact, the fighting was so close that American air and artillery fire could not support the cavalry troopers. The enemy was also aware of that fact, so they made a concerted effort to fight the Americans toe-to-toe. Like the previous day, Moore's forces had been vastly outnumbered. The upside was that his men were brave, almost to a fault. They had superior weapons, and they were excellent marksmen.

> The 7th Cavalry at Ia Drang was the first large American force to be armed with the new fully automatic M-16 assault rifle in Vietnam. Previously, U.S. ground forces had been armed with the longer, more cumbersome, semi-automatic M-14 infantry rifle.

Additionally, Moore, who would later be described as the "penultimate battle captain," had an intuitive ability to read a battlefield. Under the most intense enemy fire, he could flash his eyes across his own front and instantly know exactly when and where to plug gaps in the line. And he was determined that the 7th Cavalry, under his command, would not suffer the same fate it had under Gen. George Armstrong Custer's command at the Little Big Horn in Montana some 90 years earlier.

"By God, they sent us over here to kill Communists," Moore shouted to the reporters. "And that's what we're doing."

By noon, Moore's weary 1st Battalion was relieved by Lieutenant Colonel McDade's 2nd Battalion, which had just completed an overland march from a nearby LZ. The shattered remnants of the isolated platoon were also reached and relieved. The battered 1st Battalion was lifted out by helicopter. Moore himself was the last man to board a chopper.

On the morning of November 17, McDade's battalion was ordered to withdraw from LZ X-Ray because U.S. Air Force B-52 Stratofortress bombers were en route to the Chu Pong massif. At 11:17 A.M. the mountain mass was pummeled by the high-altitude bombers.

As the bombers were wreaking havoc on the slopes, the cavalry fell back on nearby LZ Albany. En route, McDade's troopers captured a couple of NVA soldiers. While the prisoners were being interrogated, the exhausted cavalrymen broke ranks, removed equipment, ate, and slept. Soon thereafter, they continued to march through fields of tall elephant grass.

Unfortunately, NVA forces had anticipated the march to Albany and were lying in wait. At 1:20 P.M., all hell broke loose when mortar rounds began exploding near the American column and machine-gun fire began ripping into their ranks. At once, the enemy charged, screaming battle cries, and shooting their weapons from the hip. The NVA broke the American column and quickly isolated elements of the battalion. The battle devolved into a terrible slugfest, with combatants bayoneting or clubbing one another to death with their rifles. Men were shot in the face at point-blank range.

The battle raged for most of the rest of the afternoon, slackening only after the enemy was literally beaten back by the physically tougher cavalry troopers. With the opposing forces fighting from distances of yards instead of inches, massed artillery and close air support were brought to bear. Isolated pockets of fighting continued throughout the night.

THE AFTERMATH

On the morning of November 18, the surviving troopers began the grisly task of recovering their dead buddies from the tall elephant grass. The dead Americans were surrounded by the bodies of their enemies. On November 20, the last of the survivors of the Battle of Ia Drang Valley were airlifted out. More than 300 American soldiers had been killed. The enemy suffered some 1,800 losses.

For its action in the Battle of the Ia Drang Valley, the 1st Cavalry Division was awarded a Presidential Unit Citation.

Aside from the decisive victory over the NVA at Ia Drang, the battle was the first true application of the new concept of helicopter-borne (airmobile or air assault) warfare. The battle proved that large infantry forces ferried by helicopter directly into battle were wholly effective. Prior to Ia Drang, a few naysayers feared that such operations were too dangerous—that helicopters delivering troops under fire would be too vulnerable to enemy fire. The soldiers themselves were never fully convinced. "I can't say that airmobile warfare is dangerous," said 1st Lt. John Temple Ligon, an artillery forward observer with the 173rd Airborne Brigade, years later. "On the other hand, plenty of choppers got hit, and we were happy to hump it in and truck it out. We preferred not to use choppers for insertion because it was always an announcement for all to see and hear all around."

Despite the soldiers' legitimate fears, the results proved otherwise: Throughout the war in Vietnam, huge numbers of armed infantrymen and many tons of supplies were successfully delivered to the front by helicopter. Wounded soldiers were quickly airlifted out—saving untold numbers of lives—and refugees were relocated.

Of the 59 helicopters that were hit by enemy fire in the Ia Drang, only four were shot down, and three of those were recovered.

The battle also proved that high-altitude B-52 bombers, which had been designed for strategic bombing, could also be employed as a tactical support arm for troops engaged on the ground.

For Moore, the battle was personal. "When your men die and you don't, you feel guilty," he said years later. "That's all I can say about it."

CHAPTER 23

BINH DINH

(JANUARY 28–MARCH 6, 1966)

A joint U.S.–South Vietnamese military operation, the first Battle for Binh Dinh was one of the largest combined force missions during the Vietnam War. The battle resulted in a clear victory for the Americans and their South Vietnamese allies. But Binh Dinh proved to be problematic in the coming years.

By early 1966, the Binh Dinh Province had become a haven for North Vietnamese Army (NVA) and Vietcong (VC) units. There, the enemy found sustenance and protection in the rice-growing valleys and overlooking mountains. South Vietnamese army forces had attempted to rid the region of Communist domination, but with little success.

The Americans believed that an operation in the province would be an opportunity to gain control of a strategic region with helicopter-borne forces employing a newly minted tactic known as search and destroy. But planning such an operation was a complicated matter in terms of politics and jurisdictional issues. The target area was occupied by U.S. forces, the Army of the Republic of (South) Vietnam (ARVN), and allied South Korean army forces. Gen. William Childs Westmoreland, commanding general of the

U.S. Military Assistance Command Vietnam (MACV), had command over all American forces in South Vietnam, but not over the allied forces. Moreover, the target area included the boundary between the Binh Dinh and Quang Ngai Provinces, which also separated the South Vietnamese I and II Corps Tactical Zones. Additionally, that boundary divided command sectors between U.S. Army forces and U.S. Marines. For the purposes of command and control, units were supposed to operate only within their assigned sectors, and the enemy was literally straddling the two.

In mid-January, Westmoreland arranged for a war council meeting to be held at the Da Nang headquarters of ARVN brigadier general Nguyen Chanh Thi, commander of the I Corps Tactical Zone. The meeting was, of course, attended by Westmoreland and Thi, as well as Gen. Stanley R. Larsen, who commanded the U.S. Army's I Field Force, and Maj. Gen. Lewis William Walt, who commanded the III Marine Amphibious Force. Also in attendance were Gen. Vinh Loc (ARVN), who commanded the II Corps Tactical Zone, and South Korean army general Chae Myung Shin.

WESTMORELAND'S PLAN

Westmoreland and the allied generals agreed that the enemy had to be confronted and destroyed. To do so would require a coordinated effort superceding matters of jurisdiction. The VC and NVA were concentrating their forces in the areas of Quang Ngai, along either side of the An Lao River Valley, and near the coastal town of Tam Quang. In order to make contact with and destroy those forces, Westmoreland suggested that Walt's Marines together with ARVN forces attack from the north and the coast, through the Quang Ngai Province toward the boundary with the Binh Dinh Province. Meanwhile, U.S. Army, ARVN, and South Korean army forces would attack from the south through the Binh Dinh Province toward the same boundary. All agreed that if during the attack one allied force crossed over into the other's jurisdictional boundary, it would be overlooked. The goal was to crush the enemy between the two forces in a classic hammer and anvil maneuver.

Despite the fact that the four separate forces agreed to work in harmony with one another, each element designed its own suboperation: Larsen's army force, which would serve as the primary striking force (the hammer of the anvil) would be helicopter-ferried into their area of responsibility and then launch a ground attack. If the enemy tried to escape they would be driven up against the front of an advancing U.S. Marine force.

Larsen's operation would initially be known as *Masher*. However, the name was changed when U.S. president Lyndon Johnson, a habitual reader of press tickers, caught a news wire flash on January 25 stating that 42 American soldiers and three airmen had been killed in a C-123 transport plane crash in "Masher." The doomed soldiers, a battalion of the 7th Cavalry Regiment, were killed at An Khe en route to Bong Son where they were to kick off the operation. Fearing that the rough-edged moniker might unsettle Americans back home, Johnson ordered the name changed. Major General Harry W. O. Kinnard, who commanded the 1st Cavalry Division of Larsen's I Field Force, changed it to White Wing (like a white-winged dove of peace).

The Marines, under Walt's supervision, were to conduct an amphibious landing then drive hard to link up with the cavalry. Walt's operation would be known as Double Eagle. The ARVN force would refer to its operation as Thang Phong II. And the South Koreans would call their action Flying Tiger.

A week prior to the attacks, both the U.S. Army and Marines sent out deep reconnaissance patrols to assess the enemy's strength and disposition of forces. The Marines dispatched one of its crack Force Recon companies. The army sent one of its special forces (Green Beret) teams under the watchful eye of Maj. Charles "Chargin' Charlie" Beckwith. Both the Marine Force Recon and the Army Special Forces teams encountered overwhelming numbers of enemy soldiers in the planned operations areas. And both of the scouting teams barely escaped with their skins.

> Maj. Charles Beckwith became famous as the irregular warfare specialist who established the Army's Delta Force in 1977. He also led the ill-fated 1980 hostage rescue mission into Iran.

THE BATTLE

On January 28, the attack began when the U.S. 3rd Cavalry Brigade, under the command of Col. Harold G. Moore (best-known as the victorious cavalry commander in the previous Battle of the Ia Drang Valley), launched a large-scale air assault (helicopter insertion) on the coastal plain between the provincial capital of Tam Quan and Bong Son. Positioned at Tam Quan was a South Vietnamese airborne brigade. The American cavalry was to seize the area around Bong Son and set up a forward base.

The enemy was ready when the first wave of more than 100 American helicopters thundered in from the south, flared their noses, and touched down on Landing Zone (LZ) Dog. An ancient Vietnamese cemetery, LZ Dog was so heavily defended it was later described as "kicking over an anthill." Twenty helicopters were hit and five were shot down.

Once on the ground, troopers of Lt. Col. Robert McDade's 2nd Battalion, 7th Cavalry quickly grouped into combat formations and returned fire. The fighting was hot.

McDade then leapfrogged over LZ Dog and air assaulted onto smaller landing zones farther north. Their objective was to link up with the ARVN paratroopers. Those areas were also heavily defended. The voice of Capt. John A. Fesire, one of McDade's company commanders, crackled over the radio. "We're in a hornet's nest!"

That night it rained hard. The following morning, Moore himself was airlifted to the battlefield with reinforcements. The Americans then attacked the nearby village of Cu Nghi where they encountered elements of the North Vietnamese 22nd Infantry Regiment.

The battle intensified with losses mounting on both sides. The village was ultimately taken, and on January 31, Moore opened LZ Quebec farther north as he continued his push into the hotly contested An Lao Valley.

Vast sweeps throughout the province were made over the next several weeks, in nearly constant rain. Supported by air and artillery, the cavalry troopers rode their helicopters up into the dark mountains looking for enemy strongholds. When found, the enemy positions were stormed and wiped out. The troopers then saddled up for another ride to the next ridgeline or hilltop.

As the cavalry was clearing the Bong Son area, the Marines launched their own operation, an amphibious assault along a stretch of coastline between the towns of Quang Ngai and Sa Huynh. Code-named Double Eagle, the Marine element was composed of three seaborne battalion landing teams with one floating reserve. Two Marine companies were ferried in beyond the beach by helicopter.

The Marine landings were deliberately timed to strike simultaneously with the army's primary air assault. Following a preparatory close air and naval gunfire bombardment, as well as U.S. Air Force B-52 bomber strikes farther inland, the Marines landed in classic fashion. For the next few weeks, the leathernecks fanned out across the countryside in the

Quang Ngai Province. Enemy contact was made, but quickly quashed. By mid-February, opposition in the Marine Corps area was so light that Double Eagle was terminated.

The heaviest fighting was in the Binh Dinh Province, where the NVA and VC forces were either falling back and fighting fierce rear-guard actions or standing and dying.

By February 7, Kinnard had reinforced Moore's brigade to a point wherein he had assumed direct command from Moore. Kinnard then initiated a powerful third thrust against the enemy into the Kim Son Valley. Moore's brigade spearheaded the thrust and established another landing zone, LZ Bird. In doing so, the Americans beat back elements of a company of the 2nd Vietcong Regiment.

THE AFTERMATH

When the smoke cleared in early March, 224 American cavalrymen were dead, another 834 were wounded (not including the 42 who had been in the C-123 crash). The U.S. Marines suffered 24 killed and 156 wounded. The combined enemy losses—from the cavalry, Marine Corps, and ARVN counts—were far greater: 2,232 killed, 811 captured, and 500 defected.

Despite the decisive victory at Binh Dinh, NVA and VC forces exhibited a greater capacity to fight and absorb losses than they had in previous engagements. Additionally, enemy forces uncharacteristically withdrew from the field in an orderly fashion. Making matters worse, the enemy soon returned to the region, a disturbing fact that soon became characteristic of the Vietnam War.

CHAPTER 24

OPERATION ATTLEBORO

(SEPTEMBER 14–NOVEMBER 25, 1966)

Operation Attleboro was a decisive victory for U.S. Army forces operating in the South Vietnamese backcountry. What began as a training exercise for a green American unit—the 196th Light Infantry Brigade—evolved into a major combined-arms operation wherein U.S. forces made contact with a battle-hardened Vietcong (VC) division and a North Vietnamese Army (NVA) regiment. The end result was the discovery of one of the largest weapons and equipment caches of the war, and more than 1,000 dead enemy soldiers.

By the late summer of 1966, U.S. intelligence reports had indicated that enemy forces were operating in the Tay Ninh Province near the Cambodian border in the III Corps Tactical Zone. The strength of those forces was unknown. What *was* known was that the terrain in the Tay Ninh was wholly suitable for any defending force.

The Tay Ninh landscape was rugged: It alternated from low flats and scrub brush to cultivated fields and rice paddies to densely forested hills, the latter offering excellent cover and concealment for the enemy. Dominating the province was the 3,200 foot Nui Ba Den (translated into English, "Black Virgin") mountain, which was controlled by the VC. Much of the region was rice country: The flat terrain was covered with water, making it difficult for American infantry and nearly impassable for tracked vehicles.

OPENING SHOTS

Shooting began on September 14 when elements of the newly arrived American 196th Light Infantry Brigade, of the 25th Infantry Division, were helicopter-inserted into the area between Tay Ninh and Dau Tieng. The 25th Infantry Division was under the command of Maj. Gen. Frederick C. Weyand. The 196th, a relatively inexperienced brigade, was under the command of Brig. Gen. Edward H. DeSaussure.

Code-named Attleboro, the operation was to serve a twofold purpose: First and foremost, the goal was to sweep the Tay Ninh for enemy forces, weapons and food caches, and to gather intelligence. A secondary objective was training. The 196th was composed of mostly young, green soldiers who a year earlier had been chasing girls or cramming for an algebra exam. The only action most of them had ever seen was on their high school football team. Concerned about their inexperience, their commanders wanted them to log some combat time in the bush. That way they would be better prepared for larger operations.

> The 196th Light Infantry Brigade had been activated the previous year at Fort Devens, Massachusetts; thus the operation was named Attleboro as a tribute to the Massachusetts town of the same name.

Fortunately for the Americans, opposition during the helicopter insertion was light to almost nonexistent. DeSaussure's riflemen then moved near the town of Tay Ninh City, its adjacent airfield, and the nearby Michelin rubber plantation. The VC, avoiding contact, simply melted into the backcountry. The search-and-destroy/training operation continued throughout the countryside for the next several weeks, and as the brigade began probing deeper into the backcountry, its battalions began making sharp albeit brief contact with small, isolated pockets of VC soldiers.

In late October, intelligence reports indicated that Loc Ninh was going to be the target of a major enemy attack before mid-November. By November 1, intelligence had determined that two enemy forces—the VC 9th Division and the 101st NVA Regiment—positioned at an advance base near Dau Tieng were deploying to attack the American Special Forces camp at Sui Da. The two enemy regiments were supported by a guard regiment, an artillery regiment, several independent battalions, and a handful of local VC guerillas.

THE BATTLE

After a month and a half of uneventful patrolling, occasionally interrupted by light skirmishing, U.S. troops made contact with elements of the 9th VC Division at their Dau Tieng base camp on November 3. The fighting was hot with casualties mounting on both sides of the field. One of the American companies was cut off from the main body. Attempting to save them, a second company rushed forward and directly in front of a concealed enemy bunker. All at once, the relief company was subjected to a devastating hailstorm of lead and rocket-propelled grenades. Experienced reaction force elements from the 25th Infantry Division—specifically the famed 27th Infantry Regiment "wolfhounds"—were hurried forward.

> The *nom de guerre* "wolfhounds" was bestowed on the 27th Infantry Regiment during the American expedition to Siberia in 1918. The 27th was so named by the Bolsheviks as a tribute to the regiment's fighting tenacity.

The following day, all available units from DeSaussure's brigade were heavily engaged. A company of the rescuing "wolfhounds" was also surrounded. The fighting was fierce, with the Americans having to face down numerous suicidal charges by the enemy.

Years later, a VC soldier who had been involved in the attacks against the "wolfhounds" recalled his surprise upon realizing how well the American soldiers could fight. "We were told we would meet with only light resistance, and that the company hunting for the rice did not wish to fight," said Van Khrak, a VC rifleman at Dau Tieng. "That was wrong. I was one of the many who believed this until we engaged the company and then enemy reinforcements. ... They fought like devils. We launched an assault from the bunkers. I was in the second wave. It was very dark and the jungle was thick except for our fire lines. Our orders were to fire at anyone we saw or heard moving around, even at the risk of hitting our own men, because the enemy forces had to be wiped out at all cost."

That night, helicopters attempted to evacuate the wounded Americans, but their landing lights illuminated the landing zone, which the VC hit with a mortar barrage. The helicopters continued to make pickups and offload water and ammunition, but in dangerous blackout conditions.

> Although night-vision scopes were introduced on the battlefield as early as 1964, it would be years before similar technologies would be employed in the cockpit. During Operation Attleboro's blackout landing conditions, pilots flew with only the natural light available. In some cases they landed by flashlight.

Within days, the fighting evolved into a "multi-divisional" battle, involving some 22,000 American and Army of the Republic of Vietnam (ARVN) soldiers. In addition to the 25th Infantry Division, the participating units included elements of the 1st Infantry Division (the famed Big Red One), the 4th Infantry Division, the 173rd Airborne Brigade, the 11th Armored Cavalry Regiment, a Special Forces "Mike Force" (a mobile quick-reaction team, larger than a company), and several ARVN battalions.

On November 6, overall control of the operation fell under the II Field Force, under the command of Lt. Gen. Jonathon O. Seaman. As such, Attleboro became the first U.S. Army operation in Vietnam to be managed at the corps level.

Key to the success of Attleboro was supporting air operations: From mid-October until the end of the campaign in late November, more than 1,600 air sorties were flown in direct support of the riflemen on the ground. Of those sorties, some 225 were flown by the high-altitude B-52 Stratofortress bomber. The remainder were close air support strikes by helicopter gunships, jet fighters, and propeller-driven airplanes. Transporting aircraft also played a major role with some 3,300 sorties airlifting in reinforcements and nearly 9,000 tons of cargo for the front.

By November 15, American forces were grinding down the enemy opposition and new enemy contacts were lessening throughout the Tay Ninh region. Dwindling contacts were a blessing indeed for DeSaussure's badly mauled infantry companies their first time under fire. Gen. William Childs Westmoreland, chief of the Military Assistance Command Vietnam, "reluctantly came to the conclusion that the brigade had 'cracked,'" according to Dr. Shelby L. Stanton, a historian and former U.S. Army Special Forces officer. DeSaussure was relieved as head of the 196th and posted to an artillery command. He was replaced by Brig. Gen. Richard T. Knowles.

Beginning November 20, a series of vigorous combat assaults was launched throughout the Tay Ninh area. By November 25, opposition had ceased throughout most of the region. The Vietcong forces had stood their ground stubbornly. But after suffering heavy losses, they withdrew to their sanctuary areas across the border in Cambodia.

THE AFTERMATH

Having forced the enemy from the field, the Americans discovered scores of dead enemy soldiers and one of the largest weapons and ammunition caches of the entire war. The cache included rifles, rocket launchers, machine guns, grenades, various explosive devices—including bangalore torpedoes (special cylindrical mines designed to breach the barbed wire defenses of opposing forces)—at least one crossbow, and more than 100 bicycles. Entrances to a vast underground tunnel system also led to enormous food stores and medical supplies. For the next several days, U.S. helicopters transported the foodstuffs to the town of Tay Ninh for distribution to the locals. Additionally, U.S. forces found secret documents detailing the disposition of enemy troops, among other gems of intelligence gleaned from captured enemy soldiers.

After searching the tunnels, the Americans set explosive charges and destroyed them. "They'll have a little trouble using them," General Seaman later said of the numerous tunnel systems crisscrossing South Vietnam. "But I should say right now that to destroy these vast tunnel complexes is a pretty formidable job. And we do the best we can. And I'm sure that if they're willing to go back in with just a whale of a lot of effort, and expend all that effort, they could probably rehabilitate them over a period of years, or months. But when you realize that it's taken them about 20 years to build this thing up, well, if I were a VC, I'd be somewhat discouraged."

CHAPTER 25

LOC NINH

(OCTOBER 29–NOVEMBER 8, 1967)

The Battle of Loc Ninh was largely a fight pitting American infantrymen and special forces (Green Berets) against Vietcong (VC) and North Vietnamese Army (NVA) soldiers in which more than 1,000 enemy combatants were killed.

During the summer of 1967, North Vietnamese ground forces made a concerted effort to attack and destroy isolated U.S. Army and Army of the Republic of (South) Vietnam (ARVN) outposts in the central highlands of South Vietnam. Though they often struck with near-complete surprise, the enemy forces were beaten back with great loss to their own.

By early fall, however, the U.S. Military Assistance Command Vietnam became particularly concerned when intelligence reports began indicating that substantial numbers of VC guerillas and NVA soldiers were massing near the borders of Laos and Cambodia, both sanctuary countries on the western border with South Vietnam.

What followed was a series of so-called border battles between U.S./ARVN soldiers and NVA/VC forces near the Vietnamese-Cambodian-Laotian frontier. The first was a fight between an NVA regiment and an ARVN battalion near the village of Song Be in the

III Corps Tactical Zone on October 27. Though greatly outnumbered, the South Vietnamese successfully repelled three aggressive assaults on their positions at Song Be, killing 134 of the enemy while suffering only 13 losses. The third, an engagement wherein several large American units would slug it out with an NVA regiment, would take place near the village of Dak To in the II Corps Tactical Zone beginning the first week in November. The second engagement began on the morning of October 29 at the town of Loc Ninh, about nine miles west of the Cambodian border in the III Corps Tactical Zone.

THE BATTLE

At 1:15 A.M., VC rocket and mortar fire began pummeling Loc Ninh, and enemy soldiers were spotted advancing toward the town. The enemy forces were the advance elements of the VC 9th Division, specifically the 272nd and 273rd VC Regiments, reinforced with regulars from the NVA.

At Loc Ninh, two South Vietnamese Regional Force companies, a Popular Force platoon, and two American Green Beret advisers were quartered. The defending soldiers rushed toward the town's perimeter, but a portion of the line was quickly overrun by the 273rd VC. Within an hour, the enemy had penetrated a section of ARVN captain Tran Minh Cong's command post. Refusing to surrender his colors, the ARVN captain radioed artillery fire and air strikes on his own position, while his defending infantrymen continued to slug it out with the enemy.

Just south of the town, beyond the Loc Ninh airfield, a force of South Vietnamese Civilian Irregular Defense Group (CIDG) soldiers and several U.S. Special Forces soldiers grabbed weapons and ammunition and hurried to reinforce the beleaguered town.

Hours later, the CIDG force, the Americans, and elements of the ARVN 5th Division were in place, and Loc Ninh was still holding. The fighting was close and in many cases had degraded into hand-to-hand combat.

Just after 5:30 A.M., the seriously battered VC force withdrew, leaving behind 147 of its dead comrades.

Responding to the attack, a brigade of the famous 1st Infantry Division (the Big Red One) and its supporting artillery, all under the command of Maj. Gen. John H. Hay Jr., were ferried into the region by helicopter. Once on the ground, Hay's brigade—elements of the 18th, 26th, and

28th Infantry Regiments, as well as elements from the detached 12th Infantry Regiment—deployed in an approximate square around the town's perimeter. At each corner of the square, temporary fire bases were set up that covered the most likely approaches of the enemy.

Throughout the day, additional American infantry forces were airlifted into Loc Ninh. Two companies and two artillery batteries were deployed to defend the nearby airfield and CIDG camp. In the early afternoon, the enemy returned in company strength (between 150 and 200 men), spoiling for a fight, and launched the first of several more human-wave attacks. This time they were facing down one of Hay's fresh battalions from the 18th Infantry. The VC were beaten back after losing more than 20 of their number.

The following day, fighting resumed with elements of the VC 273rd again being savaged by the American 18th Infantry. More than 80 enemy soldiers were killed. Just after midnight on Halloween, the second VC regiment, the 272nd, struck out from the northeast toward Loc Ninh's district office and the CIDG camp and airstrip. They were met by a battalion of the 28th Infantry supported by massed artillery. After nearly 10 hours of combat, and suffering more than 100 killed in action, the VC retreated. Making matters worse for the enemy, his retreat was blocked by another battalion from the U.S. 28th, which had been helicopter-ferried to a point ahead of their withdrawal route.

Two nights later, on November 2, the 18th Infantry was again struck. This time the enemy attacked from three directions and in great numbers. The assault was preceded by a mortar attack inside the 18th's perimeter. Meanwhile, outlying American ambush patrols spotted the advancing VC. After setting off claymore mines (an antipersonnel mine designed to explode in a predetermined lateral direction) into the VC ranks, the Americans withdrew toward the safety of their own lines, shooting as they went.

The VC attacked with all manner of individual and crew-served weapons, including Soviet-made flame-throwers. Fortunately, the soldiers armed with the flame-throwers were wiped out before they could unleash their fiery streams. The enemy was beaten back with overwhelming losses. And like the Halloween attack, the VC force's retreat was blocked, this time by elements of the U.S. 26th and the 12th Infantry Regiments. When the smoke cleared, 263 dead enemy soldiers were scattered around the area in front of the perimeter and along their escape route. Six were captured.

On November 7, two companies of the 26th Infantry were airlifted a few miles northeast of the town. There, they made contact with, and soundly defeated, a battalion of the VC 272nd. The following day, a second VC battalion was attacked and pummeled. In the final engagement for Loc Ninh, 93 VC were killed, and nearly a third fell victim to U.S. air strikes.

THE AFTERMATH

In each clash, the enemy was beaten back with heavy losses, and the Americans quickly fanned out into the adjacent scrub brush, jungle, and rubber tree plantations. "Cleaning out rubber plantations was always a trying assignment," Gen. William Childs Westmoreland, commander of American forces in Vietnam, would later write. "For long rows of evenly spaced trees afforded the enemy excellent concealment while leaving unobstructed fields of fire down the lanes formed by the interval between rows of trees."

Despite massed artillery fire, hundreds of close air support sorties from both jets and helicopters, and heavy bombardments from B-52 Stratofortress bombers, the VC and NVA continued to fight. After 10 days, the enemy withdrew from the field, leaving behind more than 1,000 dead and untold numbers wounded. Approximately 60 allied soldiers had been killed.

Although the enemy was decisively defeated at Loc Ninh, Westmoreland would later write that the "drab little rubber plantation town ... was destined through the years to serve as a tragic focus for enemy attack."

CHAPTER 26

DAK TO

(NOVEMBER 3–23, 1967)

The Battle of Dak To was one of the bloodiest battles of the Vietnam War and the largest fight of the war up to that point in late 1967. Oddly, however, most military history enthusiasts are only vaguely familiar with the battle. Most have heard the name of the little village in South Vietnam's central highlands. But only a few military historians—and, of course, those who fought there—have any real grasp of the utter brutality that characterized the struggle for Dak To.

LAST OF THE BORDER BATTLES

The Battle of Dak To was the third in a series of so-called border battles near the Vietnamese-Cambodian-Laotian frontier. The first was a fight between a North Vietnamese Army Regiment and a South Vietnamese Army battalion near the village of Song Be in the III Corps Tactical Zone on October 27. Though greatly outnumbered, the South Vietnamese successfully repelled three aggressive assaults on their positions at Song Be, killing 134 of the enemy while suffering only 13 losses.

The second border battle took place two days later at Loc Ninh, a U.S. Army Special Forces outpost in the III Corps Tactical Zone

where approximately 1,000 North Vietnamese soldiers (NVA) and Vietcong (VC) guerrillas were killed. As the fighting at Loc Ninh was winding
down, one of the worst struggles of the entire war was opening on the hills
and ridges around Dak To in the II Corps Tactical Zone. Located near
Pleiku, the small hamlet of Dak To was situated in a valley adjacent to
a U.S. Army Special Forces (Green Beret) outpost. The camp and its
adjoining airstrip were surrounded by commanding hills and ridges, some
as high as 6,000 feet. The slopes were thickly forested. The terrain offered
perfect points of observation as well as cover and concealment for any
attacking force. The location of the camp itself was simply a defending
force's nightmare.

Although the Battle of Dak To would not officially open until November 1967, a number of bloody related clashes had begun to take place the
previous June. That month, a Special Forces patrol had been ambushed
in the surrounding backcountry. In response, U.S. Army general William
Childs Westmoreland, commander of American forces in Vietnam, ordered the 173rd Airborne Brigade to Dak To. Within days of the brigade's
being airlifted to the outpost, the paratroops moving into the surrounding
hills ran smack into an overwhelming enemy force. The force was part of
the 24th NVA Regiment. In what would become known as the Battle of
the Slopes (so named for the hillsides on which the battle was fought), the
involved American platoons were cut off from their main body and nearly
destroyed. When the fight was over, the surviving Americans from the
main body made a grisly discovery: Many of their fellow paratroopers,
isolated and wounded, had been shot execution-style in the head at point-
blank range.

Soon, additional troops were moved into the valley, including the 3rd
Brigade of the 1st Cavalry Division under the temporary command of
Col. James O. McKenna. Additionally, three ARVN battalions were moved
into the region.

In mid-August, most of the weary paratroopers of the 173rd Airborne
Brigade were pulled out of Dak To, but only temporarily. The brigade
was rested and refitted.

The next few months was a dark period for American soldiers based
at Dak To. Patrols continued against enemy forces operating in the hills.
Casualties mounted, including the number of missing. Horrifying discov-
eries were periodically made of decomposing American bodies. On top of
it all, heavy monsoon rains turned the landscape into a sea of mud and

washed away land routes linking Dak To with the nearby town of Kontum and the rest of the world. Supplies were airlifted in, but poor weather hampered the transport runs.

THE BATTLE

Officially, the Battle for Dak To began in early November. It was an extension of a major search-and-destroy operation, code-named MacArthur, which had been launched by a brigade of the U.S. 4th Infantry Division in late October. Having been airlifted into Dak To, the 1st Brigade of the 4th—along with a detached battalion of the 173rd Airborne Brigade— began sweeping the surrounding countryside on November 3.

On November 4, U.S. forces located a heavily fortified North Vietnamese Army (NVA) position on a commanding ridge not far from where the 173rd had fought its terrible "Battle of the Slopes" in June. The American soldiers attempted to take the position frontally, but it was too well defended. Unable to dislodge the enemy with a ground attack, air strikes were called in that pummeled the NVA defenses. After some 40 strikes, the Americans advanced up the ridge and into the remnants of the enemy's works.

On November 6, the detached battalion from the 173rd made contact with an enormous force of NVA soldiers on nearby Hill 823, and a bitter fight ensued. The Americans were shot to pieces. One 164-man company was whittled down to 44 riflemen, and the battalion was ordered to fall back on Dak To.

The bulk of the 173rd Airborne Brigade, now under the command of Brig. Gen. Leo Schweiter, was rushed back into the valley. The paratroopers were also joined by a new kind of soldier—dogs. Canine teams were employed as the vanguard of any advancing elements. The dogs were able to sniff out tunnels, bunkers, and food and weapons caches. When the shooting started, the dogs were hurriedly removed to the rear. This was done not so much as a humane gesture, but to protect the dogs' most important attribute—their keen sense of hearing. Their hearing could easily have been damaged by the sound of gunfire, particularly artillery blasts.

Over the next several days, sharp fighting erupted on and around a chain of hills surrounding Dak To as American and ARVN units continued to comb the slopes of the dominant heights.

On November 13, a savage close-quarters struggle ensued between a company of the 503rd Airborne Infantry Regiment and a battalion from the crack 174th NVA Regiment. A second American company was hurried forward to reinforce their fellow paratroopers. The fighting—literally cold steel and grenades—raged throughout the night. Casualties soared on both sides. By first light, the NVA had withdrawn.

> "The fighting had been so intense that one log was found in the morning with six dead paratroopers on one side and four dead NVA sprawled out on the other side," Dr. Shelby L. Stanton, historian and former U.S. Army Special Forces officer, would later write. "At the end of the log were two more NVA, one of them an officer who still clutched an M-16 rifle taken from one of the Americans."

Fighting continued to swirl in the hills around Dak To, the Americans in a death-grip struggle to wrest the hills from the NVA's 66th and 32nd Regiments.

Meanwhile, the camp itself was subjected to frequent enemy mortar attacks. On November 15, mortar shells struck an ammunition dump near the Dak To airstrip which sent exploding ordnance whistling across the valley. Two C-130 transport aircraft were destroyed in the attack.

Three days later, as the weary 66th and 32nd NVA Regiments retreated toward the Cambodian border, a U.S. Special Forces "Mike Force" (a mobile quick-reaction team) made contact with the 174th NVA Regiment on the eastern slopes of Hill 875. The Green Berets also discovered an extensive network of tunnels connected point-to-point with bunkers and machine-gun nests.

On November 19, the 2nd Battalion of Schweiter's 173rd were ordered to take Hill 875. As the paratroopers advanced up the northern slopes, shooting began. All at once, a strong force of blackened-faced North Vietnamese soldiers, spoiling for a fight, attacked and drove the Americans back. Some of the GIs frantically tried to dig in and return fire, but were quickly overrun. Others in full retreat were relentlessly pursued by the enemy and mercilessly cut down.

At the base of the hill, an advancing American company encountered waves of charging NVA soldiers. The latter attacked in such force that, according to Stanton, "two (U.S.) platoons simply evaporated."

U.S. Air Force jets were radioed in, and soon a flight of four F-100 Super Sabre fighters were over the top and blistering the hill crest with napalm (bombs containing jellied gasoline).

The shattered airborne companies attempted to regroup and counter-attack, but the command element was overrun and wiped out in hand-to-hand combat. Supporting helicopters attempted to land reinforcements, but several were shot down. The 2nd Battalion was soon completely sur-rounded. Fighting raged throughout the night as the paratroopers held out for promised reinforcements. The following morning, the enemy began to waver under the relentless pounding of U.S. artillery and aircraft. Meanwhile, sky soldiers of Schweiter's 4th Battalion began making their way toward their besieged brothers. When the two battalions finally linked up, the physically and emotionally drained but still-holding paratroopers of the 2nd Battalion openly wept.

On November 21, the bloodied companies were helicopter-lifted from a newly cleared landing zone. As the wounded were being loaded onto the choppers, jets were roaring over the hill, blasting and burning the summit to a crisp.

That afternoon, Schweiter's regrouped force prepared for another up-hill attack. At 3 P.M., the paratroopers stepped off. As the Americans clam-bered up the smoking hill, enemy machine guns began to chatter. The fighting was close and nasty over the next 48 hours. Numerous decorations for valor were earned, including two Congressional Medals of Honor won posthumously by Pfc. Carlos Lozada and Chaplain Charles J. Watters. Lozada, a young machine-gunning paratrooper, held off an entire NVA company and killed more than 20 enemy soldiers before he himself was completely surrounded and cut down.

Watters, an unarmed chaplain, dashed from one man to the next, offering words of encouragement to the wounded and frightened and administering last rites to the dying. In several instances, he rushed between the two embattled forces to lift a wounded man onto his shoul-ders and carry him to safety. He, too, was killed.

Just before noon on November 23, the American paratroopers reached the summit, shouting their famous war cries—"Geronimo" and "Air-borne." Other GIs simply collapsed among the ruins and opened a few cans of C rations. It was their Thanksgiving Day dinner.

THE AFTERMATH

The Battle of Dak To was over, and the U.S. Army was in control of the field. Between 1,400 and 1,600 enemy soldiers were dead, and untold numbers were wounded and out of action. As a result, three badly mauled enemy regiments retreated into Laos and were unable to participate in the upcoming Tet Offensive of 1968. Had those regiments been there, the outcome might have been dramatically different. On the downside, 376 U.S. soldiers were dead, or missing and presumed dead. Another 1,441 were wounded. The greatest losses were suffered by the 173rd Airborne Brigade, which lost 208 killed and 645 wounded.

General Westmoreland referred to the Battle of Dak To as "the largest and most significant" at that point in the war. It was clearly one of the toughest battles fought by the American army in Vietnam.

TET OFFENSIVE

(JANUARY 29–MARCH 7, 1968)

The North Vietnamese Army's Tet Offensive of 1968 was a Pyrrhic American victory. But it was decisive for two reasons: Vietcong (VC) and North Vietnamese Army (NVA) forces were soundly defeated in every attack, and the battle signaled the beginning of the end of America's involvement in Vietnam. Tet included the sub-battles for the South Vietnamese capital of Saigon, the old provincial capital of Hue, and points throughout the countryside.

Launched in late January 1968, during the height of the Vietnamese holiday of Tet Nguyen Dan (translated into English, "lunar new year"), the offensive was timed to kick off during the holiday truce that both sides had honored during the previous years of fighting in Vietnam.

American and Army of the Republic of Vietnam (ARVN) forces agreed to recognize a 36-hour cease-fire beginning at 6 P.M. on January 29. The VC and NVA forces also agreed to a temporary cease-fire, theirs beginning on the morning of January 27 and lasting seven days. It was a ruse on the part of the North Vietnamese designed to catch U.S. and ARVN military forces off guard.

Tet, which opened the Vietnamese Year of the Monkey, lasted January 29 through 31. But the actually shooting didn't commence until the wee hours of the last day. In doing so, the VC and NVA hoped to slip into populated areas concealing themselves among the ongoing revelers. Then, before anyone knew they were in place, the enemy forces—numbering some 84,000—would launch a series of simultaneous attacks on major urban centers as well as government and military installations. The North Vietnamese believed that if their attacks were successful, they might be able to both destroy the South Vietnamese government's ability to wage war and rally the South Vietnamese people to the cause of the National Liberation Front (the Vietcong or Communist Party in South Vietnam). In terms of the battle, the enemy's Tet Offensive was destined to fail. Just how effective they were at surprising the American and ARVN forces has since been the subject of debate. U.S. Army general William Childs Westmoreland, commander of American forces in Vietnam, later argued that he knew the enemy was going to attack, and that was why the enemy was defeated militarily.

In fact, a full 24 hours prior to the attacks, Westmoreland dismissed the truce and placed U.S. forces throughout South Vietnam on full alert. Intelligence gleaned from Central Intelligence Agency (CIA) and National Security Agency (NSA) intercepts indicated that the Communists were planning something big. But information was not specific enough to determine when or where. ARVN forces, honoring the truce, were told that the American alert was simply a precautionary measure based on an increase in NVA activity near Khe Sanh, an isolated U.S. Marine Corps base near the Laotian border in the I Corps Tactical Zone.

The enemy activity around Khe Sanh was not a coincidence. North Vietnamese general Vo Nguyen Giap deliberately turned up the heat near the Marine base in order to lure U.S. and ARVN forces north. Giap believed that in doing so, defenses throughout the rest of the country would be weakened. That fact combined with Tet celebrations would enable VC forces, particularly in and around Saigon, to move into position easily and attack with great shock and penetration.

When the battle opened, more than 100 targets in South Vietnam were struck almost simultaneously by the VC. Those targets included Saigon and 4 other major cities, 36 provincial capitals, and nearly every military installation throughout South Vietnam. The latter included Westmoreland's headquarters at the Military Assistance Command Vietnam (MACV) facility on Tan Son Nhut Airbase. Meanwhile, NVA forces attacked Hue. Within days, the enemy was crushed in and around Saigon. Fighting in the outlying areas would continue for another month.

CHAPTER 27: TET OFFENSIVE

"We failed to seize a number of primary objectives and to completely destroy mobile and defensive units of the enemy," read a dispatch issued by VC headquarters on February 1. "We also failed to hold the occupied areas. On the political field, we failed to motivate the people to stage uprisings and break the enemy's oppressive control."

The enemy was decisively defeated militarily. He was driven off every point in the field, and most of his units were so badly mauled it would be months before they could be refitted for future action. But despite being a military victory for U.S. forces, the battle had a far-reaching negative impact in the United States. And already-wavering support for the war declined even further.

As mopping up continued throughout South Vietnam, intelligence reports indicated that VC reinforcements were gathering in outlying villages. Fearing a second series of attacks, Westmoreland ordered air strikes against the villages. One hamlet, Ben Tre, was targeted by U.S. warplanes. When a reporter asked "Why?" a U.S. Army major replied, "We had to destroy it to save it." It was an offhand remark that, when published, fueled the growing antiwar movement in the United States.

During a CNN interview in 1998, Gen. Westmoreland said:

> We saw the Tet Offensive coming and we were prepared for it, and the enemy took tremendous casualties ... The American public was caught by surprise. We were making military progress at the time— which [is] a statement of fact. If I would have to do it over again, I would have made known the forthcoming Tet Offensive. At that time, I didn't want the enemy to know that I knew what was going to happen. I did know. I made a mistake in not making that known to the American public, because they were caught by surprise and that was very much of a negative factor.

Indeed, public consensus was that in an attempt to appease dissenters back home, American politicians and military commanders had "oversold" the progress of U.S. forces in Vietnam. The credibility gap in Washington widened. By March 2, all remnants of Tet opposition throughout the back-country were snuffed out. But by the end of the month, a weary U.S. president Lyndon Baines Johnson announced, "I will not seek, and I will not accept, the nomination of my party for another term as your president."

American forces suffered some 1,000 casualties during the Tet Offensive. South Vietnamese and other allied forces combined suffered approximately 2,500 losses. The VC and NVA forces, on the other hand, suffered more than 32,000 killed and 5,800 captured. "On anybody's terms, this was a striking military defeat for the enemy," said West-more-land in a 1998 interview for *George* magazine. "Their defeat was so great that it took them years to recover. But the newspaper and television reporting gave the impression, if not of American and South Vietnamese defeat, then of an endless war that could never be won. And the only attack aimed at an American installation in Saigon was the U.S. Embassy. That particular target was hit for psychological effect. It worked. And the American reporters helped achieve it. This influenced the president and advisers so much that they ignored the maxim 'When the enemy is hurting, you don't diminish the pressure, you increase it.'"

Westmoreland's contention that reporters "helped" to achieve the enemy's psychological impact during Tet was a view that would strain soldier-reporter relations for the next two decades. American military officers believed that unwarranted criticism on the part of the media regarding Tet and the overall war resulted in America's defeat in Southeast Asia. American combat veterans would eventually depart from South Vietnam convinced that "the U.S. news media had betrayed the nation, that reporters had gone from being the Fourth Estate to acting like an enemy fifth column," former ABC and NBC News reporter Don North would write years later. "In turn, the correspondents who covered Vietnam, many of whom now assume highly influential roles in their news agencies, are more distrustful of U.S. military officials than their older or younger counterparts."

Military historians, however, have since concluded that the war was lost by senior U.S. leaders, not by disloyal journalists. Nevertheless, Tet was simply the beginning of the end.

THE TET BATTLE FOR SAIGON

On the night of January 30, the South Vietnamese capital of Saigon was filled with the sights and sounds of Tet. Fireworks were whistling and crackling, and throngs of jubilant South Vietnamese citizens were celebrating in the streets. They barely noticed when, just before midnight, heavily armed soldiers wearing helmets covered in palm leaves, black "pajama" uniforms, and sandals jogged past them and entered side streets. The Saigon partygoers might have been too caught up in the spirit of Tet, or perhaps they thought it was another shakeup in the government or a full-blown coup d'état—common occurrences in South Vietnam during the 1960s. When the enemy did attack, the initial crackling of automatic weapons fire was believed to be firecrackers.

In the wee hours of January 31, a group of some 20 VC soldiers dressed in black with identifying red armbands met at a Saigon automobile repair shop and began making final preparations. A few days before, baskets and bamboo crates supposedly containing vegetables and rice had been delivered to a house next to the garage. But instead of foodstuffs, the containers were packed with AK-47 assault rifles, rocket-propelled grenades, and satchel charges loaded with high explosive. The soldiers, part of a 250-man VC Sapper Battalion, armed themselves and crowded into a small pickup truck and a taxicab. Just after 1:45 A.M., the vehicles rolled out toward the U.S. Embassy. The sappers, having no floor plans of the building and no pre-determined escape routes, were on a one-way suicide mission to force their way into the embassy building, kill Americans, and generally make a big media splash. They accomplished the latter two only.

Around 2 A.M., the first targets were struck. The Presidential Palace was hit. The enemy then attacked public buildings and a local radio station. VC soldiers suddenly burst out of nowhere, commandeering taxicabs and privately owned cars at gunpoint.

Despite the initial dismissal of the sounds of small arms fire, the Saigon celebrants began to realize something was amiss when various points throughout the city were subjected to mortar and rocket attacks.

At 2:45 A.M., the sappers from the auto repair shop struck the U.S. Embassy. The South Vietnamese police, known to the Americans as "the white mice," broke and ran. The enemy began blasting away at the gates of the embassy compound with small arms fire. Two young U.S. Army military policemen (MPs) returned fire and closed the gates. Two minutes later, a coded enemy-attack alarm, "Signal 300," went out. All at once, a satchel charge containing plastic explosive detonated, rocking the entire six-story embassy chancery building and blowing a hole in the surrounding concrete wall. The sappers poured through the wall onto the embassy grounds. Caught in the open, one of the American MPs began shouting into his radio, "They're coming in! Help me!" They were the last words he would utter.

> The South Vietnamese police were referred to by American servicemen in Vietnam as "white mice" because they wore white uniforms and their courage under fire was often questionable.

Inside the building, noncombatant office personnel took cover as other MPs and members of the Marine Corps Security Guard Detachment returned fire with rifles, pistols, submachine guns, and 12-gauge shotguns loaded with buckshot.

The VC leaders were killed in the earliest exchanges of fire, and without clear orders the remaining sappers took cover behind large flower pots on the lawn. The American troops and a handful of civilian embassy officials continued firing from windows, doorways, and the chancery rooftop.

As dawn broke, a platoon of U.S. Army paratroopers was helicopter-inserted on the top of the building. They then began to work their way down to the first-floor lobby, clearing rooms, hallways, and stairwells along the way. But no VC were found. Despite reports that the enemy had actually entered the building, all were either killed or captured on the grounds.

Despite being beaten back at the U.S. Embassy, the VC attacked and established defensive positions throughout much of the southern and western sectors of the city. They were subsequently pummeled by helicopters, tanks, and artillery. The U.S. Army's 716th Military Police Battalion was charged with knocking out many of the enemy strongholds. Dressed in starched fatigues and wearing glossy black helmets and armbands emblazoned with the letters MP, they more closely resembled gate guards than street-fighting combatants. But they were soldiers first, they quickly adapted to the reality that they were directly involved in a full-blown battle, and they fought well.

A battalion of the U.S. 27th Infantry was inserted by helicopter into the Hon Mon district, but the American force was slowed by fierce enemy resistance.

The nearby Phu Tho racetrack had been captured by the enemy. The track, used as a primary base of operations for the VC, was a vital strategic point. Elements of the U.S. 199th Light Infantry Brigade and several ARVN units all supported by armor were rushed forward. En route, the Americans fought a series of tough street battles, advancing only a few blocks every few hours. At the track, the enemy was defeated after being frontally attacked by a battalion of the 199th. The struggle for the racetrack lasted several days. Final resistance around Saigon was not quashed until March 7.

THE TET BATTLE OF HUE CITY

The Battle for Hue City was one of the longest and bloodiest engagements between American and enemy forces during the North Vietnamese Army's Tet Offensive of 1968. It took only a few days to crush most of the primary resistance in the South Vietnamese capital of Saigon. Pockets of isolated VC continued to resist for another month. Other flashpoints were quashed in less time. The exception was the city of Hue.

Located between the port city of Da Nang and the Demilitarized Zone (DMZ) that separated North from South Vietnam, Hue had served as the imperial capital for centuries. It was situated along a primary trade route. And in 1968, it was still considered to be the cultural and intellectual center of Vietnam.

Hue was the third-largest city in South Vietnam (Saigon was the largest city, followed by Da Nang). It was old. It was respected. And with the exception of a handful of U.S. military advisers and the headquarters of the ARVN 1st Division, it was considered off-limits to both sides. Thus it had been war-free.

Hue had a population of about 100,000 residents, not including refugees. Most of that population lived within the confines of its fortresslike walls. Surrounded by multichanneled moats, the walls of the city were massive; many sections along the walls had prepared defenses. A maze of bunkers and tunnels had been constructed there by Japanese forces when they occupied Hue during World War II.

Enclosed by those walls in the early 19th century by Emperor Gia Long with the aid of French military engineers, Hue was modeled after the ancient Chinese capital of Peking (modern Beijing). It was a three-square-mile, rectangular-shaped citadel encompassing some of the world's oldest and most beautiful gardens, pagodas, finely carved stone buildings, and the old imperial palace. There were also shops, row houses, and a short airstrip.

In his book *Semper Fi Vietnam: From Da Nang to the DMZ,* author Edward F. Murphy described Hue as a "camera-toting tourist's dream," that would prove to be "a rifle-toting infantryman's nightmare."

Hue bordered the Song Houng (translated into English, "River of Perfumes") to the southeast. South of the Perfume River was Hue's new city, which also had a substantial population. The new city was connected to the old walled city by a bridge spanning the river.

Located within the new city was a small complex for the Military Assistance Command Vietnam (MACV). There, American army and Marine Corps advisers were based. The ARVN 1st Division headquarters was across the river in the old city. But the ARVN division's battalions, deliberately kept out of Hue, were deployed along South Vietnam's Highway 1 between Hue and the DMZ. The only ARVN soldiers in Hue were a company-strength reaction team that was more of a security detail than an offensive force.

In the early morning hours of January 31, word reached MACV and ARVN headquarters in Hue that Saigon was under attack from forces within the city. Then, at 3:40 A.M., points throughout Hue became the targets of mortar and rocket fire. Two battalions of NVA infantry led by sappers simultaneously attacked the ARVN headquarters.

When dawn broke, some 7,500 enemy soldiers were in control of most of the old city. There, North Vietnamese soldiers raised the gold-starred Communist flag over the ramparts and then began systematically search-ing out, apprehending, and executing some 2,800 government officials. The doomed included schoolteachers, doctors, clergymen, foreigners, government officials, and others who were suspected of aiding the Ameri-cans or who might be loyal to the South Vietnamese government.

Westmoreland and his ARVN counterparts, fearful of killing innocent civilians and not wanting to destroy any more of the ancient citadel than necessary, initially placed tight restrictions on the supporting tanks, artil-lery, and air cover desired by the ground forces. But as casualties mounted, the senior commanders were compelled to lift the restrictions.

The fighting for Hue was bitter. It was primarily a U.S. Marine and South Vietnamese army operation: Elements of the 1st and 5th Marine Regiments participated, as did numerous ARVN battalions. But before it was over, elements of the U.S. Army's 1st Cavalry and 101st Airborne Divisions were also involved. The combat was initially house-to-house, but the fighting evolved into a painful process of driving the enemy from the battlements and other fortifications along the inner walls of the old city.

Within days, the retaking of Hue took on a sort of calculated sense: The Marines would attack the enemy each morning, fight throughout the day and capture ground, try to scarf down at least one hot meal, and then hunker down in defensive positions at night.

CHAPTER 27: TET OFFENSIVE

By the beginning of the second week in February, the Americans had gained possession of most of Hue's new city. ARVN forces were in control of most of the old city. The enemy's strongholds were along the southeastern wall on the Perfume River, the west wall, and the old Imperial Palace. Along those points the fighting was bitter, with NVA forces fighting to the death. Marine snipers were deployed, as were flame-thrower teams. Other leathernecks, paratroopers, and cavalrymen picked their way through the maze of alleyways, rows of buildings, wall niches, and other deadly hideaways. The fighting was frighteningly close: Each man had a bayonet fixed to the end of his rifle. When contact was made, the two sides blasted into each other's ranks until one side no longer existed. Fortunately for the Americans, superior training and leadership overcame fanaticism.

Hue was finally declared secure on February 25, but small, isolated NVA holdouts continued to resist. All opposition ceased on March 2.

CHAPTER 28

HAMBURGER HILL

(MAY 10–20, 1969)

The Battle for Hamburger Hill was a terrible 10-day slugfest resulting in a decisive American victory. Unfortunately for those who fought and died on its slopes, the hill was abandoned one month after it had been captured, an action which reflected the overall futility of the war.

The battle was the culmination of a series of campaigns aimed at capturing the strategic A Shau Valley along the Laotian border in the I Corps Tactical Zone. After struggles in the A Shau during the early days of America's involvement in Vietnam, the valley had been abandoned to the Communists in 1965. It had since become a source of great frustration for the two Military Assistance Command Vietnam (MACV) chiefs—first Gen. William Childs Westmoreland, then Gen. Creighton Abrams.

SETTING THE STAGE

In April 1968, soon after the Tet Offensive, Westmoreland ordered the 1st Cavalry Division to the A Shau in an attempt to regain control in the region. Code-named Delaware, the mission's objectives were achieved in part. But poor weather hampered the cavalry's air mobility, and the campaign was called off.

In August, the 101st Airborne Division was ordered in under the code name Somerset Plain. Again, limited objectives were achieved. But it was quickly determined that if the valley was to be completely controlled, further operations were needed.

In January 1969, the 9th Marines launched Operation Dewey Canyon through the Da Krong Valley in the Quang Tri Province, just north of the A Shau. There fighting was heavy, but the Marines killed large numbers of enemy soldiers and uncovered large caches of weapons.

In March, the 101st again went on the offensive in the A Shau. The paratroopers were helicopter-ferried into the heart of the valley. There they fought a tough engagement forcing the enemy to fall back on the valley's northwestern sector and a steep hill known to the Vietnamese as Dong (translated into English, "mountain") Ap Bia.

THE AP BIA MOUNTAIN

Located about one mile from the Laotian border, the Ap Bia mountain was officially designated by MACV as Hill 937. Local Montagnard tribesmen referred to it as "the mountain of the crouching beast." It was dubbed "Hamburger Hill" by American soldiers because it seemed to chew up their buddies like a hamburger meatgrinder. And the North Vietnamese Army (NVA), who lost even more men attempting to defend the hill, had a similar nickname for it: Thit Bam (translated into English, "meat chopper").

Ap Bia was a steep mountain. Its slopes were covered in a tangled morass of undergrowth, vines, and thick groves of bamboo. Positioned on the heights was the 29th NVA Regiment, nicknamed the "Pride of Ho Chi Minh." The 29th was a crack force of 1,200 regulars who were dug in behind an extensive network of log bunkers. Having been there for several years, the enemy had taken great pains to ensure that the hill's defenses could withstand ground attacks from any direction. Subterranean tunnels that honeycombed the mountain offered surprisingly good protection from heavy artillery and aerial bombardment.

The A Shau was deemed to be a primary terminus on the Ho Chi Minh Trail, the vital North Vietnamese supply line that ran just inside the Laotian and Cambodian borders before turning east at various points into South Vietnam.

APACHE SNOW

The battle was part of Operation Apache Snow, a broad sweep aimed at clearing the 28-mile A Shau Valley. The operation began on May 10, when a brigade of the famed U.S. 101st Airborne Division and elements of the Army of the Republic of (South) Vietnam (ARVN) were ferried into a clearing in the northern A Shau.

The 101st, under the command of Maj. Gen. Melvin Zais, was one of the most celebrated units in the U.S. Army. Known as the Screaming Eagles, the division started out as a traditional airborne unit during World War II. But with the advent of the helicopter and air assault tactics, the 101st became "airmobile." The division's heliborne assault into the A Shau typified its new role.

To oppose the enemy, Zais had three American Airborne Infantry battalions—the 1st Battalion of the 506th Regiment, the 2nd Battalion of 501st, and the 3rd Battalion of the 187th. The three combined battalions formed the 3rd Brigade under Col. Joseph Conmy. The 3rd Brigade was to be the primary striking force. Zais also had two ARVN battalions under his direction.

As the 506th and 501st began fanning out into the A Shau back-country, Lt. Col. Weldon Honeycutt's 3rd Battalion of the 187th Infantry Regiment—known by the Japanese term Rakkasans (translated into English, "umbrella men" or "parachutists")—landed some 2,000 yards west of Ap Bia with little opposition. The Rakkasans then launched a reconnaissance in force toward the base of the mountain.

Lt. Col. Weldon Honeycutt, a North Carolina native who lied about his age to enlist as a private at 16, loved the army. He was fiercely loyal, and he believed that America's place was in Vietnam. He had once physically thrown a subordinate officer, who expressed his opposition to the war, head-first out of his headquarters building. He then accused the officer of cowardice and treason and had orders cut shipping him to another unit. The incident was not isolated, as Honeycutt was known for getting rid of those whom he deemed to be cowards, duty shirkers, conscientious objectors, or even marginal fighters. Honeycutt was a warrior. He expected every soldier under his command to be the same. Consequently, by the spring of 1969, he had honed his 3rd Battalion into one of the best combat units in South Vietnam.

Confident that his Rakkasans could defeat all comers, Honeycutt temporarily violated one of the great principles of war and divided his force over unfamiliar ground. Some elements moved around to the north and northwest of Dong Ap Bia. Others swept west toward the Laotian border. And still others moved up toward the base of Ap Bia's southern slopes. On May 11, having made virtually no contact with the enemy, Honeycutt ordered one of his companies to assault and seize the summit.

THE ASSAULTS

The first assault was beaten back. Worse, supporting Cobra helicopter gunships mistook Honeycutt's command post for an NVA unit and attacked. The friendly fire incident killed two GIs. Another 35 were wounded, including Honeycutt.

The Americans then pulled back into hastily erected defensive positions and radioed for supporting fire. American air and artillery fire pounded the hill in an attempt to knock out the NVA positions. Enemy soldiers caught in the open were killed. Most, however, remained underground and survived.

The bombing and shelling stripped the hill of its vegetation, enabling pilots and artillery forward observers to have a better visual idea of what they were hitting. But it also eliminated most of the cover and concealment needed for attacking forces. Making matters worse, heavy rains turned the hill's slopes into giant mudslides.

The following day, Honeycutt launched the second of several attempts to take Ap Bia. By May 13, it had become obvious to Colonel Conmy that there were far more NVA soldiers dug in on the hilltop than Honeycutt's force could deal with. To support the latter, Conmy dispatched the 1st Battalion of the 506th toward Ap Bia.

Known by its Cherokee Indian nickname, *Currahee* (translated into English, "stands alone"), the 506th was to launch a forced march across the backcountry toward the hill's northern slopes and attack the enemy from the rear. In doing so, the Currahees would also sever any NVA supply columns moving in that direction. Conmy had hoped that the 1st of the 506th would be in position to attack Ap Bia the following day. Instead, rugged terrain and enemy snipers delayed the marching Currahees for five days.

Honeycutt launched coordinated attacks against the heights on both May 14 and 15. Both attacks were beaten back by fierce enemy resistance.

In fact, the elusive crest began to seem impregnable to the men tasked with taking it. Each time the exhausted GIs struggled up the hill, they tripped explosive booby traps, got shot, slipped and slid back down in the mud, or were ordered to fall back short of reaching the top. Those in the advance elements who got close enough to the top were killed, maimed, or pinned down by the enemy, who poured machine-gun fire into their ranks and rolled grenades down on them. Each time, Honeycutt was hoping to be reinforced by the battalion from the 506th, but they were still battling their way across the countryside.

The precariousness of the situation quickly permeated the ranks from rifle company private to battalion commander. At no time was this more evident than when Honeycutt appealed to Conmy for help. On the night of the May 14, the two commanders held a powwow, standing in the rain as artillery fire pounded the heights above.

"Joe, this fight is getting awful rough," said Honeycutt, according to author Samuel Zaffiri in "Hamburger Hill." "I don't know how many of the bastards are up there, but I know there's a helluva lot of them. The bastards have got heavy weapons. They've got communications. They're dug in. They've got a defense-in-depth, and they're movin' fresh troops up those draws from Laos every night. Every night. And I don't have the manpower to stop them."

On May 16, elements of the 506th reached closing distance of Ap Bia and attacked. But the attack was diverted when they were forced to move against and seize nearby Hill 916. Conmy then ordered Honeycutt to halt his ongoing attacks against Ap Bia and wait for the 506th to catch up.

Meanwhile, the battle began to take on a new dimension. Reporters, having gotten wind of the numerous unsuccessful assaults to seize Ap Bia, began to question the fruitlessness of it all. Subsequent newspaper accounts began to ignite a firestorm of controversy which heaped criticism on General Zais, stirred the ire of the antiwar movement, and unsettled Washington policymakers. Moreover, journalists began flocking to rear-area headquarters and forward bases that were supporting the Ap Bia battle in an attempt to glean anything from the front. This forced commanders to divide their focused efforts between the battle and a brewing public relations nightmare.

But Zais, Conmy, and Honeycutt were determined not to fail. On May 20, the Rakkasans—now joined by the two battalions from the 506th and the 501st, as well as one of two ARVN battalions—attacked Ap Bia in force. After a bitter struggle and 11 uphill assaults, Zais's men punched through the enemy's summit defenses and became the kings of Hamburger Hill.

Rifling through the remnants of the NVA position, the Americans discovered more than 630 enemy bodies scattered along the slopes and the crest. Two NVA battalions had been virtually destroyed. More enemy soldiers may have been killed and either buried under debris after the bombings or carried across the border into Laos. Some 70 Americans were also dead. Another 372 were wounded.

> Over the years, a number of sources have erroneously claimed that 241 Americans were killed at Hamburger Hill. This information has been fostered by the fact that a month after the battle, *Life* magazine published photographs of the faces of all Americans killed in Southeast Asia during the time that the Battle for Hamburger Hill was being waged. Many readers assumed that those were the faces of the men who struggled on the slopes of the hill. It was "a misleading feature," according to the late Dr. John Pimlott, who oversaw the War Studies Department at the Royal Military Academy in Sandhurst, United Kingdom.

THE AFTERMATH

In terms of losses, Hamburger Hill had not been the bloodiest fight of the war, nor had it been the longest, but no battle of the war faced more public scrutiny. Although it was a decisive victory for the American army, commanders were roundly criticized for ordering their soldiers up the hill time and again under relentless enemy fire. Worse, the hill, located in a remote region of Vietnam, was later deemed to be of little strategic value. Thus, it was abandoned weeks after being captured.

Hamburger Hill was, in the words of outspoken Col. David H. Hackworth, a "totally useless piece of real estate," which had been assaulted by General Zais "as if he thought he was in Korea or storming Kraut positions at Normandy."

General Westmoreland was of a different opinion. In his memoir, *A Soldier Reports*, Westmoreland defended the decision to capture Hamburger Hill. "To have left the North Vietnamese undisturbed on the mountain would have been to jeopardize our control of the valley and accept a renewed threat to the coastal cities," Westmoreland wrote.

"A prolonged siege would have been costly and tied up troops indefinitely." He added that General Zais "quite properly ordered an attack."

Nevertheless, the struggle for Hamburger Hill—and other similar, though not as widely publicized, battles—resulted in a U.S. policy shift toward "Vietnamization."

> Vietnamization was a two-part policy implemented by U.S. president Richard M. Nixon in the spring of 1969. The first part outlined plans for a measured withdrawal of U.S. combat forces from South Vietnam. The second part called for ARVN forces to increasingly assume more of the military responsibilities previously held by the withdrawing Americans.

Nixon directed Gen. Creighton Abrams, who had recently replaced Westmoreland as chief of the Military Assistance Command Vietnam, to avoid engagements like Hamburger Hill in the future.

PART 5

POST-VIETNAM TO THE 21ST CENTURY

CHAPTER 29

OPERATION URGENT FURY

(OCTOBER 23–NOVEMBER 2, 1983)

The invasion of the West Indian island nation of Grenada was the first time that a joint U.S. force combining all four traditional armed services had fought together since the Vietnam War. Code-named Operation Urgent Fury, the invasion was a decisive victory for the Americans: "A whale of a good job," in the words of Army Chief of Staff Gen. John Wickham. But the operation was not without tactical and service-coordinating difficulties.

Located in the southernmost Caribbean islands of the West Indies, the 133-square-mile island of Grenada was one of the smallest independent nations in the Western Hemisphere. Its population was just under 100,000. Often referred to as the Isle of Spice, Grenada was surrounded by sandy beaches and natural harbors. Inland were lush tropical rain forests dominated by a 3,000-foot mountain ridge—beautiful, but with the potential of being a rugged and dangerous environment for any invading force.

THE SITUATION

On October 13, 1983, the army of Grenada, under the direction of former Deputy Prime Minister Bernard Coard and Grenadian general Hudson Austin, seized power of the tiny island nation in a bloody coup d'état. Martial law was immediately declared and a shoot-on-sight curfew was established. Grenada's prime minister Maurice Bishop, his wife, and most of government's senior officials were arrested and shot.

Coard was a devout Marxist. Bishop was also a Marxist, but with free-market leanings. Those facts, combined with the rapid and violent ouster of Bishop's government, were unsettling to most of the democratized nations in the Caribbean, as it was to the administration of U.S. president Ronald Reagan. The president, in fact, referred to Coard and his cronies as "a brutal group of leftist thugs."

Coard's faction was supported financially and militarily by Fidel Castro's Cuba, then considered a dangerous satellite state of the Soviet Union. The Cold War was at its zenith, and Reagan was committed to winning against the Soviets on all fronts. Closer to home, nearly 1,000 American medical students were attending school on Grenada. Their fate was an immediate concern to the White House.

On October 21, the Organization of Eastern Caribbean States, as well as Jamaica and Barbados, requested U.S. assistance. The following day, Reagan approved a directive for military force as an option to restore order on the island.

> Disaster struck when, on October 23, a smiling Muslim suicide bomber raced a five-ton truck through concertina wire and past armed sentries at the U.S. Marine barracks in Beirut, Lebanon. The sentries, armed with unloaded weapons, were unable to return fire. The truck, loaded with explosives, then crashed into the four-story headquarters building of the 24th Marine Amphibious Unit's Battalion Landing Team and erupted in an enormous orange ball of flame. The truck and driver vaporized. The building was leveled. The death toll was devastating: 218 marines, 18 sailors, 3 soldiers, 1 French paratrooper, and 1 Lebanese civilian were killed. The White House, though stunned, quickly realized that an immediate, successful operation in Grenada would alleviate some of the horrifying news coming out of Beirut.

THE OPERATION

On the night of October 23, Team 6 of the U.S. Navy SEALs (the Navy's elite sea, air, land commandos) and a handful of U.S. Air Force Combat Controllers (an elite Air Force ground combat element trained to set up drop zones and coordinate airborne assaults, among other special operations responsibilities) conducted an open-water parachute drop off Point Salines on the southern tip of Grenada.

The SEALs were responsible for reconnoitering the airfield and then determining the condition of the runway and the location and strength of nearby enemy forces. The combat control airmen were tasked with clandestinely positioning radar beacons on the airfield so that parachuting U.S. Army Rangers and Airborne forces would be able to find the drop zone. Sadly, four SEALs drowned in the heavy seas, and the others were ordered to withdraw before completing the mission. Nevertheless, the operation to seize the island was given a green light.

Vice Adm. Joseph Metcalf III, commander of the U.S. 2nd Fleet, was the overall operations commander for the invasion. His weapon to accomplish the mission was Joint Task Force 120 (JTF-120), a force comprising Navy, Marine Corps, Army, and Air Force elements. Advising Metcalf on the conduct of ground operations was U.S. Army major general H. Norman Schwarzkopf, destined to become famous as the senior field commander during the Persian Gulf War of 1991.

At Grenada, Metcalf's senior tactical commanders included U.S. Navy captain Carl Erie, commanding Amphibious Squadron 4; U.S. Army major general Edward L. Trobaugh, commanding the 82nd Airborne Division; U.S. Army major general Richard A. Scholtes, commanding the Joint Special Operations Command (JSOC) and the 75th Ranger Regiment; and Col. James P. Faulkner, commanding the 22nd Marine Amphibious Unit (22 MAU).

> The 22nd MAU was en route to relieve their weary brothers in Beirut when they were diverted toward the Caribbean.

Just after midnight on October 25, Navy SEALs were again dispatched to reconnoiter the island. This time they scouted the beach areas slated for the 22 MAU's amphibious landings. The SEALs determined that the landing points were "marginal" at best.

Around 2 A.M., Erie's squadron moved into position off Grenada. There, based on the SEALs' report, the landing points for the Marines were changed to Pearls Airport and the town of Grenville, both inland landing sites.

At 5 A.M., helicopters loaded with a heavily armed company of U.S. Marines began landing at Pearl's Airport. As the helicopters touched down, they were immediately fired upon by elements of the Grenadian People's Revolutionary Army (PRA). The leathernecks—Echo Company of the 2nd Battalion, 8th Marine Regiment—scrambled out of the choppers, hit the deck, and returned fire.

Thirty-six minutes later, a team of Air Force Combat Controllers made the first parachute jump over the heavily defended Point Salines airport. The airmen were followed by the parachuting 1st and 2nd Battalions of the Army's 75th Ranger Regiment. Their landings had been timed to take place as the marines hit Pearls, but an aircraft navigational problem forced them to land later without the protection of darkness.

Point Salines was no cakewalk. There, the Rangers encountered the toughest overall resistance of the operation and were forced to make a dangerous low-level jump from only 500 feet. They were under fire the entire time.

"The Cubans and PRA (Grenadian People's Revolutionary Army) were very well placed," said U.S. Navy captain Thomas Scott, an assistant chief of staff for the commander in chief of the Atlantic. "They had occupied the high ground and strategically placed their antiaircraft positions around the airfield before the initial assault by U.S. and Caribbean forces. They were probably where we'd have been if we'd been on the resisting side."

American medical students attending St. George's Medical College were awakened by the sounds of distant gunfire and aircraft. Jumping out of bed and peering through their dormitory windows, they saw two planes circling the edge of the Point Salines airport. Minutes later, they watched as helicopters roared in from the sea and flew through antiaircraft fire. Then there were the blossoming parachutes, hundreds of them. The students be came frightened when the blackened-faced paratroopers landed, rushed toward their complex, and began cutting through the school's chain-link fence. Believing the sky soldiers to be Coard's men coming to take them prisoner, many of the students began to panic. Some cried. But tears were soon replaced with cries of joy, when they discovered that the tough-looking paratroopers were actually U.S. Army Rangers coming to their rescue.

A second campus at Grand Anse was farther north. Retreating Cubans and PRA units blocked the Rangers from the students, but the enemy forces were eventually beaten back. The students were later picked up by helicopters on the beach.

Meanwhile, a SEALs team had been dispatched to rescue British governor-general Sir Paul Scoon, his wife, and staff—all of whom were being held hostage by Grenadian forces at the Scoons' "Government

House" residence. As two helicopters loaded with SEALs roared over the capital toward the mansion, the enemy holding Scoon prepared to fight back. Once on site, the helicopters came under heavy fire. The first of the two choppers was hit and forced to withdraw. The second, also hit, managed to hover over the mansion long enough for the SEALs to fast-rope to the ground. The SEALs quickly overwhelmed the Grenadian guards and stormed the residence. But they soon found themselves under heavy fire from enemy armored personnel carriers.

> Fast-roping is a technique wherein SEALs and other air assault-trained combatants wearing heavy leather gloves slide down thick nylon ropes from a hovering helicopter to the ground.

At 6 A.M., a second helicopter-borne force of marines—Fox Company—landed near the town of Grenville, south of Pearls. Meanwhile, Cobra AH-6 attack helicopters swarmed in and destroyed PRA artillery positions.

Meanwhile, another force of SEALs was helicopter-ferried to a radio transmitter site near the capital city of St. George. There the SEALs were to launch an assault to capture the transmitter without damaging it. They were successful in reaching the site and overpowering the guards in a brief hand-to-hand struggle. But an enemy counterattack forced the American sailors to withdraw.

As the SEALs were fighting beneath the radio transmitter, Delta Force commandos (a secret counterterrorist group known affectionately in U.S. Army circles as the "D-Boys") were preparing to conduct an air assault operation against Richmond Hill Prison, the site of an old fortress overlooking St. George. The Delta objective was to free illegally held political prisoners. It was feared that once the landings started, the prison guards would begin executing the prisoners. Delta soldiers, experts at clearing rooms and close-quarters fighting, were the tools of choice in preventing this.

Located across a small valley from Richmond Hill was Fort Frederick, which garrisoned a heavily armed force that would also have to be taken. The Delta commandos, supported by one company from the 75th Rangers and transported by nine Black Hawk helicopters from the 160th Special Operations Group "Nightstalkers," were slated to seize the prison and the fort soon after midnight. Unfortunately, interservice bickering and confusion at the senior command level delayed the assault until the early daylight hours.

Just after 6:30 A.M., the force was air-ferried up toward the prison, but quickly came under heavy and unexpected antiaircraft fire. One helicopter was shot down. Others roared in to suppress the antiaircraft batteries, but to no avail. Other close air-support aircraft were requested, but all were working over the enemy positions facing the ground forces below. The mission was aborted. It was attempted later, but again with no success.

Nearby Fort Rupert was a different story. There Delta Force assaulted and captured the complex with stunning shock and speed. The defenders did not know what hit them. The Americans quickly rounded up a number of Coard's henchmen and Austin's senior commanders and loaded them onto helicopters, which then ferried the prisoners out to the USS *Guam* for interrogation.

By midmorning, the SEALs at the governor-general's mansion were rescued by a small force of U.S. Marines. Scoon and his wife were then helicopter-ferried to the *Guam*.

By the afternoon, the Rangers were in complete control of Point Salines. There were still small pockets of resistance sniping and lobbing the occasional mortar round. But in each instance, they were spotted and knocked out. The Rangers, reinforced by elements of the 82nd Airborne Division, began moving against enemy positions near St. George's.

Meanwhile, the 8th Marines' Fox and Echo companies linked up north of St. George's and captured a stretch of ground known as the "Queen's Racecourse." It was quickly dubbed "Landing Zone Racetrack." There, the Marine command element set up headquarters.

Fighting continued for the next two days as Marines, Rangers, and paratroopers swept the island. By October 27, much of the resistance in the St. George's area had been quashed. The Americans fanned out and captured Fort Lucas, Richmond Hill Prison, and other strongholds. The Southern portion of the island was soon seized, and by Halloween, the highlands were secured.

In a secondary operation, the Marines landed on and captured the nearby isle of Carriacou on November 1. The following day, the leathernecks were relieved by the paratroopers.

THE AFTERMATH

In a televised address to the nation, President Reagan said, "It [Grenada] was a Soviet-Cuban colony, being readied as a major military bastion to export terror and undermine democracy. We got there just in time."

Indeed. In the aftermath of the battle, intelligence analysts wading through numerous captured documents discovered that the Grenadian revolutionary government had begun developing substantive political-military relationships with a variety of rogue nations, chief among them Colonel Muammar Qaddafi's Libya. Qaddafi had hoped to export his own brand of terrorism to the Western Hemisphere through Grenada. He was stopped cold by Urgent Fury. And in less than three years, the Libyan leader's direct involvement in terrorist activities throughout the world forced Reagan to launch a devastating air attack against that nation.

Compared to previous battles and campaigns, casualties suffered during the Grenada invasion were light on both sides: Nineteen American combatants were killed and another 116 were wounded. Forty-five Grenadian soldiers were killed and 358 were wounded. Nearly 30 Grenadian civilians were killed. Cuban forces suffered 25 killed, 59 wounded, and 638 captured.

Although the invasion of Grenada was a decisive victory for U.S. military forces, insiders have since argued that some of the American forces involved suffered a number of command problems that could have been disastrous. At the soldier level, the combatants fought well. At the command level, there were glitches.

That said, the Rangers—who clearly faced the stiffest opposition—performed well, as did the Marines. The special operating units—Delta Force and the SEALs—fought bravely and achieved most of their objectives. Delta was a relatively new organization, as was the SEALs' Team 6. Their missions were more complex than those tackled by the conventional forces. Consequently, they discovered glitches in their own operational methods and corrected them immediately.

The elite 82nd Airborne had a few problems. One officer monitoring radio communications later said that it sounded "as if the whole division was on the verge of panic." Speed of movement was also called into question. At one point, Gen. John W. Vessey Jr., then the outspoken chairman of the Joint Chiefs of Staff, telephoned an 82nd Airborne commander and allegedly demanded to know why there were "two companies of Marines running all over the island and thousands of Army troops doing nothing. What the hell is going on?"

Nevertheless, the Americans won the day. Nearly 600 Americans and 120 foreign nationals were rescued. The popular government was restored on the island. And the possible strategic threat to U.S. lines of communication in the Caribbean had been eliminated. In so doing, the cynical American public, still smarting after the debacle in Vietnam, had a reason to again be proud of its soldiers. More important, the troops learned valuable tactical lessons that would serve them well six years later in Panama and seven years later in the Iraqi desert.

CHAPTER 30

OPERATION EL DORADO CANYON

(APRIL 15–16, 1986)

Code-named Operation El Dorado Canyon, the 1986 air attack against Libya was a meticulously planned strike that was launched in retaliation for Libyan leader colonel Muammar Qaddafi's direct involvement in previous terrorist attacks against Americans. And like famed Colonel James H. Doolittle and his raiders who—almost 44 years to the day prior to the Libyan raid—struck Tokyo, the psychological impact of the raid far outweighed the military value.

PRIOR TO THE OPERATION

Poor relations had existed between the United States and Libya since Qaddafi had seized power in a 1969 coup d'état and ordered all foreign military forces out of the country. The following year, Wheelus Air Base, the U.S. Air Force's primary station in Libya, was returned to Libyan control and all military personnel were withdrawn.

As American-Libyan relations continued to deteriorate, Qaddafi began warming to the Soviet Union and other Eastern Bloc nations. Ironically, Libya continued to oppose the spread of communism in the Arab world.

During the 1970s and early 1980s, Western intelligence agencies began gathering information indicating that Libya was supporting global terrorism on a number of fronts. When newly elected U.S. president Ronald Reagan moved into the White House in 1981, he began focusing on what he believed was a credible threat from Qaddafi. In May, the White House expelled 27 Libyan diplomats from the United States on charges that they were directly involved in the support of international terrorism. Three months later, American F-14 Tomcats shot down two Soviet-built Libyan fighters over the contested Gulf of Sidra during a routine U.S. Navy exercise. Qaddafi claimed that the Mediterranean Gulf of Sidra was Libyan territorial waters, and he threatened to attack any foreign air or sea craft that crossed his "line of death" into the Gulf. The U.S. considered the Gulf to be an extension of international waters. In December, Reagan ordered all 1,500 American citizens still living in Libya to leave the country. Beginning in the spring of 1982, Libyan oil imports were embargoed and technology transfers halted.

Tensions between the United States and Libya increased over the next four years. In July 1985, a Trans World Airlines (TWA) airliner was hijacked in Lebanon, and in December, American airline ticket counters in Rome and Vienna were the targets of terrorist bombings. In all cases, the actions were perpetrated by terrorist mastermind Abu Nidal. But Qaddafi provided support for Nidal and his agents. That same year, Libya began upgrading its air defenses with Soviet-built surface-to-air missiles. In January 1986, Libyan assets were frozen in the United States.

In March, six Libyan surface-to-air missiles were launched against U.S. Navy fighters conducting routine maneuvers over the Gulf of Sidra. The missiles failed to hit their targets, but the jets destroyed the launch sites by homing in on the missiles' radar guidance signals. Libyan gunboats also moved against American warships in the region, but were easily destroyed by American jets.

Soon thereafter, Qaddafi wired a message to the Libyan Embassy in East Berlin, which directed terrorists "... to conduct a terrorist attack against Americans to cause maximum and indiscriminate casualties." The message was intercepted. But before Washington could react, terrorists struck twice. On April 2, four Americans were killed when a bomb exploded aboard TWA Flight 840 en route to Athens. The attack appeared to be Syrian-sponsored, but Qaddafi's fingerprints were all over it. He brazenly congratulated the terrorists and threatened an escalation of similar acts. Three days later, terrorists struck a second time: A bomb was detonated in La Belle discotheque, a Berlin dance club frequented by off-duty U.S. military personnel. Two hundred people were injured in the blast, including 63 American soldiers. One soldier and a civilian were killed.

The U.S. intelligence community determined that Qaddafi was behind both acts, and the White House feared it was the beginning of a reign of terror against American interests throughout the world. The decision was made to strike back.

AMERICAN FORCES GET THE GREEN LIGHT

Ten days after the discotheque bombing—on the evening of April 15 and early morning of April 16—the United States launched a series of air attacks against five primary Libyan ground targets. Directed by Vice Adm. Frank Kelso of the U.S. 6th Fleet, the attacking force was made up of two strike groups: one Air Force, one Navy. The first was a flight of 24 U.S. Air Force (USAF) F-111F Aardvark fighter-bombers based at the Royal Air Force base in Lakenheath, England. The second consisted of two sub-groups of U.S. Navy fighters based on the aircraft carriers USS *America* and USS *Coral Sea* operating in the Mediterranean Sea.

The Aardvarks, part of USAF colonel Sam W. Westbrook's 48th Tactical Fighter Wing, comprised the primary attack force. They were supported by 28 KC-10 and KC-135 refueling tankers and five EF-111 Raven electronic countermeasures aircraft.

The navy jets comprising the secondary strike group were part of Kelso's 6th Fleet. They included a flight of seven A-6E Intruders from the VA-34 Blue Blasters squadron and six A-7E Corsair II fighters from the CVW-1 squadron based on the *America*. The secondary strike group also included eight A-6Es from the VA-55 Warhorses squadron and six F/A-18 Hornets from the CVW-13 squadron based on the *Coral Sea*.

At exactly 5:36 P.M. (7:36 P.M. Libyan time), the first of the Aardvarks raced down the runway and lifted off into the early evening sky over Lakenheath. The jet was the first to be launched in the USAF's first fighter combat mission in more than 10 years. It was quickly followed by 23 others, 6 of which were considered "airborne spares" and would be returned to Lakenheath after the first midair refueling.

The planes flew toward their first of several refueling rendezvous on a 6,000-mile round-trip flight, which would last nearly 13 hours with a few minutes of battle during the halfway point. Both France and Spain, despite both being members of the North Atlantic Treaty Organization (NATO), had denied the United States overflight rights for the mission. Consequently, the route taken was south—skirting Portuguese airspace but remaining over international waters—then east into the Mediterranean Sea before turning south again toward the Libyan coast.

Just after midnight, the two carriers turned into the wind about 150 miles off the Libyan coast and began launching jets. Combat Air Patrol (CAP) cover was provided by F-14 Tomcats from the carriers.

A handful of the naval aviators had seen action over the Mediterranean. But for most of the USAF pilots and weapons systems operators, El Dorado Canyon was their first combat mission.

As they approached Libya, normal—occasionally lighthearted—cockpit radio chatter ceased. Conversations continued but were wholly serious and mission-focused. Crews began busying themselves with last-minute preparations from personal prayers to systems checks. If the aircraft target-guidance systems failed prior to attack, the pilots were to abort rather than estimate their targets' locations. "America fully intended to kill terrorists," U.S. Military Academy history professor Daniel P. Bolger would later write. "But nobody wanted a bloodbath in Libya's streets."

For the crews, it was a critical last few minutes between peace and war. According to Air Force colonel Robert E. Venkus, the 48th's vice wing commander, "The main benefit for many was that their physical discomfort—they had been strapped to their jets for over five hours—was all but forgotten in the accelerating schedule of critical cockpit actions. Captain M. [so-named to protect his identity from terrorists] recalls dropping a checklist page and struggling for what seemed like ten minutes to recover it from that inaccessible place where dropped pencils and pages go in jet fighters. Major M. thought that his helmet's earphone speakers had failed—his normally garrulous pilot had been quiet for so long. In every cockpit, pressure grew as they neared Tripoli waiting for the inevitable, and unpredictable, reaction of the Libyan air defenses."

ATTACK

The pilot of the lead USAF jet looked through his windscreen at the lights of Tripoli in the distance. From his vantage point, the city was positioned at 12 o'clock, level, about 10 miles ahead, and closing fast. He alternated between his instruments, the city lights, and the darkness—searching the dark sky for any telltale glows from enemy missiles his own radar might not detect. He was also trying to maintain the predetermined approach speed of nearly 600 miles per hour—9 miles per minute—so that the jets behind him wouldn't overshoot his own plane. The spacing between the warplanes was between 30 and 75 seconds.

At 2 A.M. (Libyan time), the warplanes roared in from several directions. Navy fighters attacked the Libyan air defenses, whereas three separate lines of Aardvarks bore down on the Libyan capital. Within seconds, the adrenaline-pumped Americans were over their targets and attacking.

The crews, bracing for a wall of antiaircraft fire and surface-to-air missiles, raced above downtown Tripoli as the enemy's tracers reached toward but arced far behind their planes, the enemy gunners failing to compensate for the jets' speed.

The Libyans were caught completely by surprise. They had of course anticipated the attacks sometime, but their air defense forces were wholly unprepared. Accurate Libyan antiaircraft fire proved to be virtually non-existent, and no enemy aircraft were launched against the Americans. The only batteries that did return fire failed to open up until the jets were already over their targets and moving too fast to be hit. In most cases, Libyan military officers were slow to command, and frightened soldiers were either killed or abandoned their posts amid the confusion.

Zeroing in on Qaddafi's headquarters, the lead Aardvark unleashed its ordnance, but the crew was momentarily surprised by a stream of 23 millimeter tracers that shot up from the earth toward their jet and missed. The pilot pulled hard away from the target as the weapons system operator craned his neck earthward and watched the bombs explode.

In less than 12 minutes some 60 tons of munitions hit enemy targets, including the following:

- The Aziziyah barracks, a military facility that served as a command and control center for Libyan-sponsored terrorists. The target was struck by 9 F111-Fs carrying 2,000-pound laser-guided bombs.

- Military targets at the Tripoli airport. The target was struck by 6 F111-Fs carrying 500-pound bombs.

- The Side Bilal base, a training facility for underwater sabotage operations. The target was struck by 3 F111-Fs carrying 2,000-pound laser-guided bombs.

- The Jamahiriyah barracks, a terrorist command post in Benghazi. The target was struck by 7 A6-Es carrying 500-pound bombs.

- Benina Air Base. The target was struck by 8 A-6Es carrying 500-pound bombs.
- The Tripoli and Benghazi air defenses were attacked by A-7Es and F/A-18s.

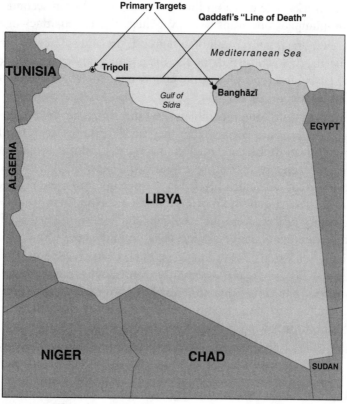

The Libyan targets.

The five targets and the Libyan air defense networks were successfully hit. The attacks severely damaged Libya's terrorist infrastructure and command-and-control capabilities. Beyond the physical damage, the psychological effect on the enemy was devastating. Qaddafi immediately went into hiding. And though terrorism was not—and will never be—eliminated completely, Qaddafi and other perpetrators of terror quickly realized that a blistering retaliation would follow any attacks on the United States or its interests.

Tragically, among the dozens of civilian casualties was Qaddafi's adopted infant daughter. It has since been suggested that Qaddafi, in a propaganda ploy, adopted the child in the wake of the attacks as she lay dying in a hospital.

The overwhelming success of El Dorado Canyon was not without American casualties, either. One of the Aardvarks, crewed by captains Fernando Luis Ribas-Dominicci and Paul Lorence, crashed in the sea. Theories have since suggested that the aircraft was struck by an undetected Libyan surface-to-air missile, or that the plane's own weapons detonated onboard. The most plausible explanation is that the crew became disoriented during the exhausting, moonless journey and simply flew the Aardvark into the sea. No one knows for sure.

THE AFTERMATH

The Libyan attack was based on five objectives:

- The strikes would deter Qaddafi from his continued support of terrorism in any fashion.
- Qaddafi's chief lieutenants would conclude that supporting terrorism would be detrimental to the security of Libya.
- The world would know that America was committed to combating state-sponsored terrorism.
- Other terrorists would view the strike as a shot across the bow.
- The United States would gain support from its allies, who would also strengthen their own efforts against terrorism.

In terms of speed, efficiency, destructive power, and conclusive results, the raid was textbook. In terms of time and distance, it was the longest fighter combat mission in military history to that point.

"Today we have done what we had to do," said Reagan in his post-attack address to the nation. "If necessary, we shall do it again."

CHAPTER 31

OPERATION JUST CAUSE

(DECEMBER 20, 1989–JANUARY 3, 1990)

The American invasion of Panama and the subsequent capture of its military strongman, Gen. Manuel Antonio Noriega, was the first battle since the end of World War II that had no connection to the Cold War. Code-named Operation Just Cause, the invasion was also the largest clash of arms in Panamanian history.

Bounded by the Caribbean Sea to the north, Colombia to the east, the Pacific Ocean to the south, and Costa Rica to the west, Panama is a 29,760-square-mile strip of a nation that essentially connects the North and South American continents. Since the early 1900s, the United States had developed something of a "quasicolonial relationship" with Panama. The Panama Canal, constructed with American money and engineering know-how across the narrow isthmus of Panama, was opened to world commerce in 1914. By agreement, the canal and the land immediately adjacent to the canal were sovereign U.S. territory. And U.S. military forces had maintained a presence in the region.

In 1977, a new agreement was signed stating that Panama would attain full ownership of the canal and the adjacent strips of land by 1999.

For years prior to the invasion, Noriega and his authoritarian rule over Panama had been developing into a major concern for the United States. Noriega was not Panama's official head of state, but as supreme commander of the Panamanian Defense Forces (PDF), he was the de facto leader of that country. Noriega was a corrupt and oppressive leader, involved in illegal drug and arms trafficking and money laundering.

But those crimes had often been overlooked as far back as the administration of president Jimmy Carter, because Noriega and his henchmen were providing information to the American intelligence community. That information was then processed into substantive intelligence related to ongoing power struggles in Latin America. Additionally, he violated American–Panamanian treaties related to the Panama Canal and constantly threatened American commercial interests and military forces in that country.

THE SITUATION

In February 1988, the U.S. government officially declared the trafficking of illegal drugs to be a major threat to American society. Noriega was simultaneously indicted in Florida on federal charges of drug trafficking and money laundering. The administrations of presidents Ronald Reagan and George H. W. Bush then began concerted efforts aimed at removing the general from power.

It was hoped that, through American-sponsored covert operations, a popular uprising or a coup d'état might unseat Noriega. But the resilient Panamanian general seemed to defy the United States at every turn. Other measures were taken including indirect negotiations, economic sanctions, and even threats of military intervention.

During the Panamanian elections of 1989, the United States was actively involved with the opposition candidate, Guillermo Endara. The U.S. Central Intelligence Agency allegedly funneled millions of dollars into Endara's campaign.

Elections were held May 7. But Endara overwhelmingly defeated Noriega's personally selected candidate for president, Carlos Duque. An enraged Noriega then nullified the elections. Thousands of Panamanian citizens marched in protest, and Noriega called out his infamous Dignity Battalions, which were essentially paramilitary "goon squads" led by thugs in Noriega's inner circle—and which served independently of the

Panamanian Defense Forces—to quash the opposition. Those opposing Noriega and Duque were seized and cruelly beaten by the Dignity Battalions. Among those brutalized was Endara.

THE OPERATION

Fearing for the safety of some 51,000 Americans living in the region as well as the security of the Panama Canal, President George H. W. Bush ordered the U.S. armed forces to begin preparing for a variety of contingencies. Four days after the volatile elections, approximately 5,000 military dependents residing in Panamanian neighborhoods moved onto nearby military bases. Soon thereafter, American civilians were airlifted out of the country, while U.S. Army and Marine Corps forces were flown in.

On October 3, a coup d'état was attempted against Noriega. It failed, and Noriega responded violently against anyone who either directly participated or was suspected of being involved. The general soon began to feel as if he and his regime were invincible. In fact, he was losing his grip on Panama: Noriega's inner circle of friends and advisers was growing increasingly smaller.

By December, it was clear to the Bush administration that the instability in Panama, combined with Noriega's desperation, was becoming a serious threat to lives and property of U.S. forces and other American citizens in that country.

On December 15, Noriega proclaimed himself "maximum leader." That same day, the Panamanian National Assembly, under the direction of Noriega, declared that Panama was in a state of war with the United States. The following day, PDF forces opened fire on a civilian vehicle, killing 1st Lt. Robert Paz, an off-duty U.S. Marine officer dressed in civilian clothes. Later, U.S. Navy lieutenant Adam J. Curtis and his wife, Bonnie, were detained by Panamanian troops. The lieutenant was beaten, and both he and his wife were threatened with death. Throughout the country, American citizens were harassed and threatened by Panamanian soldiers.

On December 17, the White House directed the Joint Chiefs of Staff to execute an invasion plan with the following six objectives:

- The operation would be launched to ensure the safety and security of American citizens and to protect key American sites and facilities in Panama.

- Noriega would be captured and delivered to "competent authority."
- PDF forces would be neutralized.
- PDF command and control would be neutralized.
- PDF forces would be restructured.
- The invasion would support the establishment of a U.S.-recognized Panamanian government.

In terms of firepower, Panamanian military forces did not pose a grave threat to U.S. forces. The entire PDF was made up of fewer than 20,000 troops, and the vast majority of those were reservists. All total, the PDF maintained 2 battalions of infantry, 10 independently operating infantry companies, 1 armored cavalry squadron, 55 aircraft (38 airplanes and 17 helicopters), air defense artillery (it was rumored that the enemy's air defenses might also include surface-to-air missiles), and a handful of small patrol boats. The PDF did not include Noriega's 18 Dignity Battalions. Overall, the marginal Panamanian force was no real threat to U.S. forces. However, they were certainly capable of killing American soldiers or taking civilians hostage. There was also a concern that a beaten PDF might withdraw into the jungle, regroup, and continue to fight as guerrillas. But the mission was on.

Just after midnight on December 20, a U.S. Air Force combat control team jumped into the darkness over Omar Torrijos International Airport and the adjacent Tocumen military airfield. On the ground, the airmen placed aircraft-navigation beacons near the end of the runway.

At 1 A.M., AC-130 Spectre gunships and Cobra helicopters roared in and began pummeling nearby PDF defenses. Within minutes, elements of both the 82nd Airborne Division, under the command of Lt. Gen. Carl W. Stiner, and the 75th Ranger Regiment, under the command of Maj. Gen. Wayne A. Downing, were parachuting onto both Torrijos airport and Tocumen airfield. As commanding general of the Joint Special Operations Task Force, Downing not only commanded the 75th Rangers, but he also directed the Army's Special Forces (Green Berets), the psychological operations and civil affairs units, the special operations helicopters, the Navy's SEALs (sea, air, land commandos) and special boat units, and the Air Force Special Operations units.

On the ground, Stiner's 1st Brigade Task Force (of the 82nd), made up of two battalions of the 504th Parachute Infantry Regiment, linked up with a third battalion which was already stationed in Panama, and the airborne-Ranger force began attacking various points in and around Panama City.

A second force of Rangers from the 75th attacked and quickly captured the Rio Hato Military Airfield. One Ranger was struck in the head by enemy antiaircraft fire before he could exit the aircraft. He survived, but five of his fellow Rangers were killed in the ensuing clash to wrest the airfield from the PDF.

AC-130 Spectre gunships were radioed in. After the gunships softened up the defending positions, the Rangers secured the perimeter of Rio Hato, and transport planes packed with ammunition, vehicles, and other combat equipment began landing on the strip.

Meanwhile, the Rangers who made the initial jump over Torrijos were tasked with moving against the PDF Commandancia headquarters in Panama City. The Rangers also seized Noriega's beach house and grounds.

As the Rangers and paratroopers were battling to achieve their day-one objectives, a U.S. Navy SEAL team attempted to move in from the sea, take Patilla airfield, disable Noriega's private jet, and wait for the Panamanian leader to arrive. But the situation began to degrade before they arrived at Patilla. Unable to make radio contact with an orbiting AC-130 gunship for fire support, the SEALs moved toward the objective. But on the airfield, they were discovered by defending PDF soldiers. Caught in the open, four SEALs were killed and eight were wounded. The sailors were forced to withdraw, but not before they destroyed Noriega's plane.

Simultaneously, Army Special Forces teams seized a key bridge in Panama City and began fanning out, looking for Noriega. Other army infantry units—including elements of the 7th Infantry Division, the 5th Infantry Division, and the 193rd Infantry Brigade—also moved in and around Panama City and seized all of their objectives, including Fort Amador.

Southwest of the city, two reinforced companies of the 6th Marine Regiment were tasked with capturing several points and protecting the U.S. Naval Station and Howard Air Force Base.

Resistance for the most part was marginal. When faced with death or surrender, the Panamanian soldiers chose the latter. When PDF resistance was stiff, it was quickly and decisively put down by the Americans' overwhelming fire superiority. New on the scene was the F-117 Nighthawk Stealth fighter, the Air Force's multi-role combat aircraft which was virtually undetectable on radar.

By the end of the first day, U.S. forces had achieved all of their D-day objectives and were able to focus on finding Noriega. On Christmas Eve, Noriega sought asylum in the Papal Nunciatura.

On January 3, 1990, after 10 days of being subjected to powerful spotlights and piercingly loud heavy-metal music blasting from the loudspeakers of a U.S. Army psychological warfare team, Noriega surrendered.

THE AFTERMATH

Just Cause was over. It had been the "largest single contingency operation since World War II," but it wasn't without cost. Twenty-three American servicemen were killed in action and another 324 were wounded. Enemy casualties were approximately 450, and civilian losses were alleged to be far greater.

"The U.S. military held a good hand in this one and had little excuse had it failed," wrote U.S. Army major David B. Haight in a report for the Naval War College. "Pre-positioned forces, technologically superior weapons, better trained and equipped troops, and established friendly installations virtually foreordained victory."

Indeed, the attacks proved to be overwhelming decisive. On the first day, 27 enemy targets were simultaneously struck by a combined force of U.S. Army infantry, paratroopers, Rangers, Marine infantry, and Navy SEALs, all supported by light armored vehicles (LAVs), attack helicopters, and jets. The PDF's command and control capabilities were knocked out and the enemy force quickly folded. Some units continued to oppose the Americans for several days after the first U.S. paratrooper landed. But for the most part, PDF resistance was eliminated in less than a day. Even before Noriega was apprehended, large numbers of American combat troops in Panama had begun the trip home.

Convicted of racketeering, drug trafficking, and money laundering, Noriega was sentenced to 40 years in prison.

CHAPTER 32

OPERATION DESERT STORM

(JANUARY 17–FEBRUARY 28, 1991)

Operation Desert Storm, also known as the Persian Gulf War (now Gulf War I), was a stunning clash of arms between an American-led allied army and Iraqi military forces in 1991. More of a large campaign or a battle than a war, Desert Storm was a one-sided victory for the Americans and their coalition partners, who decisively defeated Iraqi leader Saddam Hussein's army on his own turf.

The allies dominated from the outset, quickly overwhelming the Iraqis and suffering fewer than 200 combat casualties. The number of Iraqis killed numbered in the tens of thousands. Much of the allied victory was the result of a massive air campaign that virtually obliterated Hussein's forces in the desert. When the ground war began, soldiers equipped with state-of-the-art weapons systems quickly overran what allied pilots had not destroyed. The Iraqi army collapsed within days, and shell-shocked Iraqi survivors surrendered by the thousands. Hussein, the brutal leader of Iraq's Ba'ath Party, remained in power and continued to lord over his countrymen with an iron fist, but his ability to invade neighboring countries was all but eliminated.

IRAQ INVADES KUWAIT

Desert Storm's proverbial wheels were set in motion when, on the morning of August 2, 1990, Iraqi tanks and infantry swept across the border into neighboring Kuwait and quickly seized Kuwait City. Disregarding Kuwaiti sovereignty, Hussein contended that Kuwait was an historical province of the Iraqi state, and that the government in Baghdad was simply exerting its authority over what was by tradition Iraqi territory.

Hussein further justified the invasion by stating that Iraq had "legitimate grievances" over what the government argued was Kuwait's use of an Iraqi oil field as well as its refusal to share petroleum resources from Kuwaiti oil fields. He also argued that Kuwait was deliberately reducing oil prices by flooding the global petroleum market with surplus oil, thus damaging the Iraqi economy. Moreover, Hussein and his government and military leaders believed they had a legitimate strategic need for unimpeded access to the Persian Gulf, and that Kuwait had failed to show any tangible appreciation for Iraq's having provided a "first-line of defense against Iranian hegemony" during the 1979–1988 Iran-Iraq War.

Iraq—roughly 168,000 square miles of primarily remote desert country with rivers, lakes, and a stretch of highlands—is inhabited by some 22 million people. It is bordered by Turkey in the north, Iran in the north and east, Kuwait and a tiny Persian Gulf coastline in the southeast, Saudi Arabia in the south and southwest, and Jordan and Syria in the west. Once known as Mesopotamia, Iraq's center is cut through by the ancient and storied Tigris-Euphrates River. The country also boasts the second-largest petroleum reserves in the world. (Saudi Arabia has the largest reserves.)

The country's invasion of Kuwait was condemned almost immediately by the United Nations. Two UN resolutions were then passed: UN Resolution 660, which condemned the attack, and UN Resolution 661, which imposed a universal trade embargo on Iraq. Defiantly, Hussein responded to both resolutions by declaring the annexation of Kuwait by Iraq. His response sealed the fate of his army.

Almost immediately, the administration of U.S. president George H. W. Bush began assembling a 28-nation coalition and preparing U.S. forces for military conflict. Moreover, a massive deployment of forces, code-named Operation Desert Shield, was begun. The U.S.–led coalition comprised the nations of Afghanistan, Australia, Bahrain, Bangladesh, Belgium, Canada, Czechoslovakia, Egypt, France, Germany, Honduras, Hungary, Israel, Italy, Kuwait, the Netherlands, New Zealand, Niger, Oman, Poland, Qatar,

Romania, Saudi Arabia, South Korea, Syria, the United Arab Emirates, and the United Kingdom. The host nation for U.S. and allied troops and equipment was Saudi Arabia.

The objectives as expressed by Bush were clear:

- Iraq must withdraw or be physically extricated from Kuwait.
- The legitimate Kuwaiti government must be restored.
- The security and stability of the region must be assured.
- American citizens in the region must be protected.

COMMANDERS, PLANS, AND EQUIPMENT

Bush's two senior military commanders were destined to become famous: At the global strategic level was U.S. Army general Colin Powell, the chairman of the Joint Chiefs of Staff. Powell, a foreign affairs–savvy son of Jamaican immigrants, was destined to become Secretary of State under George W. Bush's administration 10 years later. As such he would be the senior cabinet member during Gulf War II in 2003.

At the regional strategic level was Powell's subordinate chief of the U.S. Central Command (CENTCOM), Gen. H. Norman Schwarzkopf. Described as "TV ready" and "a smooth composite of traditional and contemporary concepts of masculinity and leadership," Schwarzkopf was the overall commander of coalition military forces in the Gulf region. Schwarzkopf's deputies included Lt. Gen. Calvin Waller, CENTCOM deputy commander; Lt. Gen. John J. Yeosock, CENTCOM army commander; Lt. Gen. Charles A. Horner, CENTCOM air force commander; Vice Adm. Stanley Arthur, CENTCOM naval commander; Lt. Gen. Frederick M. Franks Jr., commander of the army's VII Corps; Lt. Gen. Gary E. Luck, commander of the army's XVIII Airborne Corps; and Lt. Gen. Walter E. Boomer, commander of the I Marine Expeditionary Force (I MEF).

Characteristically, the U.S. Army and Marine Corps disagreed over which service should be given the largest slice of the ground campaign pie. Both wanted the biggest piece. In the end, the Army, with the largest overall force—and by far the most tanks and armored vehicles—was given the task of making the sweeping end run into the Iraqi desert from Saudi Arabia. The Marines would take the shortest route and drive straight along the coast into Kuwait. Additionally, Marines offshore would conduct an amphibious feint to tie up Iraqi forces on the beaches.

U.S. troops and equipment (not including troops and equipment fielded by allied nations), included 540,000 personnel, 4,000 tanks and armored personnel carriers, 1,700 helicopters, and 1,800 fixed-wing aircraft. Iraqi forces—with only 260,000 troops, fewer than 2,000 tanks, and approximately 1,050 aircraft—were vastly outnumbered. (Hussein's troops were originally estimated at 500,000 and his tanks at 4,000.) In addition to the numerical disparity, technological superiority in weaponry rendered the Iraqis almost helpless in the face of America and her allies.

Nevertheless, Hussein, threatening to defeat the Americans in what he announced would be the "mother of all battles," rallied his troops with promises that the Americans were soft and would quickly fold after suffering a few casualties. He also banked on a broader war, with Arab nations ultimately breaking ranks with the coalition and coming to the aid of Iraq.

"THE MOTHER OF ALL BATTLES"

On January 17, 1991, at 2:38 A.M., the so-called "mother of all battles" opened when a U.S. Army Apache helicopter fired the first of many Hellfire missiles at an Iraqi radar complex.

What followed was a blistering campaign, waged with aircraft- and sea-launched weapons, aimed at knocking out Saddam Hussein's ability to both shoot down coalition aircraft and communicate with his senior commanders in the field. The first targets struck were air defense and radar stations and command-and-control facilities. Those targets were eliminated within a day or two. Hussein and his senior military commanders were essentially cut off from their most forward units and rendered strategically blind and helpless against attacking coalition aircraft. Though a few U.S. and allied pilots were shot down, most were able to prowl above the Iraqi desert with an ease not known by aircrews in previous wars.

The next series of targets—bridges, barracks, defensive positions, tanks, and troop concentrations—were hit almost hourly for nearly two weeks. Attention was focused on entrenched Iraqi ground forces in Kuwait and on the Iraqi-Kuwaiti and Iraqi–Saudi Arabian borders. Additionally, enemy air force units—which were originally positioned in the south but bugged out during the first few hours of combat—were knocked out as they regrouped on new air bases deep in the north. (Some enemy aircraft escaped into Iran.)

Highways and bridges were next. Their destruction was key to stopping troop transport and movement of supplies; moreover, the U.S. intelligence community determined that Iraqi engineers were attempting to reestablish communications with isolated units by running fiber-optic cable across bridges. That alone made bridges a priority.

As the Iraqi army was being systematically destroyed, the American-led coalition army was moving its infantry, artillery, tanks, and other vehicles into position along a 300-mile stretch of the Saudi Arabian–Kuwaiti/Iraqi border.

Within hours after the initial strikes, Iraq began launching SCUD surface-to-surface ballistic missiles against coalition forces in Saudi Arabia. Most were knocked down by U.S. Patriot air defense missiles. A number of SCUDs, however, managed to get past the Patriot screens and hit Saudi Arabian territory. In some cases they struck populated areas, killing civilians and combatants. In most cases they landed harmlessly in the desert.

SCUDs were also launched against cities in Israel. Tel Aviv was struck, as was Haifa. Hussein was hoping that by killing Israeli civilians, Israel—previously persuaded by the United States to stay out of the fight—would attack Iraq. He hoped to evolve the conflict into a general Arab-Israeli war, destroying the coalition. Fortunately, the Israelis—at the behest of the White House—held their fire and did not enter the fray. Hussein's Israel strategy failed.

On January 29, the Iraqis again pressed coalition forces by launching a reconnaissance-in-force across an isolated stretch of the Saudi Arabian border. Just after 8 P.M., approximately 700 enemy soldiers and 45 tanks moved against the Saudi coastal town of Ras Al Khafji. Two Iraqi battalions simultaneously penetrated the Saudi frontier approximately 45 miles west. Defending the region were elements of Boomer's I MEF, as well as a number of Joint Force allies.

The engagement opened when elements of three U.S. Marine infantry companies spotted a battalion of Soviet-built T-62 tanks bearing down on their positions. The Marines immediately radioed for air support and began engaging the tanks with antitank missiles. The fighting was sharp, but within a half-hour U.S. Air Force F-16 Falcon and F-15 Eagle fighters, A-10 Wart Hog tank-busters, and C-130 Spectre gunships were overhead and tearing mercilessly into the enemy tanks. The Iraqis were beaten back, but not without the tragic loss of 11 Marines, all victims of a friendly fire accident: Two misidentified armored personnel carriers were struck by American air and artillery fire.

The following day, American military leaders began boasting that coalition forces had established total air supremacy. In fact, air superiority had existed since day one.

On the ground, Hussein was deceived from the beginning. The Iraqi leader believed the invasion force would strike from Saudi Arabia in the south into the heart of Kuwait. He also feared an amphibious invasion along the Kuwaiti coastline (a slice of which was Iraqi coastline just north of Kuwait) from the Persian Gulf where thousands of U.S. Marines were hunkered down in the holds of troop ships. The Iraqis, well aware of the fighting reputation of the U.S. Marine Corps, feared the leathernecks as much or more than any of the coalition troops they were facing. They nicknamed the Marines "angels of death," a name which fueled the pride of the already proud "few good men."

Stoking the fears of the Iraqis who were convinced of a Marine landing, U.S. Navy SEALs (the Navy's vaunted sea, air, land commandos) and similarly trained Marine Force Recon (deep reconnaissance) units began conducting intelligence-gathering and sabotage operations along the Kuwaiti coastline and on nearby Faylaka Island. Moreover, U.S. warships and planes pounded the enemy's beach defenses. The bombings and the raids forced Hussein to deploy more than 100,000 of his troops along the coast in anticipation of a Marine landing which would never occur. The landings had been ruled out, except as a last resort, after U.S. military commanders determined that 10 percent of the 17,000-man Marine force would be wiped out on the beaches.

COALITION FORCES POSITION TO ATTACK

While the Iraqis were concerning themselves with the amphibious threat and the Saudi Arabian–Kuwaiti border, the primary elements of the invasion force were preparing to attack into the heart of Iraq. Two enormous U.S. Army forces—Luck's XVIII Airborne Corps and Franks's VII Corps—had positioned themselves along a stretch of the Saudi Arabian–Iraqi border. The two forces were on the allied extreme left flank and center respectively. On the extreme right flank was Boomer's I MEF made up of the 1st and 2nd Marine divisions and the detached Tiger Brigade of the U.S. Army's 2nd Armored Division.

On either flank of the I MEF were Joint Force elements of Saudis, Syrians, Egyptians, Kuwaitis, Pakistanis, Omanis, and soldiers of the United Arab Emirates.

Given the "go" command, the two army corps would launch a surprise thrust across the border deep into Iraq's Sahra al-Hijarah desert, and then make a hard right turn. The plan—from positioning along the border to the attack to the right turn—was to be known as Schwarzkopf's great "Hail Mary" attack (drawing an analogy to a football play where a receiver goes long to complete a forward pass).

As the two army corps attacked on the left and center, the MEF and the Joint Force elements on the right would race into Kuwait.

On February 22, Hussein's troops began setting fire to oil wells across the desert, thus creating an environmental disaster. At 4 A.M. on February 24, Schwarzkopf gave his corps commanders the green light and the first elements of the enormous coalition ground force began to surge forward.

The previous day, Marines on the right of the line had begun a limited push across the Kuwaiti border from Saudi Arabia—once again reaffirming the Corps' longstanding boast of being "first to fight." The Marines' engineers set charges and blew up enemy defensive berms in the path of Boomer's leathernecks. On D day, elements of the I MEF punched giant holes through the Iraqi defenses. Led by light tanks and supported by jets and helicopter gunships, the feared "angels of death" raced toward the Kuwaiti capital. They were temporarily slowed, not so much by resisting forces, but by thousands of physically and emotionally wrenched Iraqi soldiers who surrendered in droves. Still, by day's end, the leathernecks had advanced some 20 miles into the heart of Kuwait.

"I can't say enough about the two Marine divisions," Schwarzkopf later stated, "If I use words like brilliant, it would really be an under description of the absolutely superb job that they did in breaching the so-called impenetrable barrier. It was a classic—absolutely classic—military breaching of a very, very tough minefield, barbed wire, fire trenches-type barrier."

As the Marines were tearing across the Iraqi defenses, Luck's XVIII Airborne Corps on the extreme right of the coalition line attacked into the vast Iraqi desert. At the vanguard of the XVIII was the French 6th Light Armored Division which had tactical control of the 2nd Brigade of the U.S. 82nd Airborne Division. Also present were the 3rd Armored Cavalry Regiment and the 24th Infantry Division. As French tanks and American paratroopers and infantrymen advanced, their right flank was covered by a helicopter-borne force of the U.S. 101st Airborne Division.

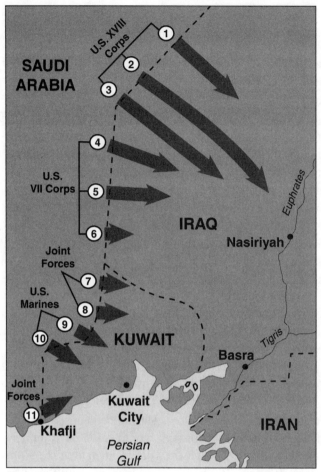

Desert Storm.

The XVIII Corps forces were tasked with attacking and seizing forward operating bases in the rear of Hussein's army. In doing so, they would be able to cut off Iraqi forces fleeing back toward Baghdad and prevent the primary American attacking force from being struck on its critical left flank.

Between the Marines on the far right and the army forces on the far the left, Franks's VII Corps—the primary attacking force—had crossed the border and was racing into the Iraqi desert. The VII Corps was made up of the 1st and 3rd Armored Divisions, the 1st Cavalry Division, the1st Infantry Division (the famed "Big Red One"), the 2nd Armored Cavalry

Regiment, and the British First Armored Division. Destroying all opposition in its path, the VII Corps trekked north 100 miles, turned east and drive straight toward the Basra Road, the infamous "highway of death." In so doing, the VII's 1,300 tanks—the largest tank corps in history—began intercepting and destroying Iraqi armored forces attempting to escape from Kuwait.

While the VII Corps was methodically killing Iraqi tanks and other vehicles, the XVIII Airborne Corps on the extreme left was also driving hard north. Several miles north of VII Corps' pivot point, the XVIII Corps also wheeled right. The trap was virtually inescapable. Thousands of Iraqis surrendered on all fronts. Those who chose to resist were annihilated.

Hussein had counted on the Americans attacking only into southern Kuwait. His army was shocked to discover that allied troops were pouring into the vast Euphrates River valley.

The primary blow against Iraq's ground forces was struck when the VII and the XVIII Corps clashed headlong into Hussein's vaunted Republican Guard in the desert west of the city Basra, as well Iraqi forces fleeing the Marine advance in Kuwait.

Attempting to escape to Baghdad, Iraqi armored forces quickly disintegrated. On the infamous "highway of death"—also known as the "highway to hell"—an enormous column of fleeing Iraqi vehicles caused a traffic jam which U.S. warplanes freely bombed and strafed with virtual impunity. Those vehicles attempting to break out and escape across the desert were also destroyed. The result was devastating for the enemy. Some 2,000 vehicles along a 60-mile stretch of road were reduced to burning hulks, and untold numbers of Iraqi soldiers were shot to death, blown up, or burned alive.

On the morning of February 28, President Bush ordered a cease-fire. The most stunningly impressive 100 hours in American military history—the ground war phase—had come to a close. Operation Desert Storm lasted a total of 42 days (38 days for the initial air campaign and 4 days for the ground campaign).

THE AFTERMATH

Casualties were amazingly low for American forces and their coalition partners. American losses included 148 killed (35 in friendly fire accidents) and 480 wounded (72 to friendly fire). Though the numbers varied widely, depending upon whose side was counting, Iraqi casualties were far greater.

An estimated 8,000 to 100,000 Iraqi soldiers were killed in the final 100 hours.

Despite the decisive victory over Iraqi forces and the extrication of the same from Kuwait, the campaign was not without some public opposition in the United States. "It has never happened in history that a nation that has won a war has been held accountable for atrocities committed in preparing for and waging that war," said former U.S. attorney general Ramsay Clark during hearings held by the independent International War Crimes Tribunal (not a UN entity) in May 1991. "We intend to make this one different. What took place was the use of technological material to destroy a defenseless country."

Others argued that Bush failed to eliminate the threat of Saddam Hussein and his Ba'ath Party regime. There were in fact whispers in some army circles that the routed Iraqis should have been pursued to Baghdad. And for the next decade, Hussein continued to thumb his nose at the United Nations by violating numerous UN resolutions aimed at keeping him in check. Nevertheless, the "mother of all battles" was over.

> As of this writing, Iraq has again been invaded by a U.S.–led coalition. American and British forces have seized a number of population centers, and are in control of most of Baghdad. The pretext for the attack was that Saddam Hussein was in violation of numerous post–Desert Storm UN resolutions, and that he was not cooperating with UN weapons inspectors tasked with determining Iraq's compliance with a UN resolution banning offensive weapons. The U.S. intelligence community also claimed it had information indicating that Hussein had in his possession, or was attempting to develop or purchase, weapons of mass destruction. Additionally, marginal intelligence indicated that he was in league with elements of Osama bin Laden's al Qaeda terrorist network.

CHAPTER 33

TASK FORCE RANGER, MOGADISHU

(OCTOBER 3–4, 1993)

Task Force Ranger was the operational name for a joint U.S. Army force of rangers, Delta Force commandos, and supporting helicopter crews tasked with snatching several senior members of warlord general Mohammed Farah Aidid's inner circle from their city center stronghold in the seaport capital of Mogadishu, Somalia. The army's air-ground team achieved its initial search-and-snatch objective, but the situation quickly degraded into the most violent firefight for American forces since the Vietnam War.

The East African nation of Somalia was a starving, disease-ridden country bordered in the east by the Indian Ocean, in the north by the Gulf of Aden, Djibouti in the northwest, Ethiopia in the west, and Kenya in the southwest. At 246,200 square miles, it is smaller than the state of Texas. In the middle of the southern half of the coastline is Mogadishu, the nation's capital, a port city, and the most populated urban center in Somalia.

Formerly governed by dictator Mohamed Siad Barre, Somalia was ruled by a motley collection of thugs who were constantly battling for control of both the nation's population centers and what little sustenance the country received from United Nations (UN) relief efforts. Barre had been forced out of power in early 1991. Clan infighting followed, which led to widespread famine: An estimated 300,000 Somalis died of starvation over the next year.

Horrified by the images of diseased and starving innocents in Somalia, the United Nations pressed the warring factions to agree to a cease-fire. The agreement also stipulated that UN officials would be allowed to enter the country and oversee international food shipments aimed at stemming the tide of starvation.

The humanitarian assistance began in the summer of 1992. But the efforts quickly deteriorated when relief flights were looted upon landing, food convoys were hijacked, and UN workers were attacked. The United Nations realized that military forces would be needed to ensure the security and equal distribution of the relief food.

THE UNITED STATES SENDS TROOPS

In December, U.S. president George H. W. Bush dispatched more than 20,000 U.S. Marines to the troubled country. The Marines served as the primary element of a new international task force, dubbed Operation Restore Hope. Once ashore, the leathernecks restored order, and food was proportionally distributed. Bush had hoped to scale down the number of American troops in Somalia within a month, thus leaving the security responsibilities with the United Nations. But when he left the White House in January 1993, American Marines were still patrolling the streets of Mogadishu. Assuming the reigns of the Oval Office, President Bill Clinton was also anxious to reduce the U.S. military presence in Somalia.

By the end of March, a UN-sanctioned multinational force moved into Somalia. The command baton was passed by the United States to the United Nations. Less than three months later, armed Somalis ambushed and killed 24 Pakistani soldiers during a routine inspection of a Somali weapons storage facility. American civilians in the country also became targets of unprovoked attacks. The UN Security Council immediately issued a resolution calling for the apprehension of "those responsible." Moreover, U.S. admiral Jonathon Howe, the special representative to the UN secretary general for Somalia, placed a $25,000 reward on Aidid's head.

Aidid—the revolutionary leader responsible for the overthrow of Barre— was the commander of Habr Gidr, one of five dominant Somali factions. As such, Aidid believed himself to be the rightful ruler of the nation.

The armed element of Habr Gidr were known simply as militiamen. (American military personnel also referred to Somali militiamen as "skinnies" because of their emaciated appearance.) Dressed in outlandish uniform items from firemen's and miners' helmets to vintage leather flying caps, the militiamen were fearless fighters. Known for disregarding their own casualties during combat, they spent time each day sitting around and chewing an hallucinogenic weed known as quat. The drug served two purposes: It suppressed hunger and it boosted courage to the point of utter recklessness. When the militiamen weren't chewing quat, they were looking for action, racing throughout the streets of Mogadishu in small cars and pickup trucks that had been fitted with machine guns. The vehicles, known as technicals, have since been described as something out of a *Mad Max* movie.

With his militiamen prowling the city and terrorizing the opposition, Aidid resisted UN efforts to force him into a shared-power coalition government. The situation deteriorated rapidly over the coming weeks, and American special operations forces were requested.

In August, Task Force Ranger arrived in country and set up a beachfront base of operations known as the Joint Task Force Center. U.S. Forces Somalia—including elements of the U.S. Army, Navy, Air Force, and Marine Corps—were under the command of U.S. Army major general Thomas M. Montgomery who also served as deputy commander, United Nations Forces, Somalia. Task Force Ranger was under the command of Maj. Gen. William F. Garrison, a career special operations officer who helped direct Operation Phoenix (the infamous program which targeted influential members of the Vietcong) during the Vietnam War. Though coordination efforts were managed between Garrison and Montgomery, Garrison was given complete tactical oversight and reported directly to Gen. Joseph P. Hoar, commander in chief of the U.S. Central Command (CENTCOM).

THE OPERATION IS LAUNCHED

On October 3, 1993, Garrison received credible intelligence indicating that several of Aidid's chief lieutenants were meeting in a three-story residence building next to the Olympic Hotel in the heart of Mogadishu. The American commander quickly called a meeting of his officers, acquainted them with the opportunity to snatch some members of Aidid's top brass, and ordered them to "go."

Just after 3:30 P.M., 19 helicopters—Sikorsky UH-60L Black Hawk helicopters loaded with heavily armed Rangers and Boeing 530F, A/MH-6 Little Birds loaded with Delta Force commandos—were launched from their beachfront base. After flying along the coastline for a short stretch, the helicopters turned inland and thundered toward the objective. A ground convoy of twelve vehicles including three five-ton trucks and nine Humvees (the Army's high-mobility multipurpose wheeled vehicle that replaced the Jeep) also raced forward toward the inner city. One hundred sixty men comprised the overall force, which included the men of Bravo Company of the 75th Ranger Regiment; a number of Delta Force commandos (a secret countererrorist group known affectionately in U.S. Army circles as the "D-Boys"); helicopter pilots and crews from the 160th Special Operations Aviation Regiment known as the "Nightstalkers"; and a couple of U.S. Navy SEALs (the Navy's elite sea, air, land commandos) from SEAL Team 6.

The onsite air commander was Lt. Col. Tom Matthews. The onsite ground commander was Lt. Col. Gary Harrell. Both officers, in a command-and-control Black Hawk, circled high above Mogadishu where they were best able to direct the operation. Three orbiting surveillance helicopters fitted with special cameras also enabled General Garrison and staff—located back at the Joint Operations Center—to watch the operation unfold via television monitors.

At 3:42 P.M., the Little Birds swooped down on their objective, landing in the street and on the rooftop. Leaping from the choppers, Delta commandos stormed the building from both ends and snatched 24 members of Aidid's inner circle. Once the building was completely cleared, the commandos rushed their prisoners downstairs and into waiting trucks.

As Delta Force was seizing the building, the Rangers were fast-roping from their Black Hawks to the street below. Four Ranger "chalks" (a squad of approximately 12 Rangers assigned to a helicopter) were deployed to set up security at each of the four corners of the target block. In the rush to get into the fight, one Ranger private missed the rope and fell 70 feet to the earth, suffering massive internal injuries.

As a few Rangers gathered around, trying to keep him alive, large numbers of Somali militiamen and armed civilians converged on the Americans and began shooting. Under terrific fire, the injured ranger was loaded into one of the vehicles and rushed from the area. Meanwhile, the force became encircled by the growing Somali mob. What was hoped would be a surgical snatch operation quickly devolved into a general street fight.

BLACK HAWK DOWN

By 4:15, the fighting had become heavy. Confusion began to permeate the Ranger ranks. Nevertheless, the prisoners were loaded into vehicles which were ready to spirit them away toward the American lines. But within minutes, the first of several frantic transmissions crackled over the radio, "We've got a Black Hawk going down! We've got a Black Hawk going down!"

A rocket-propelled grenade had hit one of the orbiting helicopters, disabling its rear anti-torque rotors. The Black Hawk, spinning wildly out of control, eventually upended itself and crashed hard on its side in an alleyway five blocks northeast of the hotel.

Garrison and his staff watched the disturbing events unfold via television. But years of preparing for such in both peace and war kept the officers focused on maintaining control of the task force. If nothing else, they had to keep the situation from completely unraveling.

Waves of frenzied Somalis rushed toward the crash site, as did the American convoy, prisoners and all.

The crash affected both sides far beyond the event itself. The Rangers who witnessed the crash immediately realized their overall situation was becoming untenable. The Somalis, already primed on quat and feeling invincible, were emboldened. Despite the U.S. technological edge, the Somalis quickly realized that the American soldiers and their aircraft could be destroyed.

Another Black Hawk roared in over the battle area, assuming the downed helicopter's place.

By 4:30 P.M., an American search-and-rescue team fast-roped on the crash site in an attempt to save the downed crew. Unfortunately, both the pilot and the copilot had been killed.

The situation degraded further when the vehicle convoy made a wrong turn and quickly became lost. Winding aimlessly through the city streets, the column was under constant heavy fire. Casualties mounted.

The Somalis fought in a manner deemed proper to themselves, but wholly inglorious to the Americans. When they attacked it was almost always in the company of women and children who themselves wielded rifles and pistols. The Rangers, averse to shooting women and children, often hesitated killing them at their own peril.

Ten minutes after the rescue team reached the first Black Hawk, the second was also fatally struck. It crashed approximately one mile southwest of the residence building and was quickly surrounded. Within minutes, two Delta Force snipers were inserted to help the downed crew fight off the surging mob. The fighting tenacity exhibited by both the air-crews and the ground forces seemed like something out of a Hollywood script. But the reality was that people were dying.

In one instance, a Little Bird helicopter landed in a narrow street in order to rescue wounded Americans. As the copilot leapt from the bird and sprinted across a fire-raked clearing toward the wounded, the pilot—at the controls of the idling helicopter—provided covering fire with his personal submachine gun. Making the rescue, the chopper lifted off and escaped with one survivor clinging to the skids.

Meanwhile, the vehicle convoy abandoned its search for the first chop-per and turned for home. It had been shot to pieces, and half of its num-ber were either dead or wounded.

In his acclaimed series for the *Philadelphia Inquirer,* reporter Mark Bowden described the desperateness of the situation at ground zero. "Some of the vehicles were almost out of ammunition," wrote Bowden. "They had expended thousands of rounds. One of the 24 Somali prisoners had been shot dead and another was wounded. The back ends of the remaining trucks and Humvees in the lost convoy were slick with blood. Chunks of viscera clung to floors and inner walls."

Constantly under fire, the second Humvee in the column was full of bullet holes and dragging its axle. The vehicle was pushed forward by a truck following it. Another badly shot-up vehicle was rolling along on three flat tires. A third was riding on four flats with a grenade hole in its side. The fighting was merciless. In one instance, an enemy rocket-launched grenade, skipped over the top of one of the American vehicles, struck a nearby concrete wall, and detonated. The concussion bouncing back from the blast lifted the vehicle up on two wheels.

Just after 5 P.M., an emergency response convoy was launched from the Joint Operations Center toward the second crash site. It, too, came under heavy fire. Thirty minutes later, the two convoy columns made contact with one another and the decision was made to forgo the first helicopter crash site. Instead they would fight their way toward the besieged crew and Delta men at the second site. An isolated force of Americans on foot—both Rangers and Delta Force—pressed on toward the first site. Greatly outnumbered, wounded, exhausted, and nearly out of ammuni-tion, the American force seemed likely to be completely destroyed.

The enemy was relentless in the quest to kill the Americans. No place was safe. The Rangers were drawing fire from every street corner, alleyway, doorway, window, and rooftop. Fortunately, the more-experienced Delta soldiers were able to keep the younger Rangers motivated and constantly moving forward.

At 5:40 P.M., the Somalis overran the second crash site, killing everyone except the wounded pilot, who was captured and carried away by Somali militiamen. For their actions in attempting to rescue the crew of the second Black Hawk, two Delta Force commandos—Gary I. Gordon and Randall D. Shugart—would be awarded the Congressional Medal of Honor, posthumously.

Just before 6, the two convoys reached the American base. Nearly 100 of their embattled brothers were trapped and dying in the city close to the first crash site. The situation was desperate. The besieged American Rangers and Delta commandos realized they could not hold indefinitely. Their annihilation seemed imminent.

An hour later, a Black Hawk thundered toward the isolated soldiers in an attempt to resupply the force and evacuate the wounded. The helicopter successfully dropped water, ammunition, and medical supplies. But severely damaged by enemy fire and unable to land, the chopper withdrew without recovering the wounded soldiers.

Throughout the night, an enormous relief force was organized from elements based in the American port base and a nearby athletic stadium, which served as a UN base. Before midnight, the force raced toward the besieged Americans.

The relief column was comprised of patched-up elements of the original Task Force Ranger, as well as the U.S. Army's 10th Mountain Division Quick Reaction Force. The latter was under the command of Lt. Col. Bill David. The effort was also directly supported by Pakistani tanks and Malaysian armored vehicles.

Just before 2 A.M. on October 4, the relief force broke through under heavy fire. One group drove hard toward the second crash site. No one was found. By dawn, the body of the pilot at the first crash site was recovered. And at 6:30 A.M., the shattered remnants of Task Force Ranger rolled into the Pakistani-held stadium.

THE AFTERMATH

"Somalis love a fight," General Montgomery later said. "Everybody grabbed their gun and came to the fight and the troops were exposed after the raid."

The result: 18 American soldiers and air crewmen dead, 73 wounded. The remaining force was barely able to escape. Untold hundreds of Somali combatants were killed, and more than 1,000 wounded. Additionally, large numbers of unarmed civilians—many women and children—were killed or wounded in the terrific crossfire.

The force achieved its "snatch" objective. But the raid, which was supposed to take no more than 60 minutes, ground on for fifteen hours. And it was far too costly.

"We face a choice," said U.S. president Bill Clinton, days after the debacle in Mogadishu. "Do we leave when the job gets tough or when the job is well done? Do we invite the return of mass suffering or do we leave in a way that gives the Somalis a decent chance to survive?"

In the end, Clinton ordered the withdrawal of all U.S. forces from that nation. The president justified the withdrawal by ordering the positioning of two seagoing U.S. Marine Expeditionary Units off the coast of Somalia. The Marines, approximately 3,600 men with supporting helicopters and armored vehicles, could fill the void left by the Rangers in a crisis. However, there were no plans to bring the leathernecks ashore.

Much of the blame for the failure of Task Force Ranger has since been placed on the White House. Prior to the battle, several requests were made by the army for supporting weapons systems like the Bradley Fighting Vehicle (a troop-carrying armored combat vehicle with heavy firepower capabilities) and the AC-130 gunship (a C-130 transport aircraft which had been specially fitted with 40 millimeter and 105 millimeter cannon for devastating close air support firepower). Each request was denied.

The disaster in Mogadishu was later said to have created a sense among America's allies that the United States would no longer be willing to absorb losses in future conflicts. Dr. Kenneth Allard, the author of one of the leading after-action reviews, said during a PBS interview that "very tight restrictions as to force protection" in Bosnia, a few years later, was a result of Somalia. Allard's contention was that the losses in Somalia may have hamstrung future operations during the remainder of the 20th century.

"This has certainly been a perception of the other multinational partners in that [Bosnian peacekeeping] coalition," said Allard. "I think that comes from Somalia, in which when the American people tuned in through their media, and they saw these poor starving kids and they saw GIs throwing bags of wheat off the back of C-130s and they sort of tuned back out again. The next time they tuned in to Somalia, they are seeing the dead bodies of our dead soldiers being dragged down the street and they ask themselves, 'What happened here? What's wrong with this picture?' The short answer is the American people were never told that we were in a de facto of state of war with the Somali clans and with the warlord Mohammed Farah Aidid."

Each year since the ill-fated mission, Somalia has officially sanctioned ceremonies celebrating their decisive defeat of the Americans. The celebration is known as Ma-alinti Rangers (translated into English, "Day of the Rangers"). General Garrison, who accepted responsibility for the disaster, retired from the Army on August 1, 1996. Ironically, that same day, Aidid died of gunshot wounds suffered during previous fighting between his militiamen and other Somali factions.

AFTERWORD

As I pen the last few lines of this manuscript, American and coalition ground forces have seized and now control enormous tracts of Iraqi territory in what I've taken to calling Gulf War II.

Officially it is known as Operation Iraqi Freedom, a code name suggesting President George W. Bush's ultimate goal of liberating the Iraqi people from the tyranny of Saddam Hussein (a goal Bush's opponents have argued should have been accomplished by his father, George H. W. Bush, in 1991). Unlike the previous Gulf War campaign, this fight is as much a ground operation as it is an air war, perhaps more so—and Hussein's forces are presently being confronted and systematically destroyed inside the city limits of Baghdad. Americans who support Operation Iraqi Freedom believe it is a just cause aimed at not only freeing an oppressed people, but finding and eliminating any weapons of mass destruction in Hussein's possession. In so doing, it is essentially a stepping-up of operations in the ongoing war against terror. Americans opposing the campaign contend it is simply a dangerous strategic move aimed at exerting influence in an unstable region and gaining control over some of the world's largest oil reserves. Further, they argue, combat operations should not have been launched without at least the tacit approval of the United Nations and the world community.

Politics aside, American military forces and their allies are there and heavily engaged, and they will no doubt carry the day. But it will surely cost the lives of many more combatants and civilians on both sides. That alone is terribly unfortunate.

The upside of it all is that, though there is still much fighting ahead for coalition forces, it has thus far been a one-sided fight in our favor. Our tactical victories are—of course—a reflection of our advantages in technology and an overwhelming superiority in firepower on land, at sea, and in the air. Beyond that, it is the individual American warrior who is responsible for any and all successes we have realized so far.

Several years ago while covering a series of clashes on the West Bank, I had the opportunity to go on patrol with an Israeli airborne squad in the city of Hebron, one of the oldest, most storied, and most contested cities in the world. In Hebron, the friction between the Israelis and the Palestinians who live in back-to-back settlements is constant. The city and its outlying communities are often combat zones. There, innocents on both sides have suffered tremendously.

As I moved through the narrow alleyways with the Israeli paratroopers, one of the younger ones looked at me and in careful, deliberate English asked, "Were you in the American army?" I replied, "Not exactly. I was in the U.S. Marines."

The paratrooper stepped back, surprised: I suppose I didn't look tough enough to have been a U.S. Marine. (I've been told that before.)

The young Israeli soldier then said something to one of his comrades in Hebrew. The other soldier looked at me and smiled that kind of cruel grin that ensures the recipient understands the pecking order.

He then stuck his chest out and said, "We are also tough like the U.S. Marines." I smiled back in agreement, and thought to myself, "Here is this young man, no doubt a veteran of many armed clashes, and serving in one of the most elite military organizations in the world. Yet he wants me to know that his unit is every bit as good as any military unit fielded by the United States."

I later discovered that other journalists who had intimate contact with foreign military forces had similar experiences.

Truth be known—whether soldier, sailor, airman, or Marine—the American warrior is respected the world over by friend and foe alike. For they know that the American warrior is armed with the finest weapons in the world. He is skilled in the use of those weapons. He is fit. He is proud. His psyche has been burnished with noble traditions stretching back to an action on a grassy Massachusetts field in 1775. And he carries with him the lessons learned by his predecessors, particularly those who fought the decisive American battles of the 20th century.

BIBLIOGRAPHY

Adams, James. *Secret Armies: Inside the American, Soviet, and European Special Forces.* New York: The Atlantic Monthly Press, 1987.

Admiral Richmond K. Turner, USN, 1885–1961. Washington, DC: Naval Historical Center, Department of the Navy, November 2, 2001.

Alexander, Joseph H. "Sulfur Island Seized." *World War II,* February 2002.

All POW-MIA Korean War Casualties. Washington, DC: Washington Headquarters Services, Directorate for Information Operations and Reports. June 1, 2000.

Ambrose, Stephen. *Citizen Soldiers—The U.S. Army from the Normandy Beaches to the Bulge to the Surrender of Germany, June 7, 1944 to May 7, 1945.* New York: Touchstone, 1997.

American Decades. Farmington Hills, MI: Gale Group Databases, 2003.

Anno, Stephen E., and William E. Einspahr. *Command and Control and Communications Lessons Learned: Iranian Rescue, Falklands Conflict, Grenada Invasion, Libya Raid.* Maxwell AFB, AL: Air War College, May 1988.

Astor, Gerald. *The Greatest War: Americans in Combat 1941–1945.* Novato, CA: Presidio Press, 1999.

———. *Operation Iceberg: The Invasion and Conquest of Okinawa in World War II, An Oral History.* New York: Donald I. Fine, 1995.

Astronaut Biographies. Houston: Astronaut Office, Johnson Space Center, National Aeronautics and Space Administration (NASA). December 1998.

Atkinson, Rick. *An Army at Dawn: The War in North Africa, 1942–1943.* New York: Henry Holt and Company, 2002.

———. *Crusade—The Untold Story of the Persian Gulf War.* New York: Houghton Mifflin, 1993.

Axelrod, Alan. *The Complete Idiot's Guide to World War I.* Indianapolis: Alpha Books, 2000.

Ballendorf, Dirk A. *The Battle for Tarawa, A Validation of the U.S. Marines.* University of Guam, Mangilao, Guam: Pacific Insights, 1997.

Bartlett, Merrill L. *Lejeune: A Marine's Life, 1867–1942.* Columbia, SC: University of South Carolina Press, 1991.

Beach, Edward L. *The United States Navy: A 200-Year History.* New York: Henry Holt & Company, 1986.

Berry, William. "Ten Days of Urgent Fury." *All Hands,* May 1984.

Blair, Clay. *The Forgotten War: America in Korea, 1950–1953.* New York: Times Books, 1987.

Blumenson, Martin. *Patton: The Man Behind the Legend, 1885–1945.* New York: William Morrow and Company, 1985.

Bolger, Daniel P. *Americans at War, 1975–1986, an Era of Violent Peace.* Novato, CA: Presidio Press, 1988.

Bonds, Ray. *The Vietnam War, the Illustrated History of the Conflict in Southeast Asia.* New York: Crown, 1979.

Bowden, Mark. "Blackhawk Down (the *Philadelphia Inquirer* series)." *Philadelphia Inquirer,* November 16, 1997–February 2, 1998.

Boyne, Walter J. "The St. Mihiel Salient." *Air Force,* February 2000.

Brigham, Robert K. *Battlefield Vietnam: A Brief History.* Alexandria, VA: Public Broadcasting System (PBS), 2003.

Brown, Ronald J. *A Few Good Men: The Fighting Fifth Marines: A History of the USMC's Most Decorated Regiment.* Novato, CA: Presidio Press, 2001.

Bruce, Anthony. *An Illustrated Companion to the First World War.* New York: Viking Penguin, 1990.

Burbeck, James. "Ia Drang: 1965 and the Defense of Landing Zone X-Ray." *War Times Journal* website, 2002. wtj.com/articles/xray/.

Burriss, Moffatt T. *Strike and Hold: A Memoir of the 82nd Airborne in World War II.* Washington, DC: Brassey's, 2000.

Bush, George Herbert Walker. *Presidential Address to the Nation.* Washington, DC: The White House, September 11, 1990.

Carter, William R. *Air Power in the Battle of the Bulge: A Theater Campaign Perspective.* Maxwell AFB, Montgomery, AL: Air Power Journal, Winter 1989.

Cerasini, Marc. *The Complete Idiot's Guide to the U.S. Special Ops Forces.* Indianapolis: Alpha Books, 2002.

Chandler, David. *Dictionary of Battles: The World's Key Battles from 405 B.C. to Today.* New York: Henry Holt and Company, 1987.

Clark, George B. *Devil Dogs: Fighting Marines of World War I.* Novato, CA: Presidio Press, 1999.

Clark, Ramsay. *War Crimes: A Report to the Commission of Inquiry for the International War Crimes Tribunal.* New York: International War Crimes Tribunal, May 11, 1991.

Cole, Hugh M. *The Ardennes: Battle of the Bulge, United States Army in World War II, The European Theater of Operations.* Washington, DC: Office of the Chief of Military History, Department of the Army, 1965.

Cole, Ronald H. *Operation Urgent Fury: The Planning and Execution of Joint Operations in Grenada.* Washington DC: Joint History Office, Office of the Chairman of the Joint Chiefs of Staff, 1997.

Collier, Richard. *D-Day, 6 June 1944, The Normandy Landings.* New York: Abbeville Publishing, 1992.

Columbia Encyclopedia. New York: Columbia University Press, 2002.

Command & Commanders in Modern Warfare. U.S. Air Force Academy, Colorado Springs, CO: Proceedings of the Second Military History Symposium, 1968.

Contemporary Authors. Farmington Hills, MI: Gale Group Databases, 2003.

Costello, John. *The Pacific War.* New York: Rawson, Wade Publishers, 1981.

Curley, Robert. *Normandy 1944.* Chicago: Encyclopedia Britannica, 1999.

Dallas, Gregor. *1918: War and Peace.* New York: The Overlook Press, 2000.

Davis, Paul K. *100 Decisive Battles from Ancient Times to the Present.* Santa Barbara, CA: Oxford University Press, 1999.

Dean, Elizabeth. "Vietnam: A Television History, The End of the Tunnel" *(1973–1975). The American Experience,* Boston: WGBH-TV, 1997.

Deighton, Len. *Blitzkrieg: From the Rise of Hitler to the Fall of Dunkirk.* New York: Alfred A. Knopf, 1980.

Dellinger, John. "Victory at El Guettar." *World War II,* March 1966.

Dictionary of American Biography. New York: American Council of Learned Societies, 1981.

Dictionary of American Naval Fighting Ships. Washington, DC: Office of the Chief of Naval Operations, Naval History Division, 2000.

Dobson, Christopher, and Ronald Payne. *The Never-Ending War: Terrorism in the '80s.* New York: Facts On File, 1987.

Donovan, James A., Jr. *The United States Marine Corps.* New York: Frederick A. Praeger Publishers, 1967.

Dorr, Robert F., Jon Lake, and Warren E. Thompson, *Korean War Aces: Aircraft of the Aces.* Oxford, England: Osprey, 1995.

Ellard, Marion L. *Operation Attleboro* website. 2000. frankandtepo.com/ attleboro.

Elliot, Florence. *A Dictionary of Politics.* Middlesex, England: Penguin Books, 1973.

Ellis, John. *The Sharp End: The Fighting Man in World War II.* New York: Charles Scribner's Sons, 1980.

Eisenhower, John S. D., with Joanne Thompson Eisenhower. *Yanks: The Epic Story of the American Army in World War II.* New York: Touchstone, 2001.

Encyclopedia Britannica. Chicago, 2000.

Federation of American Scientists website. Washington, DC: 2002. fas.org

Ferrell, Robert H. *Woodrow Wilson & World War I: 1917–1921.* New York: Harper & Row, 1985.

Frank, Benis M. *The Epic of Chosin.* Washington, DC: Naval Historical Center, Department of the Navy, February 24, 2003.

Frankum, Ronald B., Jr., and Stephen F. Maxner. *The Vietnam War for Dummies.* New York: Wiley Publishing, 2003.

BIBLIOGRAPHY

Fraser, David. *Knight's Cross: A Life of Field Marshal Erwin Rommel.* New York: HarperCollins, 1993.

Gailey, Harry A. *Historical Encyclopedia of the United States Marine Corps.* Lanham, MD: Scarecrow Press, 1998.

Garand, George W., and Truman R. Strobridge. *Western Pacific Operations, History of U.S. Marine Corps Operations in World War II, Historical Division, Headquarters, U.S. Marine Corps.* Washington, DC: U.S. Government Printing Office, 1971.

Garland, Albert N. *Infantry in Vietnam: Small Unit Actions in the Early Days: 1965–66.* Nashville, TN: Battery Press, 1967.

Gawne, Jonathan. *Spearheading D-Day: American Special Units in Normandy.* Paris: Histoire & Collections, 1998.

Gettleman, Marvin E., Jane Franklin, Marilyn B. Young, and H. Bruce Franklin. *Vietnam and America: A Documented History.* New York: Grove Press, 1995.

Gilboa, Eytan. "The Panama Invasion Revisited: Lessons for the Use of Force in the Post Cold War Era." *Political Science Quarterly,* Winter 1995–1996.

Goulden, Joseph C. *Korea: The Untold Story of the War.* New York: Times Books, 1982.

Gray, Denis D. "Hamburger Hill Looms Large: Vietnam's Pivotal Battle Still Provokes Nightmares, Debate." Associated Press, April 28, 2000.

Great War Society website. Stanford, CA: 1998–2000.

Greenfield, Kent Roberts. *Command Decisions.* Department of the Army, Center of Military History, Washington, DC: U.S. Government Printing Office, 2000.

Gregg, Charles T. *Tarawa.* Briarcliff Manor, NY: Stein and Day, 1984.

Gulf of Tonkin Resolution, Public Law 88–408; 78 Stat. 384. Washington, DC: The United States Congress, August 10, 1964.

Gwin, S. Lawrence. "Ambush at Albany." In *Vietnam: A Reader,* edited by David T. Zabecki. New York: ibooks, 2002.

Hackworth, David H. *About Face: The Odyssey of an American Warrior.* New York: Touchstone, Simon & Schuster, 1989.

Haight, David B. *Operation JUST CAUSE: Foreshadowing Example of Joint Vision 2010 Concepts in Practice.* Newport, RI: U.S. Naval War College, February 13, 1998.

Hammel, Eric. *Guadalcanal—Starvation Island.* New York: Crown, 1987.

Harkins, Michael D. "Storming the Citadel." In *Vietnam: A Reader,* edited by David T. Zabecki. New York: ibooks, 2002.

Hart, Gary, and William S. Lind. *America Can Win: The Case for Military Reform.* Bethesda, MD: Adler & Adler, 1986.

Hastings, Max. *The Korean War.* New York: Simon & Schuster, 1987.

Hay, John H., Jr. *Vietnam Studies, Tactical and Materiel Innovations.* Department of the Army, Washington, DC: U.S. Government Printing Office, 1989.

Heinl, Robert Debs, Jr. *Soldiers of the Sea: The United States Marine Corps, 1775–1962 (Great War Stories).* Annapolis, MD: Nautical & Aviation Publishing Co. of America, 1991.

———. *Victory at High Tide: The Inchon Seoul Campaign.* Annapolis, MD: Nautical & Aviation Publications, 1979.

Herr, John K., and Edward S. Wallace. *The Story of the U.S. Cavalry, 1775–1942.* New York: Bonanza Books, 1984.

Hicken, Victor. *The American Fighting Man.* New York: Macmillan, 1969.

Hickey, Michael. *The Korean War: The West Confronts Communism.* Woodstock, NY: Overlook Press, 1999.

Historical Statistics of the United States: Colonial Times to 1970 (Bicentennial Edition). Washington, DC: U.S. Department of Commerce, Bureau of the Census, 1975.

History of Marine Corps Recruit Training. Washington, DC: United States Marine Corps, History and Museums Division, Washington Navy Yard. December 2001.

History of the USS Okanogan *(APA-220).* Conover, NC: Mobile Riverine Force Association. August 28, 1999.

Holbrook, Heber A. "A Look at the Bloody Korean War." *Pacific Ship and Shore Historical Society,* March–April 1997.

Holt, Tonie, and Valmai Holt. *Battlefields of the First World War: A Traveler's Guide.* London: Pavilion Books, 1993.

Hoobler, Dorothy, and Thomas Hoobler. *Vietnam, Why We Fought: An Illustrated History.* New York: Alfred A. Knopf, 1990.

Horne, Charles F., and Walter F. Austin. *Report of Secretary of the Navy Josephus Daniels, The Great Events of the Great War, Volume VI*. United States of America: National Alumni, 1920.

Hoyt, Edwin P. *America's Wars & Military Excursions*. New York: McGraw Hill, 1987.

———. *Blue Skies and Blood: The Battle of the Coral Sea*. New York: ibooks, 2003.

———. *The GI's War: The Story of American Soldiers in Europe in World War II*. New York: McGraw Hill, 1988.

Hunter, Thomas B. *Fort Rupert and Richmond Hill Prison, Grenada, October 1983*. SpecialOperations.com, 1998.

Hymel, Kevin. *MacArthur and Patton: The St. Mihiel Offensive* (an article published on the Army Historical Foundation website and adapted from a paper presented by Hymel, AHF research assistant, for the 1997 Annual Meeting of the Society of Military History. The article describes the battlefield meeting between Patton and MacArthur.). Arlington, VA: The Army Historical Foundation, 1997.

———. *Battle on the Basra Road*. Arlington, VA: Army Historical Foundation, 2003.

Jablonski, Edward. *Airwar*. Garden City, NY: Doubleday & Company, 1979.

Jackson, Kenneth. *The Thin Red Line: Not Enough History*. Washington, DC: Perspectives Online. The American Historical Association, April 1999.

Jaco, Charles. *The Complete Idiot's Guide to the Gulf War*. Indianapolis: Alpha Books, 2002.

Jodice, II, Ralph J. *El Dorado Canyon: Strategic Strike, National Objectives*, Alexandria, VA: CSC, GlobalSecurity.org, 1990.

John Basilone, Gunnery Sergeant, United States Marine Corps. Arlington, VA: Arlington National Cemetery website, 2002. arlingtoncemetery.org.

Jones, Archer. *The Art of War in the Western World*. Chicago: Board of Trustees of the University of Illinois. Barnes & Noble Books, 1997.

Karnow, Stanley. *Vietnam: A History*. New York: Penguin, 1984.

Keegan, John. *The First World War*. New York: Alfred A. Knopf, 1998.

Keegan, John, and Andrew Wheatcroft. *Who's Who in Military History: From 1453 to the Present Day.* New York: William Morrow & Company, 1976.

King, Jennifer, and Timothy Rollins. *Pacific Theater of Operations—Sixty Years Ago, Dateline: 7 May 1942, The Battle of the Coral Sea.* Bloomfield, NY: American Partisan, 2002.

King, John. *The Gulf War.* New York: Dillon Press, 1991.

Kingseed, Cole C. "Beyond the Ia Drang Valley." *Army,* November 2002.

Knox, Donald. *The Korean War: An Oral History, Pusan to Chosin.* Orlando: Harcourt Brace Jovanovich, 1985.

Korean War: The Forgotten War. San Francisco: Military.com, Military Advantage, Inc., 2003.

Krulak, Victor H. *First to Fight: An Inside View of the U.S. Marine Corps.* Annapolis, MD: Naval Institute Press, 1984.

Ky, Nguyen Cao, and Marvin J. Wolf. *Buddha's Child, My Fight to Save Vietnam.* New York: St. Martin's Press, 2002.

Landsberg, Mitchell. "Fifty Years Later, Iwo Jima Photographer Fights His Own Battle." Associated Press, 1995.

Lanning, Michael Lee. *The Military 100: A Ranking of the Most Influential Military Leaders of All Time.* Secaucus, NJ: Citadel Press, 1996.

Leckie, Robert. *Warfare.* New York: Harper & Row, 1970.

———. *Okinawa: The Last Battle of World War II.* New York: Viking Penguin, 1995.

Lewis, Jon E. *The Mammoth Book of Battles: The Art and Science of Modern Warfare.* New York: Carroll & Graf Publishers, 1995.

Livesey, Anthony. *Great Battles of World War I.* New York: Macmillan Publishing, 1989.

———. *Historical Atlas of World War I.* New York: Henry Holt & Company, 1994.

Livingstone, Neil C. *The Cult of Counterterrorism: The Weird World of Spooks, Counterterrorists, Adventurers, and the Not-Quite Professionals.* Lexington, MA: Lexington Books, 1990.

Lopez, George. "The Gulf War: Not So Clean." Chicago: *Bulletin of the Atomic Scientists,* September 1991.

Lord, Walter. *Midway: The Incredible Victory.* Hertfordshire, England: Wordsworth Editions, 2000.

Luvaas, Jay. *Frederick the Great on the Art of War.* New York: The Free Press, 1966.

MacDonald, Charles B. *A Time for Trumpets: The Untold Story of the Battle of the Bulge.* New York: William Morrow and Company, 1985.

MacDonald, John. *Great Battlefields of the World.* New York: Macmillan Publishing, 1984.

———. *Great Battles of World War II.* New York: Macmillan Publishing, 1986.

MacGarrigle, George L. *Aleutian Islands—The U.S. Army Campaigns of World War II.* Washington, DC: U.S. Army Center of Military History, 2002.

Malinarich, Nathalie. *Flashback: The Berlin Disco Bombing.* London: BBC News, November 13, 2001.

Malkasian, Carter. *The Korean War.* Great Britain: Osprey, 2001.

Malmgren, Jeanne. *Battle of the Bulge—Nuts!* Center of Research and Information on the Battle of the Bulge website, 2002, users.skynet.be/bulgecriba/battlebul.htm

Manchester, William. *American Caesar: Douglas MacArthur, 1880–1964.* Canada: Little Brown & Company, 1978.

———. *Goodbye Darkness: A Memoir of the Pacific War.* Boston: Little Brown and Company, 1979.

The Marines in Vietnam 1954–1973. Washington, DC: History and Museums Division, Headquarters, U.S. Marine Corps, 1985.

Marling, Karal Ann, and John Wetenhall. *Iwo Jima: Monuments, Memories, and the American Hero.* Cambridge, MA: Harvard University Press, 1991.

Marshall, S. L. A. *American Heritage History of World War I.* New York: American Heritage Publishing, 1983.

———. *Bastogne: The First Eight Days.* Washington, DC: Center of Military History, United States Army, 1988.

Matloff, Maurice. *American Military History: Army Historical Series.* Washington, DC: Office of the Chief of Military History, United States Army, 1969.

McClellan, Edwin N. *The United States Marine Corps in the World War.* Washington, DC: Historical Branch, Headquarters U.S. Marine Corps, 1920.

McNamara, Robert S. *CNN Cold War* series (an interview), *Vietnam 1954–1968*. Atlanta, GA: CNN, 1998.

McNamara, Robert S., with Brian VanDeMark. *In Retrospect: The Tragedy and Lessons of Vietnam*. New York: Times Books, 1995.

Melton, H. Keith. *The Ultimate Spy Book*. New York: DK Publishing, 1996.

Millett, Allan R. *Semper Fidelis: The History of the United States Marine Corps*. New York: Macmillan Publishing, 1980.

Moore, Harold G., and Joseph L. Galloway. *We Were Soldiers Once … and Young: Ia Drang: The Battle That Changed the War in Vietnam*. New York: Random House, 1992.

Moorehead, Alan. *The March to Tunis: The North African War 1940–1943*. New York: Harper & Row, 1967.

Morelock, J. D. *The Army Times Book of Great Land Battles: From the Civil War to the Gulf War*. New York: Berkley Books, 1994.

Morison, Samuel Eliot. *History of United States Naval Operations in World War II*. Boston: Little Brown and Company, 1975.

———. "Thoughts on Naval Strategy, World War II." U.S. Naval War College, Newport, RI: *Naval War College Review*. March 1968.

Moskin, J. Robert. *The U.S. Marine Corps Story*. New York: McGraw Hill, 1982.

Murphy, Edward F. *Dak To: The 173rd Airborne Brigade in South Vietnam's Central Highlands, June–November 1967*. Novato, CA: Presidio Press, 1993.

———. *Semper Fi Vietnam: From Da Nang to the DMZ, Marine Corps Campaigns, 1965–1975*. Novato, CA: Presidio Press, 1997.

Murphy, Jack. *History of the U.S. Marines*. Greenwich, CT: Bison Books, 1984.

Night Vision and Electronic Sensors Directorate. Fort Belvoir, VA: U.S. Army website, 2003. army.mil.

Nofi, Albert A. *Marine Corps Book of Lists: A Definitive Compendium of Marine Corps Facts, Feats, and Traditions*. Philadelphia: Combined Books, 1997.

North, Don. *Tet Plus 30: A U.S.–Vietnam Turning Point*. Arlington, VA: Consortium News, The Consortium for Independent Journalism, 1998.

———. "VC Assault on the U.S. Embassy." *Vietnam*, February 2000.

North, Oliver L. *Under Fire: An American Story.* New York: HarperCollins, 1991.

Nye, Roger H. *The Patton Mind: The Professional Development of an Extraordinary Leader.* Garden City Park, NY: Avery Publishing Group, 1993.

Oxford Essential Dictionary of the U.S. Military. New York: Oxford University Press, 2001.

Page, Tim, and John Pimlott. *NAM: The Vietnam Experience 1965–75.* New York: Barnes & Noble Books, 1995.

Parrish, Thomas. *The Simon & Schuster Encyclopedia of World War II.* New York: Simon & Schuster, 1978.

Pierce, Kenneth R. *The Battle of the Ia Drang Valley.* Fort Leavenworth, KS: U.S. Army Command and General Staff College, Military Review, Vol LXIX, 1989.

Prados, John. *The Hidden History of the Vietnam War.* Chicago: Ivan R. Dee, 1995.

———. "Operation Masher—The Boundaries of Force." *Veterans*, February–March 2002.

Rangers to Exit Somalia. Washington, DC: The Associated Press (AP). October 20, 1993.

Reagan, Ronald Wilson. *Presidential Address to the Nation.* Washington, DC: The White House, October 27, 1983.

Regan, Geoffrey. *The Guinness Book of Decisive Battles. Fifty Battles That Changed the World from Salamis to the Gulf War.* New York: Canopy Books, Abbeville Press, 1992.

Reynolds, Clark G. *The Epic of Flight—the Carrier War.* Chicago: Time-Life Books, 1982.

Richmond, Peter. *My Father's War: A Son's Journey.* New York: Simon & Schuster, 1996.

Roe, Patrick C. "The Chinese Failure at Chosin" (lecture presented at 1996 Chosin Few Reunion). Portland, OR: Chosin Few Historical Committee, 1996.

Ropp, Theodore. *War in the Modern World.* Durham, NC: Duke University Press, 1959.

Ross, Bill D. *Iwo Jima: Legacy of Valor.* New York: Vanguard Press, 1985.

Russ, Martin. *Breakout: The Chosin Reservoir Campaign, Korea 1950.* New York. Penguin, 2000.

Saddam's Iraq: Key Events. Gulf War 1990–1991. London: British Broadcasting Corporation (BBC), 2003.

Scalard, Douglas P. *The Battle of Hamburger Hill: Battle Command in Difficult Terrain Against a Determined Enemy.* Fort Leavenworth, KS: Combat Studies Institute, Command & General Staff College, 1995.

Shafritz, Jay M. *Words on War: Military Quotations from Ancient Times to the Present.* New York: Prentice Hall, 1990.

Sheehan, Neil. *A Bright and Shining Lie: John Paul Vann and America in Vietnam.* New York: Random House, 1988.

Shirer, William L. *The Rise and Fall of the Third Reich: A History of Nazi Germany.* New York: Simon & Schuster, 1960.

Simmons, Edwin Howard. *The United States Marines: The First Two Hundred Years, 1775–1975.* New York: Viking Press, 1976.

———. *The Battle for Hue.* The Urban Operations Journal website, 2003. urbanoperations.com.

Smith, W. Thomas, Jr. "An Old Warrior Sounds Off: General Westmoreland, Commander of U.S. Forces in Vietnam Until 1968, Talks of War and General Giap." *George,* November 1998.

———. "Waging War: A Crash Course in the War on Terror, the Possible Expansion of That War into Iraq, and How We Fight It." Charleston, SC: *Charleston City Paper,* December 18, 2002.

Stanton, Shelby L. *The Rise and Fall of an American Army: U.S. Ground Forces in Vietnam, 1965–1973.* Novato, CA: Presidio Press, 1985.

Steinberg, Rafael. *World War II—Island Fighting.* Alexandria, VA: Time-Life Books, 1978.

Stokesbury, James L. *A Short History of the Korean War.* New York: William Morrow and Company, 1988.

Sulzberger, C. L., and Stephen E. Ambrose. *The American Heritage New History of World War II.* New York: Viking Penguin, 1997.

Summers, Harry G., Jr. *On Strategy: A Critical Analysis of the Vietnam War.* Novato, CA: Presidio Press, 1982.

Taylor, John M. *Hue: A 1989 Analysis.* Quantico, VA: Marine Corps Command and Staff College, The Urban Operations Journal website, 1989.

Thomas, Raymond A. *JUST CAUSE Revisited: Paradigm for Future Operations.* Newport, RI: U.S. Naval War College, 1995.

Toland, John. *No Man's Land 1918—The Last Year of the Great War.* Garden City, NY: Doubleday, 1980.

Tolson, John J. *Airmobility, 1961–1971, Part 15. Department of the Army: Vietnam Studies.* Washington, DC: U.S. Government Printing Office, 1973.

Turkey Trots to Water: The Battle of Leyte Gulf, October 1944. La Habra, CA: Iowa Class Preservation Association, 2000.

Uschan, Michael V. *The Korean War.* San Diego, CA: Lucent Books, 2001.

Venkus, Robert E. *Raid on Qaddafi. The Untold Story of History's Longest Fighter Mission by the Pilot Who Directed It.* New York: St. Martin's Press, 1992.

Vogel, Steve. "50 Years Later, an Army Force Gets Its Due: Ceremony to Mark Chosin Reservoir Battle in North Korea." *The Washington Post,* December 11, 2000.

Young, Charles H. *Into the Valley: The Untold Story of USAAF Troop Carrier in World War II, From North Africa Through Europe.* Dallas, TX: PrintComm, 1995.

Way, Almon Leroy, Jr. *How America Goes to War: The President, American Law, & U.S. Military Intervention into Foreign Conflicts.* The Progressive Conservative website. June 10–December 31, 1999.

Westmoreland, William C. Interview. *CNN Cold War Series, Vietnam 1954–1968.* Cable News Network, 1998.

———. *A Soldier Reports.* Garden City, NY: Doubleday & Company, 1976.

Whiting, Charles. *Ardennes, the Secret War.* Briarcliff Manor, NY: Stein and Day, 1985.

———. *The Other Battle of the Bulge, Operation Northwind.* Chelsea, MI: Scarborough House, 1990.

Willbanks, James H. *The Battle for Hue, 1968.* Fort Leavenworth, KS: Combat Studies Institute, Command & General Staff College, 2002.

Williams, Gladys. *Alvin C. York.* Jamestown, TN: Alvin C. York Institute, 1999.

Wolf, Julie. "The Invasion of Grenada." *The American Experience*, Public Broadcasting System (PBS), 1999–2000.

Woodward, Bob. *The Commanders*. New York: Simon & Schuster, 1991.

World Factbook. Langley, VA: The Central Intelligence Agency (CIA), 2002.

Wright, Derrick. *Tarawa 1943*. Great Britain: Osprey, 2000.

Zabecki, David T. "Battlefield North Africa: Rommel's Rise and Fall." *World War II*, 2000.

Zaffiri. Samuel. *Hamburger Hill, May 11–20, 1969*. Novato, CA: Presidio Press, 1988.

Zakheim, Dov S. "Civil Society: Democratization in the Arab World: Review of *Common Ground on Iraq-Kuwait Reconciliation*." Cairo, Egypt: Ibn Khaldun Center for Development Studies, January 1999.

INDEX

INDEX